CLARISSA DALLOWAY

Major Literary Characters

**THE ANCIENT WORLD THROUGH
THE SEVENTEENTH CENTURY**

ACHILLES
Homer, *Iliad*

CALIBAN
William Shakespeare, *The Tempest*
Robert Browning, *Caliban upon Setebos*

CLEOPATRA
William Shakespeare, *Antony and
  Cleopatra*
John Dryden, *All for Love*
George Bernard Shaw, *Caesar and
  Cleopatra*

DON QUIXOTE
Miguel de Cervantes, *Don Quixote*
Franz Kafka, *Parables*

FALSTAFF
William Shakespeare, *Henry IV, Part I,
  Henry IV, Part II, The Merry Wives
  of Windsor*

FAUST
Christopher Marlowe, *Doctor Faustus*
Johann Wolfgang von Goethe, *Faust*
Thomas Mann, *Doctor Faustus*

HAMLET
William Shakespeare, *Hamlet*

IAGO
William Shakespeare, *Othello*

JULIUS CAESAR
William Shakespeare, *Julius Caesar*
George Bernard Shaw, *Caesar and
  Cleopatra*

KING LEAR
William Shakespeare, *King Lear*

MACBETH
William Shakespeare, *Macbeth*

ODYSSEUS/ULYSSES
Homer, *Odyssey*
James Joyce, *Ulysses*

OEDIPUS
Sophocles, *Oedipus Rex, Oedipus
  at Colonus*

OTHELLO
William Shakespeare, *Othello*

ROSALIND
William Shakespeare, *As You Like It*

SANCHO PANZA
Miguel de Cervantes, *Don Quixote*
Franz Kafka, *Parables*

SATAN
The Book of Job
John Milton, *Paradise Lost*

SHYLOCK
William Shakespeare, *The Merchant
  of Venice*

THE WIFE OF BATH
Geoffrey Chaucer, *The Canterbury
  Tales*

**THE EIGHTEENTH AND
NINETEENTH CENTURIES**

AHAB
Herman Melville, *Moby-Dick*

ISABEL ARCHER
Henry James, *Portrait of a Lady*

EMMA BOVARY
Gustave Flaubert, *Madame Bovary*

DOROTHEA BROOKE
George Eliot, *Middlemarch*

CHELSEA HOUSE PUBLISHERS

Major Literary Characters

DAVID COPPERFIELD
Charles Dickens, *David Copperfield*

ROBINSON CRUSOE
Daniel Defoe, *Robinson Crusoe*

DON JUAN
Molière, *Don Juan*
Lord Byron, *Don Juan*

HUCK FINN
Mark Twain, *The Adventures of
    Tom Sawyer, Adventures of
    Huckleberry Finn*

CLARISSA HARLOWE
Samuel Richardson, *Clarissa*

HEATHCLIFF
Emily Brontë, *Wuthering Heights*

ANNA KARENINA
Leo Tolstoy, *Anna Karenina*

MR. PICKWICK
Charles Dickens, *The Pickwick Papers*

HESTER PRYNNE
Nathaniel Hawthorne, *The Scarlet Letter*

BECKY SHARP
William Makepeace Thackeray, *Vanity Fair*

LAMBERT STRETHER
Henry James, *The Ambassadors*

EUSTACIA VYE
Thomas Hardy, *The Return of the Native*

TWENTIETH CENTURY

ÁNTONIA
Willa Cather, *My Ántonia*

BRETT ASHLEY
Ernest Hemingway, *The Sun Also Rises*

HANS CASTORP
Thomas Mann, *The Magic Mountain*

HOLDEN CAULFIELD
J. D. Salinger, *The Catcher in the Rye*

CADDY COMPSON
William Faulkner, *The Sound and the Fury*

JANIE CRAWFORD
Zora Neale Hurston, *Their Eyes Were
    Watching God*

CLARISSA DALLOWAY
Virginia Woolf, *Mrs. Dalloway*

DILSEY
William Faulkner, *The Sound and the Fury*

GATSBY
F. Scott Fitzgerald, *The Great Gatsby*

HERZOG
Saul Bellow, *Herzog*

JOAN OF ARC
William Shakespeare, *Henry VI*
George Bernard Shaw, *Saint Joan*

LOLITA
Vladimir Nabokov, *Lolita*

WILLY LOMAN
Arthur Miller, *Death of a Salesman*

MARLOW
Joseph Conrad, *Lord Jim, Heart of
    Darkness, Youth, Chance*

PORTNOY
Philip Roth, *Portnoy's Complaint*

BIGGER THOMAS
Richard Wright, *Native Son*

CHELSEA HOUSE PUBLISHERS

Major Literary Characters

C L A R I S S A
D A L L O W A Y

Edited and with an introduction by
HAROLD BLOOM

CHELSEA HOUSE PUBLISHERS
New York ◊ Philadelphia

Inset: Title page from the first English edition
of *Mrs. Dalloway* (London: Hogarth Press, 1925).
By permission of the Newberry Library, Chicago.

Chelsea House Publishers

Editor-in-Chief Nancy Toff
Executive Editor Remmel T. Nunn
Managing Editor Karyn Gullen Browne
Picture Editor Adrian G. Allen
Art Director Maria Epes
Manufacturing Manager Gerald Levine

Major Literary Characters

Managing Editor S. T. Joshi
Copy Chief Richard Fumosa
Designer Maria Epes

Staff for CLARISSA DALLOWAY

Researcher Mary Lawlor
Editorial Assistant Katherine Theodore
Picture Researcher Debra Hershkowitz
Assistant Art Director Loraine Machlin
Production Manager Joseph Romano
Production Assistant Leslie D'Acri
Cover Illustration Daniel Mark Duffy

Library of Congress Cataloging-in-Publication Data

Clarissa Dalloway / edited and with an introduction by Harold Bloom.
p.   cm.— (Major literary characters)
Includes bibliographical references.
ISBN 0-7910-0956-4.—ISBN 0-7910-1011-2 (pbk.)
1. Woolf, Virginia, 1882-1941. Mrs. Dalloway. I. Bloom, Harold.
II. Series.
PR6045.072M734 1990
823'.912—dc20
89-35284
CIP

CONTENTS

THE ANALYSIS OF CHARACTER

Harold Bloom

"Character," according to our dictionaries, still has as a primary meaning a graphic symbol, such as a letter of the alphabet. This meaning reflects the word's apparent origin in the ancient Greek *charactēr,* a sharp stylus. *Charactēr* also meant the mark of the stylus' incisions. Recent fashions in literary criticism have reduced "character" in literature to a matter of marks upon a page. But our word "character" also has a very different meaning, matching that of the ancient Greek *ēthos,* "habitual way of life." Shall we say then that literary character is an imitation of human character, or is it just a grouping of marks? The issue is between a critic like Dr. Samuel Johnson, for whom words were as much like people as like things, and a critic like the late Roland Barthes, who told us that "the fact can only exist linguistically, as a term of discourse." Who is closer to our experience of reading literature, Johnson or Barthes? What difference does it make, if we side with one critic rather than the other?

Barthes is famous, like Foucault and other recent French theorists, for having added to Nietzsche's proclamation of the death of God a subsidiary demise, that of the literary author. If there are no authors, then there are no fictional personages, presumably because literature does not refer to a world outside language. Words indeed necessarily refer to other words in the first place, but the impact of words ultimately is drawn from a universe of fact. Stories, poems, and plays are recognizable as such because they are human utterances within traditions of utterances, and traditions, by achieving authority, become a kind of fact, or at least the sense of a fact. Our sense that literary characters, within the context of a fictive cosmos, indeed are fictional personages is also a kind of fact. The meaning and value of every character in a successful work of literary representation depend upon our ideas of persons in the factual reality of our lives.

Literary character is always an invention, and inventions generally are indebted to prior inventions. Shakespeare is the inventor of literary character as we know it; he reformed the universal human expectations for the verbal imitation of personality, and the reformation appears now to be permanent and uncannily inevitable. Remarkable as the Bible and Homer are at representing personages, their characters are relatively unchanging. They age within their stories, but their habitual modes of being do not develop. Jacob and Achilles unfold before us, but without metamorphoses. Lear and Macbeth, Hamlet and Othello severely modify themselves not only by their actions, but by their utterances, and most of all through *overhearing themselves,* whether they speak to themselves or to others. Pondering what they themselves have said, they will to change, and actually do change, sometimes extravagantly yet always persuasively. Or else they suffer change, without willing it, but in reaction not so much to their language as to their relation to that language.

I do not think it useful to say that Shakespeare successfully imitated elements in our characters. Rather, it could be argued that he compelled aspects of character to appear that previously were concealed, or not available to representation. This is not to say that Shakespeare is God, but to remind us that language is not God either. The mimesis of character in Shakespeare's dramas now seems to us normative, and indeed became the accepted mode almost immediately, as Ben Jonson shrewdly and somewhat grudgingly implied. And yet, Shakespearean representation has surprisingly little in common with the imitation of reality in Jonson or in Christopher Marlowe. The origins of Shakespeare's originality in the portrayal of men and women are to be found in the *Canterbury Tales* of Geoffrey Chaucer, insofar as they can be located anywhere before Shakespeare himself. Chaucer's savage and superb Pardoner overhears his own tale-telling, as well as his mocking rehearsal of his own spiel, and through this overhearing he is emboldened to forget himself, and enthusiastically urges all his fellow-pilgrims to come forward to be fleeced by him. His self-awareness, and apocalyptically rancid sense of spiritual fall, are preludes to the even grander abysses of the perverted will in Iago and in Edmund. What might be called the character trait of a negative charisma may be Chaucer's invention, but came to its perfection in Shakespearean mimesis.

The analysis of character is as much Shakespeare's invention as the representation of character is, since Iago and Edmund are adepts at analyzing both themselves and their victims. Hamlet, whose overwhelming charisma has many negative components, is certainly the most comprehensive of all literary characters, and so necessarily prophesies the labyrinthine complexities of the will in Iago and Edmund. Charisma, according to Max Weber, its first codifier, is primarily a natural endowment, and implies a primordial and idiosyncratic power over nature, and so finally over death. Hamlet's uncanniness is at its most suggestive in the scene of his long dying, where the audience, through the mediation of Horatio, itself is compelled to meditate upon suicide, if only because outliving the prince of Denmark scarcely seems an option.

Shakespearean representation has usurped not only our sense of literary character, but our sense of ourselves as characters, with Hamlet playing the part of

the largest of these usurpations. Insofar as we have an idea of human disinterest-
edness, we tend to derive it from the Hamlet of Act V, whose quietism has about
it a ghostly authority. Oscar Wilde, in his profound and profoundly witty dialogue,
"The Decay of Lying," expressed a permanent insight when he insisted that art
shaped every era, far more than any age formed art. Life imitates art, we imitate
Shakespeare, because without Shakespeare we would perish for lack of images.
Wilde's grandest audacity demystifies Shakespearean mimesis with a Shakespearean vivaciousness: "This unfortunate aphorism about art holding the mirror up to
Nature is deliberately said by Hamlet in order to convince the bystanders of his
absolute insanity in all art-matters." Of *Hamlet*'s influence upon the ages Wilde
remarked that: "The world has grown sad because a puppet was once melancholy."
"Puppet" is Wilde's own deconstruction, a brilliant reminder that Shakespeare's
artistry of illusion has so mastered reality as to have changed reality, evidently
forever.

The analysis of character, as a critical pursuit, seems to me as much a
Shakespearean invention as literary character was, since much of what we know
about how to analyze character necessarily follows Shakespearean procedures. His
hero-villains, from Richard III through Iago, Edmund, and Macbeth, are shrewd and
endless questers into their own self-motivations. If we could bear to see Hamlet, in
his unwearied negations, as another hero-villain, then we would judge him the
supreme analyst of the darker recalcitrances in the selfhood. Freud followed the
pre-Socratic Empedocles, in arguing that character is fate, a frightening doctrine that
maintains the fear that there are no accidents, that overdetermination rules us all
of our lives. Hamlet assumes the same, yet adds to this argument the terrible
passivity he manifests in Act V. Throughout Shakespeare's tragedies, the most
interesting personages seem doom-eager, reminding us again that a Shakespearean
reading of Freud would be more illuminating than a Freudian exegesis of
Shakespeare. We learn more when we discover Hamlet in the Freudian Death
Drive, than when we read *Beyond the Pleasure Principle* into *Hamlet*.

In Shakespearean comedy, character achieves its true literary apotheosis,
which is the representation of the inner freedom that can be created by great wit
alone. Rosalind and Falstaff, perhaps alone among Shakespeare's personages, match
Hamlet in wit, though hardly in the metaphysics of consciousness. Whether in the
comic or the modern mode, Shakespeare has set the standard of measurement in
the balance between character and passion.

In Shakespeare the self is more dramatized than theatricalized, which is why a
Shakespearean reading of Freud works out so well. Character-formation after the
passing of the Oedipal stage takes the place of fetishistic fragmentings of the self.
Critics who now call literary character into question, and who proclaim also the
death of the author, invariably also regard all notions, literary and human, of a stable
character as being mere reductions of deeper pre-Oedipal desires. It becomes

clear that the fortunes of literary character rise and fall with the prestige of normative conceptions of the ego. Shakespeare's Iago, who wars against being, may be the first deconstructionist of the self, with his proclamation of "I am not what I am." This constitutes the necessary prologue to any view that would regard a fixed ego as a virtual abnormality. But deconstructions of the self are no more modern than Modernism is. Like literary modernism, the decentered ego came out of the Hellenistic culture of ancient Alexandria. The Gnostic heretics believed that the psyche, like the body, was a fallen entity, mechanically fashioned by the Demiurge or false creator. They held however that each of us possessed also a spark or pneuma, which was a fragment of the original Abyss or true, alien God. The soul or psyche within every one of us was thus at war with the self or pneuma, and only that sparklike self could be saved.

Shakespeare, following after Chaucer in this respect, was the first and remains still the greatest master of representing character both as a stable soul and a wavering self. There is a substance that endures in Shakespeare's figures, and there is also a quicksilver rendition of the unsettling sparks. Racine and Tolstoy, Balzac and Dickens, follow in Shakespeare's wake by giving us some sense of pre-Oedipal sparks or drives, and considerably more sense of post-Oedipal character and personality, stabilizations or sublimations of the fetish-seeking drives. Critics like Leo Bersani and René Girard argue eloquently against our taking this mimesis as the only proper work of literature. I would suggest that strong fictions of the self, from the Bible through Samuel Beckett, necessarily participate in both modes, the sublimation of desire, and the persistence of a primordial desire. The mystery of Hamlet or of Lear is intimately invested in the tangled mixture of the two modes of representation.

Psychic mobility is proposed by Bersani as the ideal to which deconstructions of the literary self may yet guide us. The ideal has its pathos, but the realities of literary representation seem to me very different, perhaps destructively so. When a novelist like D. H. Lawrence sought to reduce his characters to Eros and the Death Drive, he still had to persuade us of his authority at mimesis by lavishing upon the figures of *The Rainbow* and *Women in Love* all of the vivid stigmata of normative personality. Birkin and Ursula may represent antithetical and uncanny drives, but they develop and change as characters pondering their own pronouncements and reactions to self and others. The cost of a non-Shakespearean representation is enormous. Pynchon, in *The Crying of Lot 49* and *Gravity's Rainbow*, evades the burden of the normative by resorting to something like Christopher Marlowe's art of caricature in *The Jew of Malta*. Marlowe's Barabas is a marvelous rhetorician, yet he is a cartoon alongside the troublingly equivocal Shylock. Pynchon's personages are deliberate cartoons also, as flat as comic strips. Marlowe's achievement, and Pynchon's, are beyond dispute, yet they are like the prelude and the postlude to Shakespearean reality. They do not wish to engage with our hunger for the empirical world and so they enter the problematic cosmos of literary fantasy.

No writer, not even Shakespeare or Proust, alters the available stock that we agree to call reality, but Shakespeare, more than any other, does show us how much of reality we could encounter if only we retained adequate desire. The strong literary representation of character is already an analysis of character, and is part of the healing work of a literary culture, which implicitly seeks to cure violence through a normative mimesis of ego, *as if it were stable,* whether in actuality it is or is not. I do not believe that this is a social quest taken on by literary culture, but rather that we confront here the aesthetic essence of what makes a culture *literary,* rather than metaphysical or ethical or religious. A culture becomes literary when its conceptual modes have failed it, which means when religion, philosophy, and science have begun to lose their authority. If they cannot heal violence, then literature attempts to do so, which may be only a turning inside out of the critical arguments of Girard and Bersani.

I conclude by offering a particular instance or special case as a paradigm for the healing enterprise that is at once the representation and the analysis of literary character. Let us call it the aesthetics of being outraged, or rather of successfully representing the state of being outraged. W. C. Fields was one modern master of such representation, and Nathanael West was another, as was Faulkner before him. Here also the greatest master remains Shakespeare, whose Macbeth, himself a bloody outrage, yet retains our imaginative sympathy precisely because he grows increasingly outraged as he experiences the equivocation of the fiend that lies like truth. The double-natured promises and the prophecies of the weird sisters finally induce in Macbeth an apocalyptic version of the stage actor's anxiety at missing cues, the horror of a phantasmagoric stage fright of missing one's time, of always reacting too late. Macbeth, a veritable monster of solipsistic inwardness but no intellectual, counters his dilemma by fresh murders, that prolong him in time yet provoke him only to a perpetually freshened sense of being outraged, as all his expectations become still worse confounded. We are moved by Macbeth, however estrangedly, because his terrible inwardness is a paradigm for our own solipsism, but also because none of us can resist a strong and successful representation of the human in a state of being outraged.

The ultimate outrage is the necessity of dying, an outrage concealed in a multitude of masks, including the tyrannical ambitions of Macbeth. I suspect that our outrage at being outraged is the most difficult of all our affects for us to represent to ourselves, which is why we are so inclined to imaginative sympathy for a character who strongly conveys that affect to us. The Shrike of West's *Miss Lonelyhearts* or Faulkner's Joe Christmas of *Light in August* are crucial modern instances, but such figures can be located in many other works, since the ability to represent this extreme emotion is one of the tests that strong writers are driven to set for themselves.

However a reader seeks to reduce literary character to a question of marks on a page, she will come at last to the impasse constituted by the thought of death, her death, and before that to all the stations of being outraged that memorialize her own drive towards death. In reading, she quests for evidences that are strong representations, whether of her desire or her despair. Such questings constitute the necessary basis for the analysis of literary character, an enterprise that always will survive every vagary of critical fashion.

EDITOR'S NOTE

This book brings together a representative selection of the best literary criticism that has been devoted to the analysis of Clarissa Dalloway, title character of Virginia Woolf's classic novel, *Mrs. Dalloway.* The criticism reprinted here is divided into two groups—extracts and essays—each arranged in the chronological order of their original publication. I am grateful to Mary Lawlor for her erudite skill as a researcher for this volume.

My introduction attempts to relate Woolf's representation of Clarissa Dalloway to the defense of literary character sketched in my opening essay, "The Analysis of Character." The extracts begin with Woolf herself, in her celebrated essay "Mr. Bennett and Mrs. Brown," a subtle indictment of the generation of novelists before her own. Woolf's attack upon societal context is a defense of her direct effort to represent Mrs. Dalloway's innermost being, an effort illuminated by an excerpt from her diary that sees the character vivified when "I invented her memories." Subsequent extracts, ranging from Elizabeth A. Drew through Perry Meisel, present crucial instances of what Meisel terms "the particularities that fashion privacy" in Woolfian character.

The fuller scale critical essays begin here with Reuben Arthur Brower's exegesis of Clarissa's Shakespearean sense of "the central." Geoffrey H. Hartman, as subtly as Woolf herself, emphasizes the continuities in the representation of Clarissa Dalloway's consciousness. In Blanche H. Gelfant's reading, the heroine's sense of identity is secure, precisely because her idea of love involves "letting others be."

Lee R. Edwards, in an early feminist interpretation, sees Clarissa's freedom as the art of manipulating one's socially defined role. Woolf's implicit theory of personality is the focus of Daniel Albright, while John G. Hessler stresses Clarissa's ethical stance. Robert Kiely traces Mrs. Dalloway's relation to her own marriage and to the fictive conventions of marriage, after which Kenneth Moon explores some of the deep ambiguities and ambivalences in the character.

In Howard Harper's view, Clarissa Dalloway's character is primarily defined by her dialectical relationship to her dark brother in sensibility, poor Septimus, as he moves towards madness and death. Susan M. Squier, emphasizing sexual politics, sees London as the defining web of patriarchal influence upon Clarissa in the novel.

The question of the self, of subjectivity itself, is taken up by Makiko Minow-Pinkney, who applies Julia Kristeva to the analysis of how Mrs. Dalloway is able to survive through, rather than despite, her own contradictions. Perhaps we have returned to the central dilemma addressed by my introduction: Woolf rediscovered for herself, through Mrs. Clarissa Dalloway, an ancient contradiction endemic both in human and in fictional character. Identity recedes from us most compellingly precisely to the degree that we quest for it, and seek to define it, whether in itself or in relation to others.

INTRODUCTION

Virginia Woolf conceived of *Mrs. Dalloway* as a pattern in which "every scene would build up the idea of Clarissa's character." Since Clarissa Dalloway, in subtle ways, is founded upon Woolf's sense of her own consciousness, we would have a kind of psychic self-portrait except for Woolf's intense aesthetic wariness. That wariness works so as to universalize certain aspects of Clarissa's character, which is implicitly presented as a study in a woman's developments, rather than a great woman writer's unfolding. Coming as it does out of the era in which Freud's case histories first appeared in English, and through the efforts of the Woolf circle, *Mrs. Dalloway* might seem to court the danger of being something of a case history itself. But, in aesthetic matters, Virginia Woolf was never doom-eager. Like her "absent father," Walter Pater (to adopt Perry Meisel's term for Pater's relation to Woolf), the author of *Mrs. Dalloway* perfected the art of evasion, of wavering with exquisite skill so as to avoid falling into patterns of overdetermination. Clarissa Dalloway, like her ultimate namesake, the Clarissa Harlowe of Samuel Richardson's great novel *Clarissa,* is finally a heroine of the Protestant will. This is well worth remarking at our critical moment, when interpretations stressing gender, class, and race are likely to make fictional heroines into victims. Clarissa Dalloway is nobody's victim, and her individuality transcends the social pressures that would deform or repress it.

"There was an embrace in death," Clarissa reflects as she reacts to the suicide of her dark daemon and psychic brother, Septimus. Is it Clarissa's association, or ours, or both together, if such an embrace is allied to "the radiance burnt through, the revelation, the religious feeling" of having kissed Sally Seton some thirty years before? Was such an embrace a little death for Clarissa, or is it that male embraces are death when compared to that lost radiance? I do not believe that Woolf's superb novel allows us to answer such questions. Clarissa Dalloway's world allows no Lovelace; only Peter Walsh and Richard Dalloway and Dr. Bradshaw. If Woolf has a severe aesthetic limitation as a novelist, it is that a strong male character can be admitted only if, like Mr. Ramsay in *To the Lighthouse,* his vitality can be seen as essentially self-maimed.

How nihilistic a character is Clarissa Dalloway? Associations of eros and death are High Romantic, but with Shakespearean origins, and Woolf tends to write an oblique version of Shakespearean romance, with a difference whose ideology is proto-feminist, but whose aesthetic drive is a familiar, rather Paterian sense of belatedness. Nietzsche's apprehension of the void within human existence, truth that would kill us but for the concealments of art, is also very Woolfian. Yet Clarissa, perhaps unlike the narrator in *Mrs. Dalloway*, combats nihilism with her will. Why after all did she refuse Peter Walsh, despite their preternatural rapport, and marry Richard Dalloway? Perhaps because she intuited that too perfect a communion between psyches would precipitate her into the void of the one great mind that somehow we share, a void she longs to enter but will not enter, for the sake of life. And yet there is a darker possibility; since the fullest erotic communion would have been with Sally Seton, the affinity with Peter Walsh may have seemed too acceptable a substitute, while not being the thing itself. Sometimes in reading *Mrs. Dalloway* we receive the occult suggestion that Clarissa is resisting the narrator's nihilism, but then we realize that the narrator is darkly moved to love of death by attending too devotedly to strains that pulsate through Clarissa. Here too Woolf's superb evasions, the quirk of her invention, baffle our desperate drive for interpretive probabilities.

Had Clarissa married Peter Walsh, she would have forsaken her solitude. The Protestant self, lonely and inviolate, finds a space for its survival in Clarissa's imperfect union with Richard Dalloway. But it would not still be the Protestant self if it did not go back over its decision, again and again. Doubtless the socialization of that self is the history of the British ruling class, but that history is hardly the focus of *Mrs. Dalloway*, and stands to the side of what is central in Clarissa as a literary character. What is central is Septimus, her daemon, the vulnerable or Shelleyan genius that in itself is hallucinatory, but in Clarissa hovers always as a visionary apprehension just off to the side from madness. What saves her from madness is her image of a central self, crystalline and diamond, the Paterian image of an ascetic aestheticism as familiar to us from Wallace Stevens as it is from Virginia Woolf.

The narrative of the movement from Protestant self to the ascetic version of an aesthetic self is the history of Romanticism, and Clarissa Dalloway embodies much of that history. The cost of confirmation for the Protestant personality is isolation, so that consciousness and communication become antithetical to one another. Suicide is communication; survival is consciousness. Clarissa has chosen consciousness, at a very high price, even as Septimus chooses communication. One feels the suffering in Clarissa's asceticism of the spirit at her party:

> And yet for her own part, it was too much of an effort. She was not enjoying it. It was too much like being—just anybody, standing there; anybody could do it; yet this anybody she did a little admire, couldn't help feeling that she had, anyhow, made this happen, that it marked a stage, this post that she felt herself to have become, for oddly enough she had quite forgotten what she looked like, but felt herself a stake driven in at the top of her stairs ...

Her consciousness is precisely awareness of her own isolation, which is why Septimus's suicide is a kind of vigorous atonement for her. Woolf's only alternative to Septimus's death would have been Clarissa's, and one remembers the awesome, protracted dying of Clarissa Harlowe. But the first, greater Clarissa dies as a kind of Protestant saint, since God is the third major presence of Richardson's novel, together with Lovelace and Clarissa. Woolf's Clarissa is belated, and is representative of a Protestant will that is post-Christian, and little short of desperate:

> A thing there was that mattered; a thing, wreathed about with chatter, defaced, obscured in her own life, let drop every day in corruption, lies, chatter. This he had preserved.

The strongest mark of this desperation is that Clarissa, elegizing Septimus, has no name for the inviolate, isolate will except "a thing." Woolf's genius dared to risk an essentially inarticulate Clarissa, very different from Richardson's eloquent heroine, or the bearers of the tradition in Jane Austen, George Eliot, Henry James, and Woolf's friend, E. M. Forster. Would we find Clarissa Dalloway other than quite ordinary if she ever ceased to provoke terror and ecstacy in Peter Walsh? Woolf will not give us an opportunity to ask so awkward a question. This is *my* Clarissa, Woolf in effect tells us, implying that this is as good a Clarissa as Woolf's London can afford her.

Walter Pater did not believe, with Nietzsche, that we possessed art in order not to perish of the truth. The truth, for Pater, was perception and sensation, and art alone, for Pater, held the truth for more than an interval. Perception and sensation alone scarcely can make up a novel, but *Mrs. Dalloway* is almost able to rely upon them alone. A contrast between Joyce's *Ulysses* and *Mrs. Dalloway* shows both the immense effect of Joyce's book upon Woolf's, and the advantages Joyce enjoyed by a naturalism far more comprehensive than sensation and perception. Poldy is complete, as comprehensive as the David of II Samuel or Clarissa Harlowe. Clarissa Dalloway is a complex of images; not just a heap of broken images, but still an articulation of perceptions and sensations. Virginia Woolf's triumph of representation belongs firmly to the Age of Freud. Joyce's Poldy comes out of an older world, where the reduction of the self to drives and defenses was not so pervasive. But we are still in the Age of Freud, where Poldy is archaic, and Clarissa Dalloway remains one of us.

CRITICAL EXTRACTS

VIRGINIA WOOLF

It seems to me possible, perhaps desirable, that I may be the only person in this room who has committed the folly of writing, trying to write, or failing to write, a novel. And when I asked myself, as your invitation to speak to you about modern fiction made me ask myself, what demon whispered in my ear and urged me to my doom, a little figure rose before me—the figure of a man, or of a woman, who said, "My name is Brown. Catch me if you can."

Most novelists have the same experience. Some Brown, Smith, or Jones comes before them and says in the most seductive and charming way in the world, "Come and catch me if you can." And so, led on by this will-o'-the-wisp, they flounder through volume after volume, spending the best years of their lives in the pursuit, and receiving for the most part very little cash in exchange. Few catch the phantom; most have to be content with a scrap of her dress or a wisp of her hair.

My belief that men and women write novels because they are lured on to create some character which has thus imposed itself upon them has the sanction of Mr. Arnold Bennett. In an article from which I will quote he says, "The foundation of good fiction is character-creating and nothing else. . . . Style counts; plot counts; originality of outlook counts. But none of these counts anything like so much as the convincingness of the characters. If the characters are real the novel will have a chance; if they are not, oblivion will be its portion. . . ." And he goes on to draw the conclusion that we have no young novelists of first-rate importance at the present moment, because they are unable to create characters that are real, true, and convincing.

These are the questions that I want with greater boldness than discretion to discuss tonight. I want to make out what we mean when we talk about "character" in fiction; to say something about the question of reality which Mr. Bennett raises;

5

and to suggest some reasons why the younger novelists fail to create characters, if, as Mr. Bennett asserts, it is true that fail they do. This will lead me, I am well aware, to make some very sweeping and some very vague assertions. For the question is an extremely difficult one. Think how little we know about character—think how little we know about art. But, to make a clearance before I begin, I will suggest that we range Edwardians and Georgians into two camps; Mr. Wells, Mr. Bennett, and Mr. Galsworthy I will call the Edwardians; Mr. Forster, Mr. Lawrence, Mr. Strachey, Mr. Joyce, and Mr. Eliot I will call the Georgians. And if I speak in the first person, with intolerable egotism, I will ask you to excuse me. I do not want to attribute to the world at large the opinions of one solitary, ill-informed, and misguided individual.

My first assertion is one that I think you will grant—that every one in this room is a judge of character. Indeed it would be impossible to live for a year without disaster unless one practised character-reading and had some skill in the art. Our marriages, our friendships depend on it; our business largely depends on it; every day questions arise which can only be solved by its help. And now I will hazard a second assertion, which is more disputable perhaps, to the effect that on or about December, 1910, human character changed.

I am not saying that one went out, as one might into a garden, and there saw that a rose had flowered, or that a hen had laid an egg. The change was not sudden and definite like that. But a change there was, nevertheless; and, since one must be arbitrary, let us date it about the year 1910. The first signs of it are recorded in the books of Samuel Butler, in *The Way of All Flesh* in particular; the plays of Bernard Shaw continue to record it. In life one can see the change, if I may use a homely illustration, in the character of one's cook. The Victorian cook lived like a leviathan in the lower depths, formidable, silent, obscure, inscrutable; the Georgian cook is a creature of sunshine and fresh air; in and out of the drawing-room, now to borrow the *Daily Herald,* now to ask advice about a hat. Do you ask for more solemn instances of the power of the human race to change? Read the *Agamemnon,* and see whether, in process of time, your sympathies are not almost entirely with Clytemnestra. Or consider the married life of the Carlyles and bewail the waste, the futility, for him and for her, of the horrible domestic tradition which made it seemly for a woman of genius to spend her time chasing beetles, scouring saucepans, instead of writing books. All human relations have shifted—those between masters and servants, husbands and wives, parents and children. And when human relations change there is at the same time a change in religion, conduct, politics, and literature. Let us agree to place one of these changes about the year 1910.

I have said that people have to acquire a good deal of skill in character-reading if they are to live a single year of life without disaster. But it is the art of the young. In middle age and in old age the art is practised mostly for its uses, and friendships and other adventures and experiments in the art of reading character are seldom made. But novelists differ from the rest of the world because they do not cease to be interested in character when they have learnt enough about it for practical purposes. They go a step further, they feel that there is something permanently interesting in character in itself. When all the practical business of life has been discharged, there is something about people which continues to seem to them of overwhelming importance, in spite of the fact that it has no bearing whatever upon their happiness, comfort, or income. The study of character becomes to them an absorbing pursuit; to impart character an obsession. And this I find it very difficult to explain: what novelists mean when they talk about character, what the impulse is that urges them so powerfully every now and then to embody their view in writing.

So, if you will allow me, instead of analysing and abstracting, I will tell you a simple story which, however pointless, has the merit of being true, of a journey from Richmond to Waterloo, in the hope that I may show you what I mean by character in itself; that you may realize the different aspects it can wear; and the hideous perils that beset you directly you try to describe it in words.

One night some weeks ago, then, I was late for the train and jumped into the first carriage I came to. As I sat down I had the strange and uncomfortable feeling that I was interrupting a conversation between two people who were already sitting there. Not that they were young or happy. Far from it. They were both elderly, the woman over sixty, the man well over forty. They were sitting opposite each other, and the man, who had been leaning over and talking emphatically to judge by his attitude and the flush on his face, sat back and became silent. I had disturbed him, and he was annoyed. The elderly lady, however, whom I will call Mrs. Brown, seemed rather relieved. She was one of those clean, threadbare old ladies whose extreme tidiness—everything buttoned, fastened, tied together, mended and brushed up—suggests more extreme poverty than rags and dirt. There was something pinched about her—a look of suffering, of apprehension, and, in addition, she was extremely small. Her feet, in their clean little boots, scarcely touched the floor. I felt that she had nobody to support her; that she had to make up her mind for herself; that, having been deserted, or left a widow, years ago, she had led an anxious, harried life, bringing up an only son, perhaps, who, as likely as not, was by this time beginning to go to the bad. All this shot through my mind as I sat down, being uncomfortable, like most people, at travelling with fellow passengers unless I have somehow or other accounted for them. Then I looked at the man. He was no relation of Mrs. Brown's I felt sure; he was of a bigger, burlier, less refined type. He was a man of business I imagined, very likely a respectable corn-chandler from the North, dressed in good blue serge with a pocket-knife and a silk handkerchief, and a stout leather bag. Obviously, however, he had an unpleasant business to settle with Mrs. Brown; a secret, perhaps sinister business, which they did not intend to discuss in my presence.

"Yes, the Crofts have had very bad luck with their servants," Mr. Smith (as I will call him) said in a considering way, going back to some earlier topic, with a view to keeping up appearances.

"Ah, poor people," said Mrs. Brown, a trifle condescendingly. "My grandmother had a maid who came when she was fifteen and stayed till she was eighty" (this was said with a kind of hurt and aggressive pride to impress us both perhaps).

"One doesn't often come across that sort of thing nowadays," said Mr. Smith in conciliatory tones.

Then they were silent.

"It's odd they don't start a golf club there—I should have thought one of the young fellows would," said Mr. Smith, for the silence obviously made him uneasy.

Mrs. Brown hardly took the trouble to answer.

"What changes they're making in this part of the world," said Mr. Smith, looking out of the window, and looking furtively at me as he did so.

It was plain, from Mrs. Brown's silence, from the uneasy affability with which Mr. Smith spoke, that he had some power over her which he was exerting disagreeably. It might have been her son's downfall, or some painful episode in her past life, or her daughter's. Perhaps she was going to London to sign some document to make over some property. Obviously against her will she was in Mr. Smith's hands. I was beginning to feel a great deal of pity for her, when she said, suddenly and inconsequently:

"Can you tell me if an oak-tree dies when the leaves have been eaten for two years in succession by caterpillars?"

She spoke quite brightly, and rather precisely, in a cultivated, inquisitive voice.

Mr. Smith was startled, but relieved to have a safe topic of conversation given him. He told her a great deal very quickly about plagues of insects. He told her that he had a brother who kept a fruit farm in Kent. He told her what fruit farmers do every year in Kent, and so on, and so on. While he talked a very odd thing happened. Mrs. Brown took out her little white handkerchief and began to dab her eyes. She was crying. But she went on listening quite composedly to what he was saying, and he went on talking, a little louder, a little angrily, as if he had seen her cry often before; as if it were a painful habit. At last it got on his nerves. He stopped abruptly, looked out of the window, then leant towards her as he had been doing when I got in, and said in a bullying, menacing way, as if he would not stand any more nonsense:

"So about that matter we were discussing. It'll be all right? George will be there on Tuesday?"

"We shan't be late," said Mrs. Brown, gathering herself together with superb dignity.

Mr. Smith said nothing. He got up, buttoned his coat, reached his bag down, and jumped out of the train before it had stopped at Clapham Junction. He had got what he wanted, but he was ashamed of himself; he was glad to get out of the old lady's sight.

Mrs. Brown and I were left alone together. She sat in her corner opposite, very clean, very small, rather queer, and suffering intensely. The impression she made was overwhelming. It came pouring out like a draught, like a smell of burning. What was it composed of—that overwhelming and peculiar impression? Myriads of irrelevant and incongruous ideas crowd into one's head on such occasions; one sees the person, one sees Mrs. Brown, in the centre of all sorts of different scenes. I thought of her in a seaside house, among queer ornaments: sea-urchins, models of ships in glass cases. Her husband's medals were on the mantelpiece. She popped in and out of the room, perching on the edges of chairs, picking meals out of saucers, indulging in long, silent stares. The caterpillars and the oak-trees seemed to imply all that. And then, into this fantastic and secluded life, in broke Mr. Smith. I saw him blowing in, so to speak, on a windy day. He banged, he slammed. His dripping umbrella made a pool in the hall. They sat closeted together.

And then Mrs. Brown faced the dreadful revelation. She took her heroic decision. Early, before dawn, she packed her bag and carried it herself to the station. She would not let Smith touch it. She was wounded in her pride, unmoored from her anchorage; she came of gentlefolks who kept servants—but details could wait. The important thing was to realize her character, to steep oneself in her atmosphere. I had no time to explain why I felt it somewhat tragic, heroic, yet with a dash of the flighty and fantastic, before the train stopped, and I watched her disappear, carrying her bag, into the vast blazing station. She looked very small, very tenacious; at once very frail and very heroic. And I have never seen her again, and I shall never know what became of her.

The story ends without any point to it. But I have not told you this anecdote to illustrate either my own ingenuity or the pleasure of travelling from Richmond to Waterloo. What I want you to see in it is this. Here is a character imposing itself upon another person. Here is Mrs. Brown making someone begin almost automatically to write a novel about her. I believe that all novels begin with an old lady in the corner opposite. I believe that all novels, that is to say, deal with character, and that it is to express character—not to preach doctrines, sing songs, or celebrate the glories of the British Empire, that the form of novels, so clumsy, verbose, and undramatic, so rich, elastic, and alive, has been evolved. To express character, I have said; but you will at once reflect that the very widest interpretation can be put upon those words.

⟨. . .⟩ With all his powers of observation, which are marvellous, with all his sympathy and humanity, which are great, Mr. Bennett has never once looked at Mrs. Brown in her corner. There she sits in the corner of the carriage—that carriage which is travelling, not from Richmond to Waterloo, but from one age of English literature to the next, for Mrs. Brown is eternal, Mrs. Brown is human nature, Mrs. Brown changes only on the surface, it is the novelists who get in and out—there she sits and not one of the Edwardian writers has so much as looked at her. They have looked very powerfully, searchingly, and sympathetically out of the window; at factories, at Utopias, even at the decoration and upholstery of the carriage; but never at her, never at life, never at human nature. And so they have developed a technique of novel-writing which suits their purpose; they have made tools and established conventions which do their business. But those tools are not our tools, and that business is not our business. For us those conventions are ruin, those tools are death.

You may well complain of the vagueness of my language. What is a convention, a tool, you may ask, and what do you mean by saying that Mr. Bennett's and Mr. Wells's and Mr. Galsworthy's conventions are the wrong conventions for the Georgian's? The question is difficult: I will attempt a short cut. A convention in writing is not much different from a convention in manners. Both in life and in literature it is necessary to have some means of bridging the gulf between the hostess and her unknown guest on the one hand, the writer and his unknown reader on the other. The hostess bethinks her of the weather, for generations of hostesses have established the fact that this is a subject of universal interest in which we all believe. She begins by saying that we are having a wretched May, and, having thus got into touch with her unknown guest, proceeds to matters of greater interest. So it is in literature. The writer must get into touch with his reader by putting before him something which he recognizes, which therefore stimulates his imagination, and makes him willing to co-operate in the far more difficult business of intimacy. And it is of the highest importance that this common meeting-place should be reached easily, almost instinctively, in the dark, with one's eyes shut. Here is Mr. Bennett making use of this common ground ⟨. . .⟩ The problem before him was to make us believe in the reality of Hilda Lessways. So he began, being an Edwardian, by describing accurately and minutely the sort of house Hilda lived in, and the sort of house she saw from the window. House property was the common ground from which the Edwardians found it easy to proceed to intimacy. Indirect as it seems to us, the convention worked admirably, and thousands of Hilda Lessways were launched upon the world by this means. For that age and generation, the convention was a good one.

⟨. . .⟩ I am not going to deny that Mr. Bennett has some reason when he complains that our Georgian writers are unable to make us believe that our characters are real. I am forced to agree that they do not pour out three immortal masterpieces with Victorian regularity every autumn. But, instead of being gloomy, I am sanguine. For this state of things is, I think, inevitable whenever from hoar old age or callow youth the convention ceases to be a means of communication between writer and reader, and becomes instead an obstacle and an impediment. At the present moment we are suffering, not from decay, but from having no code of manners which writers and readers accept as a prelude to the more exciting intercourse of friendship. The literary convention of the time is so artificial—you have to talk about the weather and nothing but the weather throughout the entire visit—that, naturally, the feeble are tempted to outrage, and the strong are led to destroy the very foundations and rules of literary society. Signs of this are everywhere apparent. Grammar is violated; syntax disintegrated; as a boy staying with an aunt for the week-end rolls in the geranium bed out of sheer desperation as the solemnities of the sabbath wear on. The more adult writers do not, of course, indulge in such wanton exhibitions of spleen. Their sincerity is desperate, and their courage tremendous; it is only that they do not know which to use, a fork or their fingers. 〈. . .〉

For these reasons, then, we must reconcile ourselves to a season of failures and fragments. We must reflect that where so much strength is spent on finding a way of telling the truth, the truth itself is bound to reach us in rather an exhausted and chaotic condition. Ulysses, Queen Victoria, Mr. Prufrock—to give Mrs. Brown some of the names she has made famous lately—is a little pale and dishevelled by the time her rescuers reach her. And it is the sound of their axes that we hear—a vigorous and stimulating sound in my ears—unless of course you wish to sleep, when, in the bounty of his concern, Providence has provided a host of writers anxious and able to satisfy your needs.

—VIRGINIA WOOLF, "Mr. Bennett and Mrs. Brown" [1924], *The Captain's Death Bed and Other Essays* (New York: Harcourt, Brace, 1950), pp. 94–102, 109–11, 115–17

VIRGINIA WOOLF

No, Lytton does not like Mrs Dalloway, &, what is odd, I like him all the better for saying so, & don't much mind. What he says is that there is a discordancy between the ornament (extremely beautiful) & what happens (rather ordinary—or unimportant). This is caused he thinks by some discrepancy in Clarissa herself; he thinks she is disagreeable & limited, but that I alternatively laugh at her, & cover her, very remarkably, with myself. So that I think as a whole, the book does not ring solid; yet, he says, it is a whole; & he says sometimes the writing is of extreme beauty. What can one call it but genius? he said! Coming when, one never can tell. Fuller of genius, he said than anything I had done. Perhaps, he said, you have not yet mastered your method. You should take something wilder & more fantastic, a frame work that admits of anything, like Tristram Shandy. But then I should lose touch with emotions, I said. Yes, he agreed, there must be reality for you to start from. Heaven knows how you're to do it. But he thought me at the beginning, not at the end. And he said the C.R. 〈*The Common Reader*〉 was divine, a classic; Mrs D. being, I fear, a flawed stone. This is very personal, he said & old fashioned perhaps; yet I think there is some truth in it. For I remember the night at Rodmell when I decided to give it up, because I found Clarissa in some way tinselly. Then I invented her memories. But I think some distaste for her persisted. Yet, again, that was true to my feeling for Kitty 〈Maxse〉, & one must dislike people in art without its mattering, unless indeed it is true that certain characters detract from the importance of what happens to them.

—VIRGINIA WOOLF, *Diary* (June 18, 1925), *The Diary of Virginia Woolf,* ed. Anne Olivier Bell and Andrew McNeillie (New York: Harcourt Brace Jovanovich, 1980), Volume 3, p. 32

ELIZABETH A. DREW

In a recently published essay on the technique of novel-writing, "Mr. Bennett and Mrs. Brown," Virginia Woolf throws down a challenge to the "Edwardian" novelists, and declares the arrival of a new age in England, the neo-Georgian. She explains that the same experience inspires novelists in all ages.

> Some [Mrs.] Brown, Smith or Jones comes before them, and says in the most seductive and charming way in the world, "Come and catch me if you can." And so, led on by this will o' the wisp, they flounder through volume after volume.... Few catch the phantom; most have to be content with a scrap of her dress or a wisp of her hair.

Mrs. Woolf then declares that the Edwardians (Bennett, Wells, and Galsworthy) never look directly at human nature—always at its surroundings; that their one idea has been to interpret character through environment, an idea which necessitates failure, since "novels are in the first place about people and only in the second place about the houses they live in." The Georgians, therefore, have felt that they simply cannot let "Mrs. Brown" be interpreted through environment any more, but that she must be rescued and expressed by some way which makes her more living and more real.

The Georgians, then, on their own showing, are aiming at the same thing as their predecessors—the creation of complete human character. They have no obscure and enigmatical goal which the average reader cannot understand, and they themselves challenge comparison with the older generation in the same field and on the same terms. On equal terms means, of course, that the critic must accustom himself to whatever is unfamiliar in their methods; must be receptive towards a new line of vision, and eager to recognize an extension of his own human and artistic experience through contact with a new human and artistic creation. On these terms, then, let us consider some of Mrs. Brown's new champions and their achievements.

Mr. D. H. Lawrence cannot really be introduced into the discussion, because his recent pursuit of raw vitality in the place of what the normal person means by personality, excludes any attempt at presenting "Mrs. Brown." *Ulysses,* too, must be left out of account, simply because it is impossible to criticize that book as a novel to the average reader of novels. If its aim, scope, and method are as profoundly and gigantically intellectual and emotional as its admirers claim, it requires to comprehend it a profundity of intelligence and sensibility which very few of us can hope to possess, and merely to criticize details—such as the complete success of the character of Bloom—must appear to its devotees as much of an impertinence as to praise the dramatic excellence of that old Babylonian creation myth to a Fundamentalist. Of the method of creating character and interpreting life invented by Dorothy Richardson, that method by which we never pass out of the realm of one person's immediate experience, and one person's consciousness is the standard of reference for the whole of existence, I have already said something in a previous chapter. Virginia Woolf herself pushes "the stream of consciousness" method further still. She gives it far more suppleness and dramatic force by not limiting it to a single individual, and her experiments stand at present as the most complete achievements in giving artistic form to the Georgian vision of "Mrs. Brown." In her latest books, *Jacob's Room* and *Mrs. Dalloway*, she illustrates methods of suggesting action and personality, atmosphere and experience which are original in fiction. They are, as is natural, the antithesis of the method by which people are described through a description of the houses they live in. No place that Jacob lives in is ever described: he is built up wholly out of suggestion and implication and fleeting glimpses mirrored in the eyes and remembrance of all who come in contact with him. He lives because he is present in the consciousness of the people who see him in the street, or sit near him in the British Museum, or on the top of a bus: of the charwoman who "does" for his friend, of the don whom he lunches with on Sunday at Cambridge, of the painter he talked to in Paris, of the chambermaid who dusted his room in a Greek hotel. We feel him because he is implicated in the episode of Mrs. Flanders losing her garnet brooch on the hilltop, and of the girl leaving her umbrella in the tea-shop, and trying to read *Tom Jones* and being late for an appointment with her lover. On just such a fine-spun thread of connection and significance is his reality sustained; his portrait stippled in with a thousand subdued touches, in a pose with his full face turned away from the reader. The form and scope of *Mrs. Dalloway* is original and different in yet another mode. It seems to spring from a moment of pregnant vision into the strangeness of life, such as the heroine of Stella Benson's *Pipers and a Dancer* has at a tea party.

> Ipsie, looking at her three friends, was conscious all at once of the little occasion as a queer junction of lives. Trailing their innumerable threads behind them, the four faced one another mysteriously. The threads behind them, joining at the tea table, spread outwards in a net over half the world, secret threads into lost lives, lost places and stories, days and delights and disasters. She imagined their four lives like a map of trade routes, their lines converging to a knot.

In Mrs. Woolf's book, the knot is one day, during whose course the fates of several flimsily related characters blend, and are made intelligible to the reader by a very sensitive "feeling backwards" along those secret threads into the past of each. Again, there is no direct statement, but this time it is the pattering drops of all the thoughts and impressions as they shower down on the mind of the various personalities, their spoken and unspoken comments on each other, which construct their outlines. But one must confess that the outlines are a little wavering and misty. Can it be that the houses which people live in do tell us more about them than Mrs. Woolf thinks, tell us something which makes us know, with a sure and satisfying knowledge, the personalities of the Baines sisters and Edwin Clayhanger and Jolyon Forsyte and Babbitt? It is obvious, of course, that the use of environment may be purely artificial and external—as it is, for instance, in Hugh Walpole's *The Old Ladies*—or it may be a mere laborious transcription of the insignificant as it so often is in the work of Theodore Dreiser; but it is the abuse, not the use, of the method which produces failure. It is necessary, of course, constantly to remind ourselves that criticism depends on collaboration between reader and writer. The artist uses his own temperament, experience, and sense of form to achieve the effect he holds in his mind, and whether that effect is conveyed or not conveyed to the reader depends largely on the temperament, experience, and sense of form of that reader. It may, therefore, simply be that we have not so spiritual a sense of life as Mrs. Woolf, and that we cannot apprehend life in any completeness when it is presented to us so immaterially. But the fact remains that we cannot. It is not merely that there is no plot in these novels: we quite agree with Mrs. Woolf that "life is not a series of gig lamps symmetrically arranged; life is a luminous halo, a semi-transparent envelope surrounding us from the beginning of consciousness to the end," but life is nevertheless made manifest to us by the colouring of personality which stains that halo, and that colouring manifests itself to a great extent through externals—through the houses we live in and the clothes we wear and our life day by day with our intimates and with our acquaintance. Surely one of the "essential principles" on which Dr. Johnson insists must be, that human existence is inexorably welded with the surroundings it lives with, and if not actually described, their reality must in some way be unmistakably suggested to the reader, for an impression of the solidity of men and women to appear. Life is not only inner life. Wraithlike humanity inevitably leaves the impression of anaemic humanity. It is noticeable, I think, that the most vivid picture in *Mrs. Dalloway* is that of Miss Kilmer, who is presented unabashed against a firmer background of externals than any other character. The whole of her is there, with her gooseberry-coloured eyes and her mackintosh and all her forty years of ugly, clumsy, shabby spinsterhood: we can feel her in Clarissa's drawing-room, looking at Clarissa's beautiful things, hating Clarissa, feeling cheated, and we can see her in the Army and Navy Stores with Elizabeth, buying a hideous petticoat, eating her tea greedily, or praying self-consciously in Westminster Abbey. But so many of the other figures have, as Mr. Mantilini said of the ladies of fashion, "no demned outline": the writer seems so afraid of suggesting only externals, that they have hardly any externals at all, and we feel rather as if we were trying to construct the plot of a Greek play from nothing but the remarks of the chorus.

This new technique of presenting characters from oblique angles with nothing but the play of glancing lights and shadows upon its half tones, does convey, however, a particular flavour of life on the emotional palate, which is most significant of the present day. It transmits a sense of great intensity to detached moments of experience; it emphasizes the sudden, revealing emotional and intellectual stroke; it probes with searching perception into fugitive and flickering mood, and reminds the reader on every page that as matter is made up of invisible individual electrons, so is experience made up of the silt of unremembered fleeting instants of passing consciousness. It is peculiar in stressing the importance of those individual instants *in themselves* to the almost total neglect of the importance they may have in relation to a general survey of human life—hence the effect of inconsequence which all this kind of writing leaves. Can we interpret this insistence on the "discontinuousness" of experience, as we interpret most of the character-istics, social and literary, of the present-day intelligentsia, by its renunciation of a definite point of view, by its dislike of embodying any activity, cosmic or human, within the bounds of a fixed outline? Is this technique a literary parallel to those painters who attempt to suggest energy by breaking up figures and projecting their parts on to different planes so as to give an impression of movement; who strive to suggest the infinity of design by leaving patterns incomplete; whose ideal is abstract form? The aim of such writers is, presumably, to give an impression of the ceaseless activity of life, while at the same time suggesting the sense of its inconclusive character—its inexorable habit of merely adding day to day instead of building itself into the convenient symmetry of a plot. We are to feel as the heroine of *Streamers Waving* feels: "Circumstances wheel me along like a baby in a perambulator, clutching with ridiculous hands at the lamp posts." This is the emblem of life left by *Jacob's Room* and *Mrs. Dalloway,* and it is accentuated by Mrs. Woolf's repeated emphasis on the irrelevance of the working of the human mind. Over and over again, sometimes with artistic relevance, sometimes surely, without, we find illustrations of how thought will stream from its original source, sweeping the mind far away in the space of a few seconds. An example is the scene of Jacob and Mrs. Wentworth Williams on the Acropolis at night.

> Now the agitation of the air uncovered a racing star. Now it was dark. Now one after another lights were extinguished. Now great towns—Paris—Constantinople—London—were black as strewn rocks. Waterways might be distinguished. In England the trees were heavy in leaf. Here perhaps in some southern wood an old man lit dry ferns and the birds were startled. The sheep coughed; one flower bent slightly towards another. The English sky is softer, milkier than the Eastern. Something gentle has passed into it from the grass-rounded hills, something damp. The salt gale blew in at Betty Flanders's bedroom window, and the widow lady, raising herself slightly on her elbow, sighed like one who realizes, but would fain ward off a little longer—oh, a little longer!—the oppression of eternity.

The craftsmanship of these novels embodies to perfection all the sharp, shifting sense of the disconnection, the irrelevance in the facts and experiences of life, in the emotions and thoughts of man's heart and mind, and the uncontrolled impulses of his unconscious being, on which there is so obvious an emphasis to-day. Its interpretation of this vision of existence is elaborate and striking, but with all its brilliance of workmanship, its sensitive use of word and cadence, its feeling for the shapely structure of language, and the exquisite keenness of its human and intel-

lectual comment and criticism, I wonder if it will ever catch a very solid and substantial "Mrs. Brown" in its delicate cobwebs.

—ELIZABETH A. DREW, "A Note on Technique," *The Modern Novel:
Some Aspects of Contemporary Fiction* (New York: Harcourt, Brace,
1926), pp. 254–62

WYNDHAM LEWIS

Well then, when Mrs. Woolf, the orthodox "idealist," tremulously squares up to the
big beefy brute, Bennett, plainly the very embodiment of commonplace *matter*—it
is, in fact, a rather childish, that is to say an over-simple, encounter. It is a cat and
dog match, right enough: but such "spiritual" values as those invoked upon Mrs.
Woolf's side of the argument, are of a spiritualism which only exists upon that
popular plane, as the complement of hard-and-fast matter. The one value is as
tangible, popular and readily understood by the "plain reader" as the other. I doubt
if, at bottom, it is very much more than a boy and girl quarrel (to change the
metaphor from dog-and-cat). I believe it is just the old incompatability of the eternal
feminine, on the one hand, and the rough footballing "he" principle—the eternal
masculine—on the other. There is nothing more metaphysical about it than that.

"If we tried to formulate our meaning in one word we should say that these
three writers [Wells, Bennett, Galsworthy] are materialists. It is because they are
concerned not with the spirit but with the body that they have disappointed us,"
writes Mrs. Woolf. Is it so simple? Or rather, were we compelled to decide upon
the respective merits of a person, of the same calibre as, say, Bennett, but who was
as delicately mental as he was grossly material, and of Bennett himself, should we
not have to say, that in their respective ways, their masculine and feminine ways,
they were much of a muchness—indeed, *a good match?* The preoccupations of
Mrs. Dalloway are after all not so far removed from the interests of Mr. Bennett's
characters. One is somewhat nearer to "the Palace," the other to the "Pub." But
does not that even suggest a subtle kinship, rather than an irreconcilable
foreignness? ⟨. . .⟩

I must assume that you do not know, or I must recall to your mind, the parable
of Mrs. Brown and Mr. Bennett. Mrs. Woolf tells us, in a skilful little sketch, how she
enters the carriage of a suburban train, and in so doing intrudes unwittingly upon
a rather passionate conversation of two people—one, *very large,* a blustering,
thick-set, middle-aged bully of a *man:* the other, *very small,* a very pathetic, poor
little old lady (not *quite* a lady—"I should doubt if she was an educated woman,"
says Mrs. Woolf—but none the less to be pitied for *that!*). The big bully had
obviously been bullying the weaker vessel: and Mrs. Woolf calls the former Mr.
Smith, the latter Mrs. Brown. As to make conversation before the inquisitive
stranger in the other corner, or else dreaming aloud, the little old woman asks her
vis-à-vis if he could tell her whether, after being the host for two years running of

caterpillars, an oak-tree dies. And while Mr. Smith (who is a shamefaced coward, as are all big bullies come to that) is eagerly replying to this impersonal question, glad to be able to mask beneath an irrelevant stream of words his blackguardly designs upon the defenceless old lady, Mrs. Brown begins, without moving, to let fall tear after tear into her lap. Enraged at this exhibition of weakness on the part of Mrs. Brown (which he probably would refer to as "waterworks" or something brutal of that sort) the big bully, ignoring the presence of a third party, leans forward and asks Mrs. Brown point blank if she will do, yes or no, what he asked her to do just now, and poor Mrs. Brown says yes, she will. At that moment Clapham Junction presents itself, the train stops, and the big bully (probably jolly glad to escape from the eye of public opinion, as represented by Mrs. Woolf we are told—for he had little streaks of decency left perhaps) hurriedly leaves the train.

Now the point of the story is, we are told, that Mrs. Woolf, being born a novelist of course, and this episode occurring apparently before she had written any novels (1910 is the date implied), is in a quandary as to what to do. She would have *liked* to write a novel about Mrs. Brown, she tells us. But how was she to do it? For after all Wells, Galsworthy and Bennett (the only novelists apparently that, true child of her time, she knew about) had not taught her how to do it: the only tools (she apologizes for this professional word) available were those out of the tool-box of this trio. And alas! they were not suitable for the portrayal of Mrs. Brown. So what was poor little she to do?

She then enlarges upon her dilemma—which she tells us was also the dilemma of D. H. Lawrence, of E. M. Forster and the rest of the people she recognizes as the makers and shakers of the new-age (*all*, to a man, ruined by the wicked, inappropriate trio—I need not repeat the names).

Finding himself in the same compartment with Mrs. Brown, Wells would have looked out the window, with a blissful faraway Utopian smile on his face. He would have taken no interest in Mrs. Brown. Galsworthy would have written a tract round her: and Bennett would have neglected her "soul" for her patched gloves and stockings.

This was really a terrible situation for a novelist to be in, in 1910: and everything that has happened since, or to be more accurate, that has *not* happened since, is due to the shortcomings of this diabolical trio (but especially, we are led to understand, to the defective pen of the eminent Fivetowner).

And what this has meant for the novelist, it has meant also for the poet, essayist, historian and playwright. *The sins of the fathers shall be visited*—it is the old old story: it is the instinctive outcry of the war-time Sitwells and Sassoons, that it was their fathers and grandfathers who had caused the war—which, as I have been at pains to point out elsewhere (*The Great Blank of the Missing Generation*), is very much neglecting the fact that there were many other and more formidable persons in the world at the same time as the amiable and probably inoffensive old gentlemen who were responsible for this recriminating offspring; and that probably those progenitors of a "sacrificed" generation were just as powerless as their sons, or fathers, to cope with the forces, visible and invisible, which precipitated the World-War—although they no doubt deserve a curse or two, just as we do ourselves, for being so short-sighted, and so ill-equipped for defence, against all the dangers that beset a modern democracy.

What Mrs. Woolf says about the three villains of this highly artificial little piece is perfectly true, as far as it goes: "the difference perhaps is," she writes, "that both Sterne and Jane Austen were interested in things in themselves; in character in itself: in the book in itself." Of course, of course! who would not exclaim: it is not "perhaps" the difference—is as plain as the nose was on Hodge's face. Of course Sterne and Jane Austen were a different kettle of fish, both to Mrs. Woolf's three sparring partners or Aunt Sallies, and to Mrs. Woolf herself.

And then Mrs. Woolf goes on to tell us that we must not expect too much of Messrs. Eliot, Joyce, Lawrence, Forster, or Strachey either. For they all, in their way, were in the same unenviable position. All were boxed up with some Mrs. Brown or other, longing to "bag" the old girl, and yet completely impotent to do so, because no one was there on the spot to show them how, and they could not, poor dears, be expected to do it themselves! Do not complain of *us,* then, she implores her public. Show some pity for such a set of people, born to such a forlorn destiny! You will never get anything out of us except a little good stuff by fits and starts, a sketch or a fragment. Mr. Eliot, for instance, gives you a pretty line—a solitary line. But you have to hold your breath and wait a long time for the next. There are no "Passion flowers at the gate dropping a splendid tear" (cf. *A Room of One's Own*)—not in *our* time. There are just disjointed odds and ends!

"We must reconcile ourselves to a season of failures and fragments. We must reflect that where so much strength is spent on finding a way of telling the truth the truth itself is bound to reach us in rather an exhausted and chaotic condition. Ulysses, Queen Victoria, Mr. Prufrock—to give Mrs. Brown some of the names she has made famous lately—is a little pale and dishevelled by the time her rescuers reach her."

There you have a typical contemporary statement of the position of letters today. Its artificiality is self-evident, if you do no more than consider the words: for *Ulysses,* however else it may have arrived at its destination, was at least not *pale.* But here, doubtless, Mrs. Woolf is merely confusing the becoming pallor, and certain untidiness of some of her own pretty salon pieces with that of Joyce's masterpiece (indeed that masterpiece is implicated and confused with her own pieces in more ways than one, and more palpable than this, but into that it is not necessary to enter here). As to the "strength spent in finding a way," that takes us back to the fable of Mrs. Brown, and the fearful disadvantage under which Mrs. Woolf laboured. Anyone would suppose from what she says that at the time in question Trollope, Jane Austen, Flaubert, Maupassant, Dostoievsky, Turgenev, Tolstoy, etc., etc., etc., etc., were entirely inaccessible to this poor lost "Georgian" would-be novelist: it is as though she, Bennett, Wells and Galsworthy had been the only people in the world at the time, and as if there had been no books but their books, and no land but England.

The further assumption is that, prior to *Prufrock, Ulysses* and Mr. Lytton Strachey's biographies, there had been either (1) no rendering of anything so exclusive and remote as the "soul" of a person: or else (2) that the fact that there was not much "soul" in the work of Mr. Bennett made it very very difficult for Mr. Joyce to write *Ulysses:* and that by the time he had succeeded in some way in banishing Mr. Bennett, he had only strength enough left to concoct a "pale" little "fragment," namely *Ulysses.*

But, again, it is obviously the personal problems of Mrs. Woolf getting mixed up with the problems of Mr. Joyce above all people! For it is quite credible that Clayhanger, astride the island scene—along with his gigantic colleagues, Forsyte and Britling—was a very real problem for the ambitious budding pre-war novelist (especially as she was a little woman, and they were great big burly men—great "bullies" all three, like all the men, confound them!).

But let us at once repudiate, as false and artificial, this account of the contemporary situation in the "Mrs. Brown" fable. Joyce's *Ulysses* may be "a disaster"—a failure—as Mrs. Woolf calls it in her Plain Reader. But it is not a fragment. It is, of its kind, somewhat more robustly "complete" than most of the classical examples of the novel, in our tongue certainly. It is not the half-work in short, "pale" and "disheveled," of a crippled interregnum. Nor is there anything *half-there* about D. H. Lawrence's books. Far from being "pale," they are much too much the reverse.

If you ask: Do you mean then that there is nothing in this view at all, of ours being a period of *Sturm und Drang,* in which new methods are being tried out, and in which the artistic production is in consequence tentative? I reply: There is nothing new in the idea at all, if you mean that the present time differs from any other in being experimental and in seeking new forms: or if you seek to use that argument to account for mediocrity, or smallness of output, or any of the other individual "failures" that occur as a result of the natural inequality of men, and the certain precariousness of the creative instinct—subject, in the case of those oversusceptible to nervous shock, to intermittency of output, and, in extreme cases, to extinction.

Then why, you may enquire, is it an opinion that is so widely held?—Because—I again make answer—the people who have been most influential in literary criticism, for a number of years now, have been interested in the propagation of this account of things—just as the orthodox economists have, consciously or not, from interested motives, maintained in its place the traditional picture—that of superhuman *difficulty*—of some *absolute* obstructing the free circulation of the good things of life.

Those most influential in the literary world, as far as the "highbrow" side of the racket was concerned, have mostly been minor personalities, who were impelled to arrange a sort of bogus "time" to take the place of the real "time"—to bring into being an imaginary "time," small enough and "pale" enough to accommodate their not very robust talents. That has, consistently, been the so-called "Bloomsbury" technique, both in the field of writing and of painting, as I think is now becoming generally recognized. And, needless to say, it has been very much to the disadvantage of any vigorous manifestation in the arts; for anything above the *salon* scale is what this sort of person most dislikes and is at some pains to stifle. And also, necessarily, it brings into being a quite false picture of the true aspect of our scene.

So we have been invited, all of us, to instal ourselves in a very dim Venusberg indeed: but Venus has become an introverted matriarch, brooding over a subterraneous "stream of consciousness"—a feminine phenomenon after all—and we are a pretty sorry set of knights, too, it must be confessed,—at least in Mrs. Woolf's particular version of the affair.

I saw pale kings, and princes too,
Pale warriors, death-pale were they all . . .

It is a myopic humanity, that threads its way in and out of this "unreal city," whose objective obstacles are in theory unsubstantial, but in practice require a delicate negotiation. In our local exponents of this method there is none of the realistic vigour of Mr. Joyce, though often the incidents in the local "masterpieces" are exact and puerile copies of the scenes in his Dublin drama (cf. the Viceroy's progress through Dublin in *Ulysses* with the Queen's progress through London in *Mrs. Dalloway*—the latter is a sort of undergraduate imitation of the former, winding up with a smoke-writing in the sky, a pathetic "crib" of the firework display and the rocket that is the culmination of Mr. Bloom's beach-ecstasy). But to appreciate the sort of fashionable dimness to which I am referring, let us turn for a moment to Mrs. Woolf, where she is apeeping in the half-light:

"She had reached the park gates. She stood for a moment, looking at the omnibuses in Piccadilly." She should really have written *peeping* at the omnibuses in Piccadilly!—for "She would not say of anyone in the world now that they were this or were that. She felt very young: at the same time unspeakably aged. She sliced like a knife through everything: at the same time was outside, looking on. She had a perpetual sense as she watched the taxicabs, of being out, out, far out to sea and alone; she always had the feeling that it was very, very dangerous to live even one day." To live *outside*, of course that means. Outside it is terribly *dangerous*—in that great and coarse Without, where all the he-men and he-girls "live-dangerously" with a brutal insensibility to all the *risks* that they run, forever in the public places. But this *dangerousness* does, after all, make it all very *thrilling*, when peeped-out at, from the security of the private mind: "and yet to her it was absolutely absorbing; all this, the cabs passing."

Those are the half-lighted places of the mind—in which, quivering with a timid excitement, this sort of intelligence shrinks, thrilled to the marrow, at all the wild goings-on! A little old-maidish, are the Prousts and sub-Prousts I think. And when two old maids—or a company of old maids—shrink and cluster together, they titter in each other's ears and delicately tee-hee, pointing out to each other the red-blood antics of this or that upstanding figure, treading the perilous Without. That was the manner in which the late Lytton Strachey lived—peeping more into the past than into the present, it is true, and it is that of most of those associated with him. And—minus the shrinking and tittering, and with a commendable habit of standing, half-concealed, but alone—it was the way of life of Marcel Proust.

But it has also, in one degree or another, been the way of life of many a recent figure in our literature—as in the case of Marius the Epicurean, "made easy by his natural Epicureanism ... prompting him to conceive of himself as but the passive spectator of the world around him." Some, not content with retreating into the ambulatories of their inner consciousness, will instal there a sort of private oratory. From this fate "the fleshly school" of the last century was saved, not much to its credit certainly, by the pagan impulses which still lingered in Europe. And it became ultimately the "art-for-art's-sake" cult of the Naughty Nineties. Walter Pater was, of course, the fountain-head of that cult. And he shows us his hero, Marius—escaping from that particular trap, waiting upon the introverted—in the following passage:

> At this time, by his poetic and inward temper, he might have fallen a prey to the enervating mysticism, then in wait for ardent souls in many a melodramatic revival of old religion or theosophy. From all this, fascinating as it might actually be to one side of his character, he was kept by a genuine virility there, effective in him, among other results, as a hatred of what was theatrical, and the instinctive recognition that in vigorous intelligence, after all, divinity was mostly likely to be found a resident.

That is, from the horse's mouth, the rationale of the non-religious, untheo-sophic, pleasure-cult, of which—in that ninetyish pocket at the end of the nineteenth century, in full, more than Stracheyish, reaction against Victorian manners—Oscar Wilde was the high-priest. And there is, of course, a very much closer connection than people suppose between the aesthetic movement presided over by Oscar Wilde, and that presided over in the first post-war decade by Mrs. Woolf and Miss Sitwell. (Miss Sitwell has recently been rather overshadowed by Mrs. Woolf, but she once played an equally important part—if it can be called important—in these events.) It has been with considerable shaking in my shoes, and a feeling of treading upon a carpet of eggs, that I have taken the cow by the horns in this chapter, and broached the subject of the part that the feminine mind has played—and minds as well, deeply feminized, not technically on the distaff side—in the erection of our present criteria.

—WYNDHAM LEWIS, "Virginia Woolf: 'Mind' and 'Matter' on the Plane of a Literary Controversy," *Men without Art* [1934] (Santa Rosa, CA: Black Sparrow Press, 1987), pp. 133–40

DOROTHY M. HOARE

Mrs. Dalloway represents the first complete triumph of technique—in its way it is very near perfection. In it Virginia Woolf is not so much at the mercy of urgent associations which clamour to be expressed at the expense of proportion. Behind the figure of Clarissa, who is the central point of radiation, the background is gradually filled in—the sounds and sights of her familiar London—the slow mellow booming of Big Ben, the crisp air of Bond Street on a fresh summer morning, the rustle of children in the parks, the good-humoured bustle of the town as the buses begin to swing up and the traffic becomes heavy. Richard Dalloway, Clarissa, Peter, move against this background; and because they are people with memories it shifts and changes momentarily with their swaying thoughts. Nowhere in her work is there a better example of the co-ordination of time and place than in this book. Within the twelve hours of a waking day and in the limits of London we have been shown, by their own physical movements in a confined space and their mental movements in a comparatively unlimited field, three full-length portraits and an agonizingly accurate and piercing analysis of the state of mind which borders on lunacy. The contrast between Clarissa's world and that of Septimus is not fortuitous. By it Virginia Woolf achieves the same kind of impression of relativity as had been strikingly outlined in *Jacob's Room* (Fanny Elmer, Clara Durrant, Florinda revealed successively in a series of illuminating flashes). People and occurrences at different levels touch each other slightly, as the ripple cast by a stone in water trembles into the arc of another, and is vaguely disturbed.

Perhaps one quotation will serve to bring out the striking way in which one event is made as it were to focus all that is going on outside it—an achievement in effect similar but more subtle than that attained by Katherine Mansfield in the most exquisite of her short stories. The passage comes when Mrs. Dalloway is sitting in her drawing-room delicately mending her frock for the party:

> Quiet descended upon her, calm, content, as her needle, drawing the silk smoothly to its gentle pause, collected the green folds together and attached them, very lightly, to the belt. So on a summer's day waves collect, overbalance and fall; collect and fall; and the whole world seems to be saying "that is all" more and more ponderously, until even the heart in the body which lies in the sun on the beach says too, that is all. Fear no more, says the heart, committing its burden to some sea, which sighs collectively for all sorrows, and renews, begins, collects, lets fall. And the body alone listens to the passing bee; the wave breaking; the dog barking, far away barking and barking.

The rhythm of life has somehow managed to creep into the rhythm of that passage.

The close of *Mrs. Dalloway* is a masterpiece of technical excellence, the final appearance of Clarissa to those who love her being almost a symbol of the reason for the book's existence. Yet, if one is to criticize it fully, *Mrs. Dalloway* is not

Virginia Woolf's highest accomplishment nor her most important work. The reason for this is that there is in it (unconsciously as far as the author is concerned) an unresolved contradiction in values. The passages which are meant to have most importance are those dealing with Clarissa and her world. The parts about Septimus, one suspects, were put in almost purely for the sake of contrast—in order to throw up the brightness and sparkle of Mrs. Dalloway's world, and also of course to reveal the general truth that brightness and shadow are co-existent. But by some curious and unintended process, the shadow of Septimus affects our attitude to the rest of the book, and finally makes us doubt the value of the other world so delicately displayed before us—in fact the charge against the non-Septimian parts of a book which contains Septimus, is that they are almost too well done for what they represent.

—DOROTHY M. HOARE, "Virginia Woolf," *Some Studies in the Modern Novel* (London: Chatto & Windus, 1938), pp. 50–53

N. ELIZABETH MONROE

The bent of Mrs. Woolf's genius became apparent very early. She is interested in experimenting with the form and substance of fiction, not to escape the demands of tradition or to compensate for lack of tradition but in order to describe character completely. She criticizes Bennett, Galsworthy, and Wells for their limited and materialistic descriptions of man. They confine their observations to man's material surroundings and apply a meticulous art to trivial subjects. Bennett, in particular, describes his characters through their environments, recording a multiplicity of realistic details that are assumed to add up to the truth about human life. To Virginia Woolf the truth about human life is at best relative. It is to be approached through intuition and involuntary associations and is to be suggested through images and symbols rather than directly described.

In a sense Mrs. Woolf's criticism of her contemporaries is a criticism of the classical attitude toward life, which the realistic novel has simply adapted to its own purpose. Aristotle recognized humanity in the abstract—a definite knowable humanness—and the possibility of arriving at exact knowledge through long observation. Nineteenth-century realists paid little heed to humanity in the abstract but transferred the Aristotelian method of observation to a new and lower level than their forbears had used. Mrs. Woolf's rejection of the old certainties is of the same kind. She has transferred the field of observation from the outside world to the inside, and, in spite of her belief that nothing can ever really be known, her whole work is based on the assumption that the truth about mental states can be known.

Mrs. Woolf is concerned with two experiments—one with character, the other with time. She does not trace the stream of consciousness as an end in itself, as some of her imitators have done, but in order to illuminate the inner recesses of character and to show the disparity between clock time and time as it is recorded on the mind. In *Jacob's Room,* the first novel to depart radically from traditional modes, she employs a cinematographic technique to portray Jacob. We catch glimpses of Jacob playing on the beach, lounging in his rooms at Cambridge, looking at the Parthenon, falling in love; we see him through the eyes of his mother, his tutor, an old lady riding in his compartment to Cambridge. Time is deciphered on the tablets of Jacob's mind, and place is restricted to an extension of his personality into various environments.

While these scenes and impressions are vivid—almost too vivid—Jacob never emerges as a complete personality. There is something arbitrary about the way details are chosen, and there is no point of reference in Jacob or his room to draw the varied aspects of his life together. Jacob's room is meant to be the integrating principle but fails as a symbol because it does not correspond to a known reality.

Mrs. Dalloway employs a more delicate and complicated technique than *Jacob's Room* and for that reason and others is more successful in its delineation of character. Mrs. Woolf is in complete control of her medium here; she makes a scrupulous pattern of consciousness, which she has explored with subtlety and grace, holding a nice balance between revery and observation and indicating with skill the transition from one person's consciousness to another's and the movement from one place to another. Moreover, time and place are circumscribed, the story covering one day though recapturing a whole lifetime in memory, and the movement in space is limited to London. The integrating principle here becomes Mrs. Dalloway's personality—nothing unrelated to her is allowed to enter the story—and as she is a charming woman of fifty, who has had a varied if not deep experience, she is more complete as a central figure than Jacob, who is hardly grown at the end of his story, and more convincing as a symbol of unity than Jacob's room.

—N. ELIZABETH MONROE, "The Inception of Mrs. Woolf's Art,"
College English 2, No. 3 (December 1940): 218–20

E. M. FORSTER

Mrs. Dalloway has the framework of a London summer's day, down which go spiralling two fates: the fate of the sensitive worldly hostess, and the fate of the sensitive obscure maniac; though they never touch they are closely connected, and at the same moment we lose sight of them both. It is a civilised book, and it was written from personal experience. In her work, as in her private problems, she was always civilised and sane on the subject of madness. She pared the edges off this particular malady, she tied it down to being a malady, and robbed it of the evil magic it has acquired through timid or careless thinking; here is one of the gifts we have to thank her for. ⟨. . .⟩

Now there seem to be two sorts of life in fiction, life on the page, and life eternal. Life on the page she could give; her characters never seem unreal, however slight or fantastic their lineaments, and they can be trusted to behave appropriately. Life eternal she could seldom give; she could seldom so portray a character that it was remembered afterwards on its own account, as Emma is remembered, for instance, or Dorothea Casaubon, or Sophia and Constance in *The Old Wives' Tale.* What wraiths, apart from their context, are the wind-sextet from *The Waves,* or Jacob away from *Jacob's Room!* They speak no more to us or to one another as soon as the page is turned. And this is her great difficulty. Holding on with one hand to poetry, she stretches and stretches to grasp things which are best gained by letting go of poetry. She would not let go, and I think she was quite right, though critics who like a novel to be a novel will disagree. She was quite right to cling to her specific gift, even if this entailed sacrificing something else vital to her art. And she did not always have to sacrifice; Mr. and Mrs. Ramsay do remain with the reader afterwards, and so perhaps do Rachel from *The Voyage Out,* and Clarissa Dalloway.

—E. M. FORSTER, "Virginia Woolf" [1941], *Two Cheers for Democracy*
(New York: Harcourt, Brace, 1951), pp. 247, 250

JOAN BENNETT

Mr. E. M. Forster writes of Virginia Woolf

> she could seldom so portray a character that it was remembered afterwards on its own account, as Emma is remembered, for instance, or Dorothea Casaubon, or Sophia and Constance in *The Old Wives' Tale.*

Nor is Mr. Forster alone in feeling that Virginia Woolf's mature novels fail to provide a gallery of memorable portraits, such as can be derived from the works of other great novelists. However that may be, it is certain that she developed a different method of characterization from theirs, and one that produces a different effect.
⟨. . .⟩ After 1919 the aspects of life in which Virginia Woolf could "believe with conviction" ceased to include the clearly definable human character. The people in her later books frequently express her own unwillingness to circumscribe human beings within the compass of a *character.* Mrs. Dalloway, for instance: "She would not say of anyone in the world now that they were this or that." [*Mrs. Dalloway*] ⟨. . .⟩
From the conviction here expressed about the incompleteness of our knowledge of one another; and from the certainty here communicated that our fellow-beings do nevertheless arouse in us profound and valued feelings, springs Virginia Woolf's individual art of creating human beings. The method is cumulative, and it is therefore impossible to isolate from her books a portrait which epitomizes a particular character, either by means of description or dramatization. Nevertheless, it seems to me false to suggest, as Mr. Forster does, that the beings she creates

are less memorable than the persons in other great works of fiction. Mrs. Ramsay, Mrs. Dalloway, Eleanor Pargiter, each of the main personalities in *Between the Acts,* and many others from her books, inhabit the mind of the reader and enlarge the capacity for imaginative sympathy. It is sympathy rather than judgment that she invokes, her personages are apprehended rather than comprehended. Increasingly the writer eliminates herself from her books, the illusion of the all-seeing eye is replaced by the illusion that we are seeing by glimpses, with our own imperfect vision. Far more, however, is set before our eyes in the books than in normal experience. Not only are we given the impression made upon other minds, but also the impressions received and formulated by the divers persons whose lives are interwoven for us and from the pattern of the book. ⟨. . .⟩

Like most novelists, Virginia Woolf can only fully communicate the experience of a limited number of human types. Some great novelists have a wider, some a narrower range than hers. By enriching her technique of character drawing in *Between the Acts,* she was able to extend her range; but in the main, because she focused her vision of human beings upon the indefinable, fluid personality, rather than on the definite and settled *character,* she concentrated upon those kinds of people into whose minds she could most fully enter and through whose eyes she could imagine herself looking out upon the world. For her central characters she limits herself to one large social class, the class of those who have incomes or earn salaries. Around that centre she creates the poor whom Eleanor visits in *The Years,* Mrs. Potter, old, deaf and bedridden, or Mrs. Dempster and other typical Londoners in *Mrs. Dalloway,* and they are often created with the same insight and sureness of touch as the central characters, though with less fullness. Mrs. Dempster has a long monologue, of which the following is a sample:

> For it's been a hard life, thought Mrs. Dempster. What hadn't she given to it? Roses; figure; her feet too. (She drew the knobbed lumps beneath her skirt.)
>
> Roses, she thought sardonically. All trash, m'dear. For really, what with eating, drinking, and mating, the bad days and good, life had been no mere matter of roses, and what was more, let me tell you, Carrie Dempster had no wish to change her lot with any woman's in Kentish Town! . . . [*Mrs. Dalloway*]

And Virginia Woolf creates also those who are in more direct touch with her centre; Mrs. Dalloway's maid Lucy; Crosby, the faithful retainer in *The Years;* the two charwomen in *To the Lighthouse;* the butler, the cook and the villagers in *Between the Acts.* She lives centred, as most people do, in one social sphere and looks outward from it, with sympathy and understanding, but with inevitably diminishing vision, to the spheres outside it.

Like many other novelists, Virginia Woolf also creates a limited range of intellectual and moral types. Jane Austen, for instance, has her intelligent, quick-witted young women, of Elizabeth Bennet's sisterhood, and also those who like Anne Elliot and Fanny Price are more notable for their gentle thoughtfulness; and she has her silly girls and silly women; her vulgarians and her social snobs, both of the climbing and of the condescending, variety. It would be possible also to classify her male characters under some half-dozen heads. Yet she never repeats herself; no individual within the class is mistakable for another. Similarly with Virginia Woolf. There are the disinterested scholars, like Mr. Ramsay, Mr. Hilbery or Edward Pargiter; there are the intellectuals, who cannot fall in love with the other sex, Bonamy in *Jacob's Room,* Neville in *The Waves,* Nicholas in *The Years* and William Dodge in *Between the Acts;* there are the women with a gift for creating harmony, women of exquisite tact and sensibility like Mrs. Ramsay, Mrs. Dalloway and Mrs. Hilbery; and there are those who create works of art, like Lily Briscoe or Miss La Trobe; and those who work for a cause, like Rose Pargiter in *The Years* and Lady Bruton in *Mrs. Dalloway.* These and some few other kinds of person recur in different books; but though they can be roughly classified in this way the individuals within each kind are more unlike than they are like one another. Her range is limited in so far as she sees most clearly, because she sympathises most fully, with men and women who are either sensitive or intelligent or both, and the dimmer wits and, above all, blunter sensibilities are further removed from her centre of vision.

—JOAN BENNETT, "Characters and Human Beings," *Virginia Woolf: Her Art as a Novelist* (New York: Harcourt, Brace, 1945), pp. 24, 29–30, 33, 47–49

EDWARD A. HUNGERFORD

Virginia Woolf did not herself use the term "stream of consciousness" to describe the characteristic style of her best-known novels, *Mrs. Dalloway* and *To the Lighthouse.* If we search her *Diary,* we find a great many allusions to her own style—or styles, for she had, as Ben Ray Redman long ago observed, several styles rather than a single manner to which she constantly returned. The term which she does apply to her method of composition for *Mrs. Dalloway* should consequently be carefully observed.

Mrs. Woolf was writing at her most intensive pace in the summer of 1923 while she had still conceived of *Mrs. Dalloway* as *The Hours.* While thus engaged, she cut down on the amount of literary criticism or reviewing which had been one of the bulwarks of her finances before she achieved fame. And it was during this period of intensive creative activity that she came upon a "discovery" as she terms it in the *Diary.* In the entry for August 30, 1923, she casually inserted this comment: "I have no time to describe my plans. I should say a good deal about *The Hours* and my discovery: how I dig out beautiful caves behind my characters: I think that gives exactly what I want; humanity, humour, depth. The idea is that the caves shall connect and each comes to daylight at the present moment."

Later in the same year she clarified this entry slightly as she discussed her work on "the mad scene in Regent's Park." It is interesting to note that she here credits her real beginning of *Mrs. Dalloway* from August, 1923, though she had worked on it for more than a year previously. And then: "It took me a year's groping to discover what I call my tunnelling process, by which I tell the past by instalments, as I have need of it. This is my prime discovery so far; and the fact that I've been so long finding it proves, I think, how false Percy Lubbock's doctrine is—that you can do this sort of thing consciously."

Her words, "my prime discovery so far," suggest that the metaphorical term, "my tunnelling process," was intended to suggest a style that transcended earlier techniques of fiction—especially her own methods in *The Voyage Out, Night and Day, Jacob's Room,* and the short stories, but also perhaps the experiments of other novelists. Although she had felt moderate success with "Kew Gardens" and "The Mark on the Wall," and then had put her new-found technical experiments into fuller play in *Jacob's Room* (1922), she continued to search for newer ways of conveying her perceptions. Thus to see in the "caves" of past time and the "tunnelling process" merely an indication of the influence of Proust as Frank Baldanza does (*Modern Fiction Studies,* February, 1956), is to miss the point of the uniqueness of her discovery.

Those who wish to distinguish among her several styles and who have found the generic term "stream of consciousness" a mere starting-point would do well to adopt the author's own metaphor, the tunnelling process, as a descriptive term for the style of *Mrs. Dalloway.* Although it is a shorthand term, the metaphor is carefully chosen. The term recurred to Mrs. Woolf at other times and explained much that seemed on the verge of being lost through the inadequacies of language—its general fuzziness—as two of her later utterances will illustrate.

In an introductory "Foreword" to a brief descriptive catalogue of "Recent Paintings by Vanessa Bell" (London, 1930), Mrs. Woolf attempts to explore the psychology of the painter. She finds herself baffled on all sides because she can learn nothing of the artist (who incidentally was her sister)—that is, nothing of the artist's state of mind as she produced the painting. Nothing of the artist's past can be deduced by the spectator. This amusing paradox puzzles the novelist: "Mrs. Bell is as silent as the grave. Her pictures do not betray her. Their reticence is inviolable." Yet Virginia Woolf must explore a step beyond; for their reticence itself presents an intellectual problem. "That is why," she continues, "they intrigue and draw us on; that is why, if it be true that they yield their full meaning only to those who can tunnel their way behind the canvas into masses and passages and relations and values of which we know nothing—if it be true that she is a painter's painter—still her pictures claim us and make us stop. They give us an emotion. They offer a puzzle."

The personal sensibility of those viewers who can "tunnel their way behind the canvas" may be compared to the sensibility of those perceptive readers (or writers) who can tunnel their way behind the printed page. In literary terms, the metaphor might be further extended. The novelist uses a "tunnelling process" which is his technique. This very technique, involving "masses and passages and relations and values [of words, not paint] of which we [the readers] know nothing" may at first seem puzzling. But as Virginia Woolf hoped, the difficult technical labor will sometimes be rewarded: "The idea is that the caves shall connect and each comes to daylight at the present moment." The present moment in *Mrs. Dalloway,* then, is the moment of revelation. It is the moment when Clarissa identifies herself with Septimus Warren Smith and sees that his death is related to her life: "She felt somehow very like him—the young man who had killed himself." And the moment of revelation comes finally to Peter Walsh, filled with extraordinary excitement by the mere fact of seeing Clarissa at the last few moments of her party. By *being,* rather than by acting, Clarissa Dalloway gives Peter his moment of vision. This moment (the present moment, for that novel) had been arrived at only after all the caves, carefully tunnelled out behind the characters in the earlier part of the book, had interconnected. The past relationships, when fully revealed, illuminated the present for Peter Walsh and continue to illuminate that moment for readers today.

In addition to the statement in Mrs. Woolf's "Foreword," where the image of tunnelling behind the canvas of a painting is found, a still more explicit statement concerning the method of "digging out beautiful caves" occurs in an essay which she wrote in 1925 for *The New Republic.* This essay, "Pictures," as later reprinted in *The Moment and Other Essays* (London, 1947), also, significantly, concerns itself with the attitudes and impressions to be gained from looking at modern paintings. Here, furthermore, she discusses her impressions specifically from the standpoint of the novelist's art. The visual image, she says, has for many modern writers (Proust, Hardy, Flaubert, Conrad) stimulated the other senses to creative activity. "The whole scene, however solidly and pictorially built up, is always dominated by an emotion which has nothing to do with the eye. But it is the eye that has fertilised their thought; it is the eye, in Proust above all, that has come to the help of the other senses, combined with them, and produced effects of extreme beauty, and of a subtlety hitherto unknown" (*The Moment,* p. 141).

After this suggestive statement, Mrs. Woolf develops the connected idea which resembles her earlier statement in the *Diary* about her "tunnelling process":

> Here is a scene in a theatre, for example. We have to understand the emotions of a young man for a lady in a box below. With an abundance of images and comparisons we are made to appreciate the forms, the colours, the very fibre and texture of the plush seats and the ladies' dresses and the dullness or glow, sparkle or colour, of the light. At the same time that our senses drink in all this our minds are tunnelling logically and intellectually into the obscurity of the young man's emotions, which as they ramify and modulate and stretch further and further, at last penetrate too far, peter out into such a shred of meaning that we can scarcely follow any more, were it not that suddenly in flash after flash, metaphor after metaphor, the eye lights up that cave of darkness and we are shown the hard tangible material shapes of bodiless thoughts hanging like bats in the primeval darkness where light has never visited them before. (p. 141)

The hints in her *Diary* have here been expanded and clarified still more than, perhaps, was possible for her in 1923. The tunnelling metaphor and the cave metaphor, so obviously inter-related in her understanding of how *Mrs. Dalloway* was being written, now have taken more definite shape. We find several important insights about her style combined in this passage. First, the visual impressions of the young man are given, in as subtle detail as possible, not through narration and description of a conventional sort, but rather through "an abundance of images and comparisons." The quality of the light, its dullness or glow, is important. When the tunnelling begins, it is a logical and intellectual process for getting at the young man's emotions.

But the logical and intellectual analysis after refining to a certain point will at last "penetrate too far, peter out into such a shred of meaning that we can scarcely follow . . ."; and here the poet's art takes over from the novelist's in order to penetrate the unconscious mind of the young man. Is not this process precisely what Mrs. Woolf has used to give us the insane consciousness of Septimus Warren Smith in *Mrs. Dalloway?* Shift the background scenery from the theatre box to Regent's Park, and the explanation fits her method perfectly. As Baldanza has suggested, and as her *Diary* reveals, "her own experience with nervous derangement" enabled her to tunnel behind the facade of objective appearance and to give a convincing picture of the insane consciousness. Unlike Wordsworth's "Idiot Boy," however, Septimus appears to us a far from ludicrous person. His thoughts have "hard tangible material shapes," which hang "like bats in the primeval darkness where light has never visited them before."

—EDWARD A. HUNGERFORD, " 'My Tunnelling Process': The Method of
 Mrs. Dalloway," *Modern Fiction Studies* 3, No. 2 (Summer 1957): 164–67

DAVID DAICHES

The aeration of her style which was one of the many ways in which Mrs. Woolf tried to free herself from the inhibiting features of the traditional novel—an aeration which *Night and Day* showed her to be much in need of, and which is shown in process in *Monday or Tuesday*—was perhaps carried a little too far in *Jacob's Room,* and in her following novel, *Mrs. Dalloway* (1925), there is a successful attempt to redress the balance. By this time the "stream of consciousness" technique had become almost a commonplace in fiction, and the problem was not so much to win freedom to employ it as to find a way of disciplining it. It is one thing to have the relation between your characters' impressions clear in your own mind and quite another to have them objectively clear in the form of the work itself. Virginia Woolf seems to have grappled carefully with the latter problem in *Mrs. Dalloway:* she limits its scope in time and place; her characters are few and their relations to each other clear-cut; impressions and thought processes are assigned clearly to those to whom they belong, even at the risk of losing some immediacy of effect; the time scheme is patterned with extraordinary care; and altogether the novel represents as neat a piece of construction as she has ever achieved. It is therefore an excellent example to take for a more detailed technical analysis.

Just as Joyce in *Ulysses* takes one day in the life of Leopold Bloom and enlarges its implications by patterning its events with sufficient care, so Virginia Woolf takes from morning to evening in the life of Mrs. Dalloway and builds her story through the events of this short time. (Events, of course, include psychological as well as physical happenings.) Being a far shorter and less ambitious work than *Ulysses, Mrs. Dalloway* employs a simpler and more easily analyzable technique. The whole novel is constructed in terms of the two dimensions of space and time. We either stand still in time and are led to contemplate diverse but contemporaneous events in space or we stand still in space and are allowed to move up and down temporally in the consciousness of one individual. If it would not be extravagant to consider personality rather than space as one dimension, with time as the other, we might divide the book quite easily into those sections where time is fluid and personality stable or where personality is fluid and time is stable, and regard this as a careful alternation of the dimensions. So that at one point we are halted at a London street to take a peep into the consciousness of a variety of people who are all on the spot at the same moment in the same place, and at another we are halted within the consciousness of one individual moving up and down in time within the limits of one individual's memory. The two methods might be represented diagrammatically as shown below.

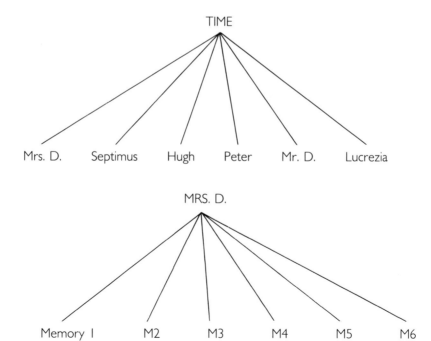

*   *   *

In the first case time is the unifying factor, making, without the knowledge of anyone except the omniscient author, significant patterns out of chance. (But, Is it chance? and What is chance? Mrs. Woolf would ask).

Here personality is the unifying factor, seeking a pattern in time by means of memory. Taking A, B, C, etc., to represent characters, T to represent the present moment (in terms of the action of the novel) and T_1, T_2, T_3, etc., to represent past moments, we might diagrammatically represent the movement of the novel as a whole as shown below.

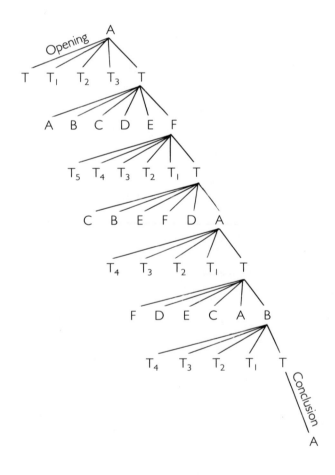

The groups of T's are, of course, different, as being presented through the consciousness of different characters. And the book does not proceed in the straightforward mathematical way indicated by the diagrams; but that is its general movement. The plot is carried forward through the line ATFTATBTA, beginning and ending with the principal character on the day whose action is described. Of course, T in the diagram is not a unique moment of time, but simply any moment of the day in question; actually, T progresses from morning to night through each stage in the diagram. The fact that the line ATFTATBTA, though it represents the carrying-forward of the chronological action (the plot, in the vulgar sense), represents only discrete fragments of thought and action and gives no adequate view of the real story is partly the measure of Mrs. Woolf's deviation from traditional methods in her construction of the story.

It would be simple to go through *Mrs. Dalloway* to show how first we get the "stream of consciousness" of a particular character; then we pause to look over the character's environment and take a glance inside the minds of other characters who are in or relevant to that environment; then we come to rest within the mind of one of those other characters and investigate his consciousness for a while; and then again we emerge to contemplate the environment, etc. And each time we pause to investigate the mind of any one character in some detail, that mind takes us into the past, and we escape altogether from the chronological time sequence of the story. As in *Ulysses,* though on a much smaller scale, the past figures more than the present, even though the action covers one single day.

Mrs. Woolf, although her scope is much more limited than Joyce's, takes much more care than Joyce does to put up signposts. When we are staying still in time and moving rapidly through the minds of various characters, Mrs. Woolf is very careful to mark those points of time, to see to it that the unifying factor which is holding these quite disparate consciousnesses together is made clear to the reader. That is why the clocks of London chime right through the book, from start to finish. When we wander through different personalities, we are kept from straying by the time indications, and, conversely, when we go up and down in time through the memory of one of the characters, we are kept from straying by the constant reminder of the speaker's identity. There is nothing haphazard about the striking of the clocks:

> "The time, Septimus," Rezia repeated. "What is the time?"
> He was talking, he was starting, this man must notice him. He was looking at them.
> "I will tell you the time," said Septimus, very slowly, very drowsily, smiling mysteriously. As he sat smiling at the dead man in the grey suit the quarter struck—the quarter to twelve.
> And that is being young, Peter Walsh thought as he passed them.

We pass from Septimus Smith to Peter Walsh, and the striking of the hour marks the transition. If we are not to lose our way among the various consciousnesses, we must understand why we are taken from one to another: because they impinge in time, and that impingement is symbolized by the striking of the clock. Almost every fifteen minutes is indicated by a clock chiming, or in some other way, throughout the book. We can always find out, at most by looking a page ahead or consulting the previous page, just what time of day it is. And these indications of time are most clearly given when we are about to go from personality to personality—through one of the ABCD rather than the T_1 T_2 T_3 lines.

Similarly, when we pause within the consciousness of one character only to move up and down in time within that consciousness, the identity of the thinker, which this time is the unifying factor, is stressed. The opening paragraphs provide a characteristic example:

> Mrs. Dalloway said she would buy the flowers herself.
>
> For Lucy had her work cut out for her. The doors would be taken off their hinges; Rumpelmayer's men were coming. And then, thought Clarissa Dalloway, what a morning—fresh as if issued to children on a beach.
>
> What a lark! What a plunge! For so it had always seemed to her, when, with a little squeak of the hinges, which she could hear now, she had burst open the French windows and plunged at Bourton into the open air. How fresh, how calm, stiller than this of course, the air was in the early morning; like the flap of a wave; the kiss of a wave; chill and sharp and yet (for a girl of eighteen as she then was) solemn, feeling as she did, standing there at the open window, that something awful was about to happen. . . .

The compromise between reported and direct thought here seems to be due to Mrs. Woolf's desire to keep the unifying factor always present to the reader's mind, but it has some interesting results. The "I" of the reverie becomes an indeterminate kind of pronoun midway between "she" (which it would have been had Mrs. Woolf used the straight objective reporting of the traditional novel) and the first personal pronoun employed naturally by the real "stream of consciousness" writer. It is not suprising to find Mrs. Woolf frequently taking refuge in "one," as in the following very characteristic sentence: "For having lived in Westminster—how many years now? over twenty—one feels even in the midst of the traffic, or waking at night, Clarissa was positive, a particular hush, or solemnity. . . . "

Here the movement is from a suppressed "I" (in the parenthetical clause) to a "one" and then, on account of the necessity of stressing the unifying factor, namely the identity of Clarissa Dalloway, to a straight third-person use of "Clarissa." We might note, too, the frequent use of the present participle (". . .she cried to herself, pushing through the swing doors"; "she thought, waiting to cross," ". . . she asked herself, walking towards Bond Street"), which enables her to identify the thinker and carry her into a new action without interrupting the even flow of the thought stream; and the frequent commencement of a paragraph with "for," the author's conjunction (not the thinker's), whose purpose is to indicate the vague, pseudo-logical connection between the different sections of a reverie.

   The plot in *Mrs. Dalloway* is made to act out the meaning of the reverie in a most interesting manner. As the heroine reflects on the nature of the self and its relation to other people, on the importance of contact and at the same time the necessity of keeping the self inviolable, of the extremes of isolation and domination, other characters in London at the same time—some encountered by and known to Mrs. Dalloway, and others quite unknown to her—illustrate in their behavior, thoughts, relations to each other, and so on, different aspects of these problems. Hugh Whitbread, whom she meets early in her morning shopping, is the perfect social man, handsome, well-bred, "with his little job at Court," who has almost lost his real personality in fulfilling his social function; though, Mrs. Dalloway reflects, he is "not a positive imbecile as Peter made out; not a mere barber's block," there is an element of glossy unreality about him. It is significant that at this stage Peter Walsh should come into Mrs. Dalloway's mind, for Peter (the man she had loved and who had loved her but whom she had refused to marry because he made too many claims on her individuality and wished to dominate her personality with his own) is at the other extreme, the individual who never really adjusts to society; he stands in some ways for the independent and assertive self, all the more vulnerable for its independence. Later on in the novel he turns up at Mrs. Dalloway's (having conveniently just returned from India) and is invited to her party that evening, where he takes his place both as part of the pattern of Mrs. Dalloway's past and as a particular kind of sensibility recording appropriate impressions. The delicate working-out of differing degrees of selfhood and social adjustment can be compared and contrasted with the same sort of thing as it is done by a great novelist working in an assured social world through public symbols. In Jane Austen's *Pride and Prejudice* we are also shown differing degrees of selfhood and of adjustment, but the degrees have moral implications and there is an ideal adjustment in which morality as well as happiness resides. Elizabeth Bennet, who at first depends too impulsively on personal impressions and personal desires, learns to modify her individualism in response to the demands of the social world of other people, while Darcy, who at first leans too much on his place in society, learns to modify his social pride and to trust also the claims of individuality: flanking each of them at the extremes of immoral absurdity is the self-indulgent individualism of Lydia and the preposterous snobbery of Lady Catherine de Bourgh. Such a moral pattern, depending on the belief (shared with her readers) that an ideal adjustment between self and society was both desirable and possible, was unavailable to Virginia Woolf, who sees the problem as psychological rather than as moral.

   Nevertheless there are moral implications, of a much more personal kind, in *Mrs. Dalloway*. Septimus Warren Smith, whose experience in the war has led him to a state of mind in which he cannot respond at all to the reality of the existence of other people, is driven mad by this meaningless isolation of the self, and his madness is exacerbated into suicide by the hearty doctors who insist that all he has to do is to imitate the public gestures of society (eat porridge for breakfast and play golf) and he will become an integrated character again. That this ideal of integration is mechanical and false is made clear by the picture of Lady Bradshaw (the wife of the specialist whose visit drives Septimus to his death) as a creature bullied into nothingness by the public face of her husband. And, even more significantly, Virginia Woolf brings the Bradshaws to Mrs. Dalloway's party that evening, and when Sir William Bradshaw tells her of the young man who had committed suicide that afternoon, Mrs. Dalloway feels a pang of sympathy and understanding for the victim and a revulsion against Sir William. She sees Sir William as "obscurely evil," "extremely polite to women, but capable of some indescribable outrage—forcing your soul, that was it"; and she sees herself for a moment as the doomed young man, associating his death with themes in her own meditations that have already been traced throughout the novel. At the same time as this kind of plot-weaving is going on, we are also shown characters and actions who weave a pattern of the moment and the flux, the self standing like an upright sword amid the waters of the time and the flow of consciousness and the world of other selves. Mrs. Dalloway watches through her window an old lady in the house opposite getting ready for bed, and as she looks at her through glass this becomes a symbol of how we are related to others—through an invisible glass wall (a device used more conspicuously in *To the Lighthouse*). The old lady puts her light out and goes to bed, and contact is lost. Mrs. Dalloway returns to the party, and as she reappears Peter Walsh is seized by "extraordinary excitement." The reality of Mrs. Dalloway's personality, her actual presence at that time and place, suddenly overwhelms him:

> It is Clarissa, he said.
> For there she was.

That is how the novel ends, with the emphasis on identity. But this is not a solution, or a resolution; it is simply a phase of an endless pattern of which the elements are personality, consciousness, time, relationship, and the basic theme, the relation of loneliness to love.

—DAVID DAICHES, "Virginia Woolf," *The Novel and the Modern World* (Chicago: University of Chicago Press, 1939; rev. ed. 1960), pp. 202–12

MORRIS BEJA

The number of moments of vision in *Mrs. Dalloway,* Virginia Woolf's first truly major achievement, is amazing; almost every section (there are no chapters) has at least one, usually more. Everyone, like Peter Walsh, is "a prey to revelations," and like him all the characters are fully conscious of this susceptibility and reflect upon it with an uncanny "power of taking hold of experience, of turning it round, slowly, in the light." Septimus Warren Smith notes his "revelations on the backs of envelopes," and his "sudden thunder-claps of fear" that he has lost the power to feel are what have driven him mad. Less an actual "prey" to them than

Septimus, Elizabeth Dalloway calmly muses upon those moments when the most surprising and trivial objects have the power "to stimulate what lay slumbrous, clumsy, and shy on the mind's sandy floor, to break surface, as a child suddenly stretches its arms; it was just that, perhaps, a sigh, a stretch of the arms, an impulse, a revelation, which has its effects for ever, and then down again it went to the sandy floor." Elizabeth's thoughts are interrupted by her desire to know, "what was the time?—where was a clock?" In the same way Septimus' revelation that beauty and truth are the same and are "made out of ordinary things" is interrupted by Rezia's remark, for they have an appointment, that "it is time." In quiet desperation, Septimus persists:

> The millions lamented; for ages they had sorrowed. He would turn round, he would tell them in a few moments, only a few moments more, of this relief, of this joy, of this astonishing revelation—
> "The time, Septimus," Rezia repeated. "What is the time?"

Septimus is forced to keep the revelation to himself, though eventually his vision seems to be shared with Mrs. Dalloway, and to that extent his essential isolation overcome.

Clarissa Dalloway is the person most sensitive to what she calls her "secret deposit of exquisite moments." In the principal account of moments of vision in this novel, her hidden revelatory experience is cryptically yet unmistakably described as sexual; feeling "like a nun who has left the world," she thinks of how she has never been able to dispel from her personality "a virginity preserved through childbirth which clung to her like a sheet" and because of which she has sometimes failed her husband:

> . . . yet she could not resist sometimes yielding to the charm of a woman, not a girl, of a woman confessing, as to her they often did, some scrape, some folly. And whether it was pity, or their beauty, or that she was older, or some accident—like a faint scent, or a violin next door (so strange is the power of sounds at certain moments), she did undoubtedly then feel what men felt. Only for a moment; but it was enough. It was a sudden revelation, a tinge like a blush which one tried to check and then, as it spread, one yielded to its expansion, and rushed to the farthest verge and there quivered and felt the world come closer, swollen with some astonishing significance, some pressure of rapture, which split its thin skin and gushed and poured with an extraordinary alleviation over the cracks and sores. Then, for that moment, she had seen an illumination; a match burning in a crocus; an inner meaning almost expressed. But the close withdrew; the hard softened. It was over—the moment.

In one sense, Clarissa's revelations of "what men felt" correspond to an experience Virginia Woolf had herself undergone, and which she recorded in *A Room of One's Own*. She had seen a man and a woman get into a taxi and depart together, and the sight, "ordinary enough" in itself, had an extraordinary effect on her imagination (so extraordinary, in fact, that she later used a very similar scene as the climax of *The Years*). As a result of this vision, Mrs. Woolf sketched a view of the soul as a fusion between male and female elements in which one or the other sex predominates. When there is a complete balance, we have the utmost power, and this, she believed, may be what Coleridge meant by saying that the great mind is "androgynous."

In *Mrs. Dalloway,* however, there is a quality to Clarissa's experience that is not simply androgynous, but displays an actual if latent homosexuality. This fact becomes more evident when Clarissa goes on to recall the feeling she used to have many years ago for Sally Seton: "Had not that, after all, been love?" At first Clarissa is unable to recapture her old emotion, but as she removes her hairpins she recalls how once, while doing her hair, she had felt a moment of ecstasy upon realizing that she and Sally were under the same roof. She then remembers another moment, "the most exquisite moment of her whole life," when "Sally stopped; picked a flower; kissed her on the lips. The whole world might have turned upside down! . . . the radiance burnt through, the revelation, the religious feeling!" This incident was innocently cut short by Peter, who was in love with Clarissa; but, fiercely indignant at his interruption, she imagined she could feel "his hostility; his jealousy; his determination to break into their companionship. All this she saw as one sees a landscape in a flash of lightning . . ." In the end, however, it was not her love for Sally that separated Clarissa and Peter, but rather her new and greater love for Richard Dalloway (who, Clarissa tells Rachel in *The Voyage Out,* "gave me all I wanted. He's man and woman as well"). For the rest of the novel, the subject of Clarissa's latent homosexuality is dropped, and the main interest of this very significant passage finally lies in the Proustian way in which the past experience is revived.

Virginia Woolf realized how, in the "perfect rag-bag of odds and ends" of which our memory is the seamstress, "the most ordinary movement in the world . . . may agitate a thousand odd, disconnected fragments" (*Orlando*). Thus Clarissa, by performing such a commonplace act as doing her hair, experiences sensations similar to the ones she had felt many years before, and these sensations lead to a complete recapture of the past—significantly, a past which itself had contained a moment of revelation. It is not only the manner of recapture that is Proustian; so is the use to which the recapture is put, for it starts a flashback that provides us with some very important facts about Clarissa's life.

Flashbacks occur more frequently in *Mrs. Dalloway* than in any of Virginia Woolf's other novels—as might be expected, since one of its major themes is the complexity of the relationship between the present and the past. Indeed, recollections of the past are so frequent that the action of the novel may be regarded as taking place on two different time levels: the present day in London, and the summer at Bourton thirty years before. At the beginning of the novel Clarissa realizes that what she loves is "life; London; this moment of June."

However, she does not live entirely in the present moment, much as she may love it. Throughout the book we are shown her many memories, and in fact only a few pages later she thinks with pleasure of those moments when friends, from whom one may have been parted for years, "came back in the middle of St. James's Park on a fine morning." She does shortly say to herself that anyone can remember, and that "what she loved was this, here, now, in front of her"; but not everyone can remember as vividly as Clarissa Dalloway can. Nevertheless, her feelings about the value of the present moment are sincere; she has an unusual ability to live in both the memory of the past and the here and now.

This characteristic is shared by Peter, who after a number of passages during which he recaptures scenes from the past—"it was extraordinary how vividly it all came back to him"—can still say that life "here, this instant, now . . . was enough." Clarissa and Peter would both prefer to stress the present, but they are in middle age and worried about growing old, so their minds almost involuntarily turn to their youth. "If you are young," Mrs. Woolf writes elsewhere, "the future lies upon the present, like a piece of glass, making it tremble and quiver. If you are old, the past lies upon the present, like a thick glass, making it waver, distorting it" ("The Moment: Summer's Night," in *The Moment and Other Essays*). In *Mrs. Dalloway,* this remark is verified by the fact that most, though not all, of Clarissa's and Peter's moments of vision now recall the past, while the ones they had experienced when young—such as his "sudden revelation" that she would someday marry the stranger, Dalloway—had anticipated the future, just as Elizabeth's do now. An exception is young Septimus, whose disturbed mind cannot forget the war.

Clarissa's fears of old age and her "horror of death" cause her to develop a transcendental theory which allows her to believe that, once having had contact with people or things, we may survive after death in the memories of this or that person, or even haunt certain places—a notion which anticipates *To the Lighthouse* and Mrs. Ramsay's continuing presence after her death. Peter's skeptical refinements on this theory produce fanciful thoughts on immortality that seem based on "retrospective" epiphanies:

> Looking back over that long friendship of almost thirty years her theory worked to this extent. Brief, broken, often painful as their actual meetings had been, what with his absences and interruptions . . . the effect of them on his life was immeasurable. There was a mystery about it. You were given a sharp, acute, uncomfortable grain—the actual meeting; horribly painful as often as not; yet in absence, in the most unlikely places, it would flower out, open, shed its scent, let you touch, taste, look about you, get the whole feel of it and understanding, after years of lying lost. Thus she had come to him; on board ship; in the Himalayas; suggested by the oddest things (so Sally Seton, generous, enthusiastic goose! thought of *him* when she saw blue hydrangeas).

Such grasping at straws for some sort of survival results from Clarissa's and Peter's intense love of life, a love that is even shared by the suicide, Septimus, who immediately before he kills himself decides to "wait till the very last moment. He did not want to die. Life was good."

And perhaps we are meant to feel that Septimus does achieve a strange, vicarious immortality through a union with other people. After his death, the ambulance rushing to the scene is heard by Peter, who experiences a moment "in which things came together; this ambulance; and life and death." That evening, at one of her frequent parties—parties which she gives because "what she liked was simply life"—Clarissa leaves her guests for a few minutes and goes into a little side room; looking out of the window, she is surprised to see the old woman she had seen climbing upstairs earlier in the day now going to bed and staring "straight at her." The scene resembles a previous one: at the window just before Septimus had jumped, "coming down the staircase opposite an old man stopped and stared at him." Clarissa cannot know of this similarity, but as she reflects that death is "an attempt to communicate," that there is "an embrace in death," she sees the old woman and remembers that someone has mentioned that a young man has committed suicide:

> There! the old lady had put out her light! the whole house was dark now with this going on, she repeated, and the words came to her, Fear no more the heat of the sun. She must go back to them. But what an extraordinary night! She felt somehow very like him—the young man who had killed himself. She felt glad that he had done it; thrown it away while they went on living. The clock was striking. The leaden circles dissolved in the air. But she must go back. She must assemble. She must find Sally and Peter. And she came in from the little room.

Although Septimus is dead, the revelation to Clarissa of her identity with him paradoxically emphasizes life and stills her fears of death. As so often in Mrs. Woolf's novels, the climax of the book is an integrating epiphany that brings together many of the important themes and characters; and here it serves the specific purpose of revealing the triumph of life and the value of love, of what Sally despairingly calls "human relationships." As Clarissa deserts the vacant little room and comes into the party among her friends, her symbolic force does not go unnoticed:

> "... What does the brain matter," said Lady Rosseter, getting up, "compared with the heart?"
>
> "I will come," said Peter, but he sat on for a moment. What is this terror? what is this ecstasy? he thought to himself. What is it that fills me with extraordinary excitement?
>
> It is Clarissa, he said.
>
> For there she was.

—MORRIS BEJA, "Virginia Woolf: Matches Struck in the Dark,"
Epiphany in the Modern Novel (Seattle: University of Washington
Press, 1971), pp. 133–39

JEREMY HAWTHORN

Mrs Dalloway said she would buy the flowers herself.

'I will come,' said Peter, but he sat on for a moment. What is this terror? what is this ecstasy? he thought to himself. What is it that fills me with extraordinary excitement?
It is Clarissa, he said.
For there she was.

In between the 'Mrs Dalloway' of the first line of Virginia Woolf's novel, and the 'Clarissa' of the concluding lines of its last page, the reader is led to an awareness of the enormous complexity of the character in question. On a simple level we can say that we move from a view of 'Mrs Dalloway'—the married woman bearing her husband's name and thus seen in terms of her relationship with other people—to 'Clarissa', a person in her own right. But this ignores the fact that the final, extraordinarily striking, view of Clarissa's 'full selfhood' is achieved through the eyes of another person, Peter Walsh. It is also worth noting that although this powerful perception of Clarissa's human distinctness is presented in terms of an epiphany, a sudden illumination, the progression through the tenses (I will come, It is Clarissa, For there she was), suggests that this view of her full selfhood that Peter Walsh obtains is dependent upon a knowledge of Clarissa's existence over time, from the days of his acquaintance with her at Bourton to the contact with her which he knows is to come after her party.

Mrs. Dalloway, I would argue, is an extended investigation of the paradoxes contained implicitly in the opening and closing lines of the novel. Clarissa Dalloway is seen as an individual whose identity varies according to the situation in which she finds herself; at different times, and with different people, she appears to be a different person. And yet 'there she was'. Along with Peter Walsh, the reader feels that in spite of the multiple, even contradictory, aspects of her personality which are revealed to him, Clarissa Dalloway is *there*, distinct, unique. In the pages that follow I want to suggest that there were—and are—particular reasons why this paradoxical nature of human identity should have fascinated Virginia Woolf so much, and that these are connected with the social phenomenon which we call alienation.

We generally assume that although different people may have different, and contradictory, views of us, we ourselves have some conception of the integrity and unity of our own personalities. It is true that different characters (not to mention critics) see Clarissa Dalloway in very different ways. But it is not true that she herself has a clear conception of any well-defined self of which she is possessed. She distinguishes between selves appropriate, it appears, to different social circumstances:

. . . this being Mrs Dalloway; not even Clarissa any more; this being Mrs Richard Dalloway.

and she seems to see within her self aspects of her youth and her maturity which do not necessarily combine to produce a unified or unambiguous identity:

> She would not say of any one in the world now that they were this or were that. She felt very young; at the same time unspeakably aged.

And yet Peter Walsh feels that 'there she was', that he has an insight into her which is somehow complete, which *does* say that she is 'this or that'.

Looking at her own reflection in the mirror, Clarissa sees:

> . . . the delicate pink face of the woman who was that very night to give a party; of Clarissa Dalloway; of herself.
>
> How many million times she had seen her face, and always with the same imperceptible contraction! She pursed her lips when she looked in the glass. It was to give her face point. That was her self—pointed; dart-like; definite. That was her self when some effort, some call on her to be her self, drew the parts together, she alone knew how different, how incompatible and composed so for the world only into one centre, one diamond, one woman who sat in her drawing-room and made a meeting-point . . .

It is worth noting the distinction between 'herself' and 'her self' that this passage presents us with—a distinction, incidentally, obscured in the Penguin edition of *Mrs. Dalloway*, which alters 'her self' to 'herself'. The distinction is important, because although Clarissa seems able to use the term 'herself' without quibble, the term 'her self', which suggests something much more fixed and distinct, is something that she sees as artificial, produced only for other people. It is in fact another person—Peter Walsh—who, at the end of the novel, perceives Clarissa's distinct self. Clarissa, on the other hand, thinks that she is composed of incompatible parts, and the connotations of artificiality brought to mind by the word 'composed' are focused more sharply by the diamond image, calling to mind artificiality and the Philistine display of wealth, as well as a certain hardness not suggestive of the sympathetically human.

The image of the diamond is an ambiguous one, and in its ambiguity we see the central paradox of human personality with which Virginia Woolf is attempting to grapple. Immediately before the 'composing' passage the diamond image is associated with the kiss given to the youthful Clarissa by Sally Seton—a moment of purity and integrity. But the single person that Clarissa 'assembles' on the landing before descending is seen as 'that diamond shape', and here it is an artificiality that seems to be being stressed. Perhaps most striking is a much later description of Lady Bruton, in which certain distinct echoes from the 'composing' passage can be detected. For the sinister Lady Bruton, emigration (her pet obsession), has become an object:

> . . . round which the essence of her soul is daily secreted [and] becomes inevitably prismatic, lustrous, half looking-glass, half precious stone; now carefully hidden in case people should sneer at it; now proudly displayed.

In Lady Bruton we see fully developed those negative aspects of the 'diamond' aspect of Clarissa: hard, self-regarding, artificial and unamenable to real human contact and mutual adaptation.

'Together and Apart' is the title of one of Virginia Woolf's short stories which is concerned with the same central paradox to which I have already made reference in talking about *Mrs. Dalloway*. Virginia Woolf seems to be fascinated by the fact that a human being's distinctness only reveals itself through contact with other people, and can only be fully perceived by another person. We exist simultaneously in terms of but distinct from other people—together with and apart from them. Thus on the one hand Clarissa can feel that Peter Walsh 'made her see herself', and that:

> ... to know her, or any one, one must seek out the people who completed them; even the places ... [and] since our apparitions, the part of us which appears, are so momentary compared with the other, the unseen part of us, which spreads wide, the unseen might survive, be recovered somehow attached to this person or that, or even haunting certain places, after death.

But on the other hand the novel suggests, paradoxically, that human beings are possessed of a central irreducible core of identity, which exists independently of other people. Throughout the novel the words 'self' and 'soul' are used to suggest this irreducible centre.

In her diary Virginia Woolf commented on the 'peculiar repulsiveness of those who dabble their fingers self approvingly in the stuff of others' souls', and in spite of the expressed belief of Clarissa's that to know her one must search out the people who completed her, *Mrs. Dalloway* also insists on the importance of a respect for the privacy of the soul. Sir William Bradshaw wants to dabble his fingers in Septimus's soul: he is introduced, ironically we feel, as one who has 'understanding of the human soul', but Clarissa feels that he is capable of 'forcing your soul'. Miss Kilman's desire to subdue Clarissa's soul and its mockery is likewise seen as an inexcusable desire to intrude into the privacy of another person's inner-self.

Again, we come face to face with a paradox. The soul is private, and must not be 'forced', but it can be destroyed by being made *too* private, by too much protection. We know that Peter Walsh talked to Clarissa about the defects of her soul at Bourton, and he associates the death of her soul with her symbolic rejection of sexuality when she left the table in confusion in response to Sally Seton's 'daring' remark. Sally, on the other hand, feared that the Hughs and the Dalloways and all the other perfect gentlemen would stifle Clarissa's soul. When Dr Holmes bursts into Septimus's room he is involved in a symbolic action similar to Peter Walsh's bursting in on Clarissa; both are guilty, in different ways, of wanting to force the soul of another person. Septimus kills himself rather than surrender the privacy of his soul, and Clarissa rejects Peter Walsh, for:

> ... with Peter everything had to be shared; everything gone into. And it was intolerable, and when it came to that scene in the little garden by the fountain,

she had to break with him or they would have been destroyed, both of them ruined . . .

Yet in attempting to preserve that necessary privacy Clarissa may, the reader suspects, have stifled her own soul. Unlike Peter, who at one point in the novel comes to the conclusion that he no longer needs people, Clarissa needs her privacy to be tempered with human contact:

> She had a sense of comedy that was really exquisite, but she needed people, always people, to bring it out . . .

In cutting herself off from Peter, we feel that she may have cut herself off from a necessary contact with others. Thus when Richard leaves her to lunch with Lady Bruton, she feels of Peter that:

> . . . If I had married him, this gaiety would have been mine all day!
>   It was all over for her. The sheet was stretched and the bed narrow. . . . Richard, Richard! she cried, as a sleeper in the night starts and stretches a hand in the dark for help. Lunching with Lady Bruton, it came back to her. He has left me; I am alone for ever, she thought, folding her hands upon her knee.

A parallel scene to this describes Septimus's feeling of terror at being left alone when Rezia leaves him, immediately before his suicide. Both characters—although on different levels—need other people whilst fearing the threat to their privacy that contact with others involves.

How is such a paradoxical combination of needs to be reconciled? One way of reconciling two contradictory or apparently irreconcilable pressures is to alternate between them. It would appear that in a number of different areas this alternation between irreconcilables presented itself to Virginia Woolf as the most effective solution to various problems. In her essay 'Life and the Novelist', she writes that:

> [The novelist] must expose himself to life . . . But at a certain moment he must leave the company and withdraw, alone . . .

Clarissa, like the novelist, feels the need both to expose herself to life, and to withdraw, alone. Her party is, for her, an exposure, but in the middle of it she feels the need to withdraw alone to the privacy of her room.

Thinking about Clarissa's party, Peter Walsh comes to a conclusion about the nature of the soul:

> For this is the truth about our soul, he thought, our self, who fish-like inhabits deep seas and plies among obscurities threading her way between the boles of giant weeds, over sun-flickered spaces and on and on into gloom, cold, deep, inscrutable; suddenly she shoots to the surface and sports on the wind-wrinkled waves; that is, has a positive need to brush, scrape, kindle herself, gossiping.

⟨. . .⟩ Clarissa leads a life that is full of contradictions, and so her self too is lacking in consistency. Now it is arguable that in *any* social situation men and women will have both public and private lives. What needs to be added to this assertion is that the extent of the privacy that men and women need will vary from situation to situation, and that the existence of contradictions between these different aspects of a single life is by no means universal. To put the argument the other way round, it seems hard to deny that one of the characteristics of capitalist society is that the distinction between public and private lives is magnified, and that there is a qualitative change from a *distinction* to a *contradiction* between the two. Clarissa is forced to be one person in one situation, and another person in a different situation, because there are fundamental contradictions in the society of which she is a part and in the human relationships which constitute it. Any search for the 'real' Clarissa on the part of either the reader, or of a character such as Peter Walsh, is thus doomed to failure. Peter Walsh's Clarissa is different from Richard Dalloway's Clarissa. Clarissa herself would like to 'compose' a unified and consistent self. The question that she has to answer before she does this, however, is the question that is posed explicitly in the novel on a number of occasions: 'to whom?'

—JEREMY HAWTHORN, "Together and Apart," *Virginia Woolf's* Mrs. Dalloway: *A Study in Alienation* (London: Sussex University Press/Chatto & Windus, 1975), pp. 9–17

JUDITH P. SAUNDERS

Like the novel *Mrs. Dalloway* (1925), Virginia Woolf's short story "Mrs. Dalloway in Bond Street" (1923) relies on literary allusion for its central structuring metaphor. However, the most important allusions in the "Bond Street" story are to Shelley's *Adonais* rather than to Shakespeare's *Cymbeline*. The lines from *Adonais* connect Clarissa's meditations on life and death with her conflicts about gender and sexuality. In the course of the story Clarissa arrives at no resolution of these conflicts; she is a woman in retreat from what she sees as all-pervasive female impurity.

Setting out to buy a pair of gloves "above the elbow," Clarissa Dalloway finds her thoughts straying to subjects apparently out of tune with her lighthearted errand. The topics of early death and wasted talent emerge when she begins remembering "dear Jack Stewart," of whom Sir Dighton had remarked, "Oh, the country will never know what it has lost." Almost immediately Clarissa contrasts Jack Stewart's fate with her own, measuring the sudden disappointment of a life cut short against the slower disappointments of a life gradually fading. As she remembers her youth, riding and dancing, a time when "one had conviction," her pity for the dead young man changes to a kind of envy: "Middle age is the devil. People like Jack'll never know that, she thought; for he never once thought of death, never, they said, knew he was dying. And now can never mourn—how did it go?—a head grown grey.... From the contagion of the world's slow stain.... Have drunk their cup a round or two before.... From the contagion of the world's slow stain! She held herself upright." In this passage Clarissa fixes on death as an escape from bodily decay. The lines running brokenly through her mind come chiefly from Stanza 40 of Shelley's *Adonais,* immediately following a major transition in the speaker's attitude. In Stanza 39 he breaks off his laments for the dead Adonais, exclaiming "Peace, peace! he is not dead.... *We* decay...." The sudden recognition of the paradox of process (life is growth, and growth implies decay) exactly parallels Clarissa's train of thought in connection with herself and Jack Stewart, who, like Keats, has been spared the experience of aging. Her musings focus on three sequential lines, which her memory fragments and disorders:

> From the contagion of the world's slow stain
> He is secure, and now can never mourn
> A heart grown cold, a head grown grey in vain.   (Stanza 40)

In choosing the word "mourn," the poet points out that, paradoxically, it is the living who are dying and who must grieve over their own ever-changing condition. The lines offer consolation not so much by hinting that the dead youth has gone to a better world as by emphasizing that he is well out of this one. There is a ring of certainty and comfort in the declaration that now "he is secure." Secure from what?—"the contagion of the world's slow stain." Shelley's remarkable metaphoric description of the on-going process which is life exudes a wearied revulsion. "Contagion" and "stain" suggest the disease and defilement which the dead have happily escaped. Clarissa feels there is also good fortune in being cut off unexpectedly, before the inevitability of one's own death has become evident. That Jack had not had time even to recognize his own mortality ("he never once thought of death") is an added boon.

She indicates that the words "contagion of the world's slow stain" particularly engage her attention, repeating them emphatically before allowing her thoughts to move off in a new direction. In fact, this phrase takes on new metaphoric significance in the context of Woolf's story, for Clarissa has been thinking about menstruation—a peculiarly female mortal "stain." Meeting Hugh Whitbread at the start of her expedition and hearing he has brought his wife up to London to see doctors for "that sort of thing," Clarissa reflects to herself:

> Of course ... Milly is about my age—fifty—fifty-two. So it is probably *that.* Hugh's manner had said so, said it perfectly—dear old Hugh, thought Mrs. Dalloway, remembering with amusement, with gratitude, with emotion, how shy, like a brother—one would rather die than speak to one's brother—Hugh had always been, when he was at Oxford, and came over, and perhaps one of them (drat the thing!) couldn't ride. How then could women sit in Parliament? How could they do things with men? For there is this extraor-

dinarily deep instinct, something inside one; you can't get over it; it's no use trying.

Clarissa's impatience with the monthly interruption of normal activities seems at first low-keyed, even coy, when she exclaims "drat the thing!" and remembers the embarrassing secrecy associated with it ("one would rather die . . ."). But when she goes on to ask, "How then could women sit in Parliament?" her question becomes an outcry against biologically imposed limitations of gender. The monthly period is far more than an embarrassing interruption: it is the source and sign of women's inferiority. "How then could they do things with men?" she asks, clearly pointing to the female sexual cycle as an insurmountable weakness ("you can't get over it"), one preventing rational, adult activity and placing women on a plane of aspiration distinctly below that of men.

Later in the story Clarissa follows up her outburst against female biology with a sudden solicitude for the shop-girl, who trots back and forth to find exactly the right pair of gloves: "The glove hardly came to the elbow. Were there others half an inch longer? Still it seemed tiresome to bother her—perhaps the one day in the month, thought Clarissa, when it's an agony to stand." This purely random guess tells the reader that Clarissa continues to be preoccupied with the subject of menstruation and female weakness. It is a subject connected in her mind, moreover, with that of aging and death. Jack Stewart will "never know" the problems of middle age, but Milly must consult doctors about her menopausal symptoms ("*that*"), and the shop-girl awakens Clarissa's solicitude on two counts, for she appears unaccountably aged: "—but this was not the girl she remembered? She looked quite old. . . . Yes, thought Clarissa, it's the girl I remember, she's twenty years older. . ." Within the space of ten lines, Clarissa moves from noticing the girl's aging ("the shop-girl, who looked ever so much older") to speculation about her possible dysmenorrhea ("perhaps the one day in the month . . ."). The cycle of growth and decay which Shelley names "the contagion of the world's slow stain" identifies itself in Clarissa's mind with the special burdens of the menstrual cycle. This female "stain" epitomizes the defilement which threatens all flesh. Consistently, Clarissa associates menstruation with disability and illness ("contagion"). In her reflections it becomes a symbol of bodily corruption and spiritual contamination.

Menstruation becomes, in fact, a symbol of mortality in the largest sense. The *Adonais* allusions, repeated several times in the course of the story, serve to connect Clarissa's revulsion from the universal "contagion" of life processes with her revulsion from the particular "contagion" of the female sex. To be female, it appears, is to be more than ordinarily subject to disease and disintegration. In *Adonais* the poet suggests that the dead are in a world which is desirable because it is incorruptible—changeless. Thus Clarissa views the monthly changes in her body as an effectual barrier between her and any kind of higher striving. Men, although they must age and die, can still hope to "do things": they "sit in Parliament"; they may work at least for some sort of earthly permanence. Irrevocably marked with earthly stain, sign of intellectual and spiritual impurity, women are debarred from endeavors which Clarissa characterizes chiefly through "Parliament" and books: i.e., history and ideas, power and responsibility, cultural and political tradition. "For all the great things, one must go to the past, she thought. From the contagion of the world's slow stain.... Fear no more the heat o' the sun.... And now can never mourn, can never mourn, she repeated, her eyes straying over the window; for it ran in her head; the test of great poetry; the moderns had never written anything one wanted to read about death, she thought; and turned." The "great things" of the past, preserved primarily by means of art, represent humankind's best attempts to create permanence in a transitory world. Reading great poetry, one can step aside from the rushing pace of life and feel that one need "fear no more" earthly ravages, need "never mourn" the passing of time. But Clarissa can only stand on the fringes of the realm of art and parliament. She has declared women unable to "do things" with men; the "great things" which lend consolation to mortal existence are evidently not theirs to accomplish.

The dirge from *Cymbeline* which Clarissa calls to mind in the passage just quoted with the line "Fear no more the heat o' the sun" suggests, like the lines from *Adonais,* that death offers a respite from the hardships of temporal change. The "heat o' the sun" and the "furious winters rages" point specifically to seasonal extremes which are, of course, cyclical. Instead of taking comfort—like a Wordsworth—in the steady recurrences of earth's diurnal course, Clarissa shrinks from the pattern of ceaseless change. She "fears" the power of the elements and of time, just as she "mourns" the maturation which necessitates decline ("a heart grown cold, a head grown grey"). Her mind fixes on different examples of natural cycles—seasons, generations—cycles which she views as leading nowhere: the head grows grey "in vain": " 'From the contagion of the world's slow stain,' thought Clarissa holding her arm stiff, for there are moments when it seems utterly futile (the glove was drawn off leaving her arm flecked with powder)—simply, one doesn't believe, thought Clarissa, any more in God." In Clarissa's mind menstrual flow is one more example of cyclical futility; she makes no connection between sexuality and regeneration. Trapped in a ceaseless round of temporal corruption, women are more bound to natural cycles than men ("this extraordinarily deep instinct, something inside one; you can't get over it"). Clarissa's preoccupation with age and death is infused with the sad recognition of her own contamination: she, as a woman, has the mark of mortality indubitably upon her.

The theme of female "stain" is reinforced by other details: Clarissa's arm is "flecked" when the glove is removed, and near the end of the story while waiting for the shop-girl she notices her arm once again: "Fear no more the heat o' the sun. Fear no more, she repeated. There were little brown spots on her arm." These "little brown spots"—presumably age spots—result quite literally from a lifetime of exposure to "the heat o' the sun." The gloves she is purchasing will hide this staining of her flesh; in fact, the whole glove-buying expedition reflects her special obligations as a woman to cover up the process of aging in her all too earthly self. For "a lady is known by her gloves and shoes," as she reminds herself at one point.

The action of the story shows Clarissa carefully fulfilling her duties as "lady," even telling herself she is bound on an "errand of happiness" in buying the gloves, but her thoughts return again and again to her feeling of being soiled. Life is reduced to a joyless round of self-effacing duty: "she would go on. But why, if one doesn't believe? For the sake of others, she thought taking the glove in her hand." Taking up the glove here evidently signifies Clarissa's reluctant acceptance of the destiny which her gender has predetermined.

Her attitude of resigned acceptance must be attributed at least in part to her feelings about the war and, in particular, to her mixed feelings about being a survivor. The war is present throughout as an undercurrent in her thoughts: it provides occasion for her meditations on early death and wasted lives. Her life, and the aging shop-girl's life, and Lady Bexborough's life (who "had nothing to live for and the old man is failing and they say she is sick of it all") are possible only because many young men sacrificed theirs. "Dear Jack Stewart" and "that nice boy [who] was killed" are only two of the countless youths who died so that she, Clarissa, might continue to live—and to live precisely in this way. Just after noticing the "little brown spots" on her arm she tells herself firmly, "Thousands of young men had died that things might go on." Her duty is ironically clear: she must grow grey in vain so that those youths might not have died in vain. She must accept her existence, with its spots and stain, as a gift dearly bought. How different her attitude is from that of the Clarissa we know from the novel *Mrs. Dalloway*. In the novel Clarissa rejoices in Septimus' gesture of "throwing away" his life; imaginatively experiencing his death, she achieves, as Professor ⟨Jean M.⟩ Wyatt observes, a "final perception of the unity of life and death." In the "Bond Street" short story, however, Clarissa regards the war deaths as a kind of unasked for ransom, committing her to a life she would otherwise gladly yield up. Because "thousands" of soldiers (young and male) are dead, she (middle-aged and female) is doomed to decay. Clearly the irony of this situation increases the polarity the story sets up between male purity and female corruption.

She looks to the Queen and to Lady Bexborough for models in her duty-bound efforts to "go on." The Queen "went to hospitals, opened bazaars" and this "matters so much to the poor ... and to the soldiers." Lady Bexborough "opened the bazaar, they say, with the telegram in her hand—Roden, her favorite killed," demonstrating the qualities of "character ... something inborn in the race," of "breeding, self-respect" which Clarissa clings to admiringly. She associates herself with this tradition of Empire and class consciousness when she prods herself to "go on" for the sake of the shop-girl, who "would be much more unhappy" if Clarissa should falter in her path. Determinedly she holds herself "upright"—a gesture she unconsciously makes once while reflecting on the character of the English race and the importance of the Queen's bazaar work, and then again when the lines from *Adonais* first drift into her mind. Seeing no way to overcome the disadvantages of gender to which all the women around her have either succumbed or adapted, she resigns herself to a life of wearing gloves and patronizing bazaars.

Superficial attempts at brisk cheerfulness notwithstanding, the predominant mood of "Mrs. Dalloway in Bond Street" is one of futility and resignation. Regarding herself as soiled, weak and unfit, Clarissa concludes that "one doesn't live for oneself," that woman is doomed to the role of spectator in all the grandest of life's enterprises. Despite its clear relationship to *Mrs. Dalloway,* the "Bond Street" story denies the connections between death and life which triumph in the novel. Instead, Clarissa looks to death to free her from the bodily and spiritual degradation of being female. Her revulsion from our common mortality goes hand-in-hand with her rejection of her tainted gender, as she shrinks from sexuality and life processes—"the contagion of the world's slow stain." Providing focus and leitmotif for Clarissa's apparently scattered thoughts, the allusions to *Adonais* serve as organizing metaphor and running refrain in Clarissa's elegy for her living, female self.

—JUDITH P. SAUNDERS, "Mortal Stain: Literary Allusion and Female
Sexuality in 'Mrs. Dalloway in Bond Street,'" *Studies in
Short Fiction* 15, No. 2 (Spring 1978): 139–44

PETER CONRADI

Harry Levin has argued that the history of the novel might usefully be approached as if it were the history of the novel's prevailing myths. These are those recurrent forms around which the novel has accreted its special expertise: the novel arranges its partial imaginative colonization of those societies it inhabits and vivifies around such myths as, for example, the *Femme Incomprise,* whose quest for feminine roles takes her beyond the sexual or familial. One such myth, at the turn of the century, is Pan. The erotic is conceived, for example by Forster and Lawrence, as a threatened if not a lost zone: our last pastoral; and it is significantly embodied in a series of libidinous gypsies, Italian dentists, vernacular speaking gamekeepers, and other "Romantic," outlaw gardengods. The figures are, like Pan himself, always Male. There is a case for arguing that another new form makes its appearance in the English novel around the early twentieth century: for which I suggest the term the "metaphysical hostess." She is related to the *femme incomprise* though it could be argued that she does not really get beyond a hypostatized version of the sexual and familial: the world is her family. In the four great Bloomsbury novels she is the local demi-goddess of the cult of personal relations, the demi-goddess of accommodation and reconciliation. She may not *physically* entertain: Forster's heroines don't. Like Pan she of course goes back to the Romantic Revival and to a view of woman as dangerous but redemptive; or redemptive because dangerous. A demi-goddess has of course a better than average chance of immortality but it is not a sure thing. Two of these heroines die in the first third of the books in which they appear (Mrs. Ramsay in *To the Lighthouse;* Mrs. Wilcox in *Howards End*). Mrs. Moore dies at a later stage of *A Passage to India.* Woolf originally intended Mrs. Dalloway to die at her party. Septimus Warren-Smith who was invented late in the preparatory stages of writing as Mrs. Dalloway's *alter ego* could be seen as dying in her place. Both Forster and Woolf exhibit a rehearsed casualness about physical death which demands explanation. It appears usually in literal or figurative parentheses. After their deaths the first three of these may be seen as playing at least as important a role as they did during their lives.

The appearance of the hostess at this juncture, in the guises that she now takes on, coincides both with the incomplete Victorian emancipation of women and also with a newly crisis-ridden cultural pessimism. This can be seen if we look at the hostess's forbears. For all the scruples that Emma Woodhouse must learn about justly and variously accommodating Mrs. Bates, Harriet, and Mrs. Elton, we don't feel that Highbury, as a working culture, would collapse without Emma herself. In the same way virtue would exist in *Bleak House* in however attenuated a form without Esther Summerson. But the party in *To the Lighthouse* would not have occurred without Mrs. Ramsay and its success is precarious even with her: so diminished, Woolf feels, are the possibilities of comity; and in the necessarily reduced area which those possibilities now inhabit, the compression seems to have given them a more critical and symbolic energy. At the same time, while the novel has always addressed itself to the theme of personal relations, and *Emma* is no exception to this rule, it would be odd indeed to speak of Miss Woodhouse as having a *"cult"* of personal relations. The phrase properly belongs to the later post-theistic world whose devotional energies are, as it were, going spare: the age of substitute religions which, it appears, has now superseded organized Christianity. For the writer such a cult can afford a set or community which may have no other warranty.

The history of the novel is of course much bound up with that of women, and within the Victorian novel's liberal humanist critique of industrial Society the position of women is (implicitly as well as sometimes explicitly) much debated; it may therefore be that women come subconsciously to represent those forces which an overreaching, Faustian and wholly Male hegemony has neglected at its peril. Woman's realm is the realm of a lost Gemeinschaft: she enshrines the lost wholeness of life. Thus, against the cult of business, money, and power, the cult of personal relations. Its rewards and disciplines can offer themselves as a last, separate realm of value; unsponsored, innocent, and difficult: the world of love, intuition, friendship: *and also of power.* For the public and private modes cannot of course stand in a relationship of pure opposition: alienation and reification, if they exist, interpenetrate throughout. So "love" too, as we have already seen, can be a guise of power. But the hostess brings people together in a relation which offers a transcendence of other available modes—pedestrian or hostile—of communication.

In a world betrayed by manufacture, and an overdetermined history, the fictional manufacture of Virtue is bound to *appear* by contrast an especially arcane business. Its etiology will be a lost one. While the nature of the epoch as it was experienced by its writers is a conditioning factor, venerable and Platonic reasons may also here come into play—especially with Bloomsbury who we remember got its neo-Platonism via G. E. Moore. Good, here, is an old mystery. It is autochthonous, gratuitous, endlessly surprising. Thus we have the paradox: with the secularization of the novel-form's theological background comes, as one possible consequence, the importation of the supernatural.

There are further and related paradoxes: the novel's "globalizing" tendencies at the turn of the century may be a sign, in some sense, of a self-consciously incomplete grasp. The decay of society-as-a-whole as a nourishing idea, its recession and fragmentation as a background, lies behind the creation of those portentous and highly symptomatic model societies of, for example, *Howards End* or *Tono-Bungay*. Again, the human person begins increasingly to be both exalted and dwarfed: as in mock-heroic, mock-epic: the preciousness and uniqueness of the individual has to be particularly insisted upon exactly because so little outside the novel any longer supports the idea of this uniqueness: liberalism with both small and large L's is in decline. The business of characters becoming *symbolic* is here integral, and of the highest significance. At the simplest level this is rightly discussed by Woolf and Forster as a symptom of the crisis experienced by the work's aesthetic. That is, there is an attempt to superannuate "character" along with "plot" and the other devices of nineteenth-century Realism, to demote it from its former position of glory as chief vector of the work's meaning; and to locate new, alternative sources of energy within the whole; or rather to see character as one only among many of the ways in which the work "means."

So the "metaphysical hostess" is at once an organizational principle—like Antonia at the centre of a centripetal eddy—and a powerful and often ambivalently portrayed cultural symptom. History is now perceived as a centrifugal force which is meaningless, inhospitable, and fragmented; conducing to a Balkanization of the human spirit. Man (as opposed here to woman) has collaborated. He has created as in *Howards End* the anomic and destructive energy of cities, motorcars, the civilization of luggage and pointless mobility. In *A Passage to India* he has perpetrated the crime of racialism: muddle and false order. And women—the grosser sort—have colluded (Turtons and Burtons). In *To the Lighthouse* the male world has a "fatal sterility," and women stand in ambiguous relation to this sterility. In *Mrs. Dalloway,* that chronicle of social over- and under-adaptation, it is a man, Sir William Bradshaw, who stands for the unimaginable zero stupidity of having totally vanished within his social persona.

But in each of these novels there is also a woman who is presented as suggesting a way—however heavily ironized this way is—and that is often very heavily indeed—in which things *might* be held together or *might* cohere. Why not merely, one might here ask, call these women exemplary (or in the words of the title of a Barbara Pym novel: *Excellent Women*)? Because they do seem very much more *numinous* than that. Each portrait (Mrs. Wilcox, Mrs. Moore, Mrs. Ramsay, Mrs. Dalloway) is a celebration. But what is celebrated is a more-than-earthly power of accommodation and reconciliation: the hostess stands for the life force, dissolving differences. These women exist at a critical point in the symbolic orderings the books make, and at a pitch of difficulty. Mrs. Dalloway is perhaps even by the book's own values a little too worldly; Mrs. Wilcox with Forster's full approval insufficiently so; Mrs. Moore becomes quite blank, before dying and turning into a minor Hindu Goddess; Mrs. Ramsay is not without egoism.

Yet the possibility of transcendence, perhaps the message of all art, is nonetheless here, we feel, the special function of these ladies. They hold together a côterie or set in the case of Mrs. Brookenham in *The Awkward Age* (she is a brilliant, early negative version of the type), a family or two as in the case of Mrs. Wilcox in *Howards End,* high society perhaps in the case of the Duchesse de Guermantes in *A la recherche du temps perdu,* and the bourgeois parody of it under Mme. de Verdurin, a party in town in Mrs. Dalloway's case, a meal at a house-party in the country (Boeuf-en-daube) in the case of Mrs. Ramsay in *To the Lighthouse.* But the hostess may represent more than she actually does: that is to say she may stand for more than her *domestic* self; or the domestic, to argue slightly differently, may itself be more than it seems. History having become the arena of determinisms of various kinds—and this naturally includes personal history—the metaphysical hostess is privy to the ideal world of the author's own incorporeal and essential values. Like Ariadne in J. Hillis Miller's essay, the metaphysical hostess suggests the possibility of a centre to the book-maze of meaning: and as in the case of Miller's Ariadne also, there may be no determinate meaning for her to lead us to. There may be no unity for her to uncover or represent ⟨. . .⟩

Society in *Mrs. Dalloway* is performance which may be both life-enhancing and -destroying; too great an absorption in social role (like Bradshaw), or too brutal a separation from it (Septimus) make each for a different kind of unhealth. Mrs. Dalloway has been ironically deified by her maid Lucy who "handles her parasol as if it were that of a goddess," simultaneously thinking, "How the gentry love!" The dramatic irony this occasions is due to our knowledge that the goddess Mrs. Dalloway at this moment most resembles, if any, is Eris goddess of strife: she is full of pique and hurt vanity at not, unlike her husband, having been invited to Lady Bruton's luncheon party.

When news of Septimus' death reaches her party she thinks, "It was her disaster, her disgrace." His death triggers a painful self-recriminating state of mind in which she sees herself as less than admirable. There is, perhaps, a small death in her own egoism, but Septimus would seem to be that part of the Self which is "taken," herself that part which abides. She physically disappears from the scene and is reincarnated only with her final triumphal entry. She has a psychic theory not unlike that which is a part of the description of Mrs. Wilcox, or attributed to Mrs. Ramsay, a commonplace version of a doctrine of transmigration of souls. It is evoked in a passage whose rhythms are carefully hesitant.

> Odd affinities she had with people she had never spoken to, some woman in the street, some man behind the counter—even trees, or barns. It ended in a transcendental theory which, with her horror of death, allowed her to believe, or say that she believed (for all her scepticism), that since our

apparitions, the part of us which appears, are so momentary compared with the other, the unseen part of us, . . . the unseen might survive, be recovered somehow attached to this person or that, or even haunting certain places, after death. Perhaps—perhaps.

Thus, Mrs. Dalloway as hostess elicits a community deeper than that of the worldly set over which she presides. She is perhaps head of a mystical body.

—PETER CONRADI, "The Metaphysical Hostess: The Cult of Personal Relations in the Modern English Novel," ELH 48, No. 2 (Summer 1981): 432–36, 445–46

JANE MARCUS

As virgin mother, Clarissa lives the life of a nun in her attic room, her narrow white bed. Her "virginity preserved through childbirth" and the memory of her blissful love for Sally make Clarissa a very attractive figure. She may lack "something central which permeated" in her relations with her husband, but she is erotically inflamed by memories of Sally, by Miss Kilman's threat to steal her daughter, and by listening to the confidences of other women. She is the lesbian who marries for safety and appearances, produces a child, cannot relate sexually to her husband, and chooses celibacy within marriage, no sex rather than the kind she wants. Denial of desire is easier than living Miss Kilman's life, she feels.

It is interesting regarding Clarissa's celibate marriage that, in Caroline Stephen's history of sisterhoods, one of the groups studied is the *Clarrisan* nuns, an order of women who were married but signed vows of celibacy with their husbands, lived at home, and were secret nuns. They performed good works without threatening the family by living in groups.

On the Clarissans, the Third Order of Saint Francis, Caroline Stephen quotes her father's *Essays in Ecclesiastical Biography*. (Virginia Woolf read her grandfather's essays when she was fifteen.) As lay nuns, the Clarissans were allowed to hide the scapulary and cord; they needed only the "tacit consent" of their husbands to their vows of celibacy. As "poor ladies" the Clarissans cared for the insane and "fallen women." Woolf also felt the appeal of the secret life of a nun under the protection of marriage, and her Clarissa is like "a nun withdrawing." Clarissa's call is even clearer in her relationship with the "insane" Septimus Smith. There is really only a difference of degree between Septimus's voices and Clarissa's, between her desire for celibacy in marriage and his. The historical relationship of nuns to the mad, the ill, and prostitutes is an interesting one, outsiders caring for outsiders.

—JANE MARCUS, "The Niece of a Nun: Virginia Woolf, Caroline Stephen and the Cloistered Imagination," Virginia Woolf: A Feminist Slant, ed. Jane Marcus (Lincoln: University of Nebraska Press, 1983), p. 10

MARK HUSSEY

"I" is, as Martin Buber put it, "the true shibboleth of humanity" (*I and Thou*), but the word can be uttered in many different ways. Woolf's novels inquire into the status of "I" as it is spoken by various characters in various contexts, and from this we may draw her concepts of identity and self, the distinction between which will emerge as we proceed.

Frequently, there is a moment in the novels when, with a feeling either of exhilaration or anxiety, a character is suddenly overcome by a sense of being unique, of being "I." In *The Voyage Out,* that Rachel Vinrace has little sense of individual identity is emphasized from the start: she would "believe anything she was told, invent reasons for anything she said." Friendless, inexperienced, and sheltered, Rachel's ordinariness is the most striking thing about her. She has had no social intercourse, and any impulse toward an individual attitude has been quickly suppressed by her father or aunts; she thus believes that "to feel anything strongly was to create an abyss between oneself and others who feel strongly perhaps but differently."

For Rachel, what can be called the experience of self-discovery is fascinating; prompted by Helen Ambrose, there comes a moment when she sees herself for the first time standing out against a background composed of all other people:

> The vision of her own personality, of herself as a real everlasting thing, different from anything else, unmergeable, like the sea or the wind, flashed into Rachel's mind, and she became profoundly excited at the thought of living.
> "I can be m-m-myself," she stammered, "in spite of you, in spite of the Dalloways, and Mr. Pepper, and Father, and my Aunts, in spite of these?" She swept her hand across a whole page of statesmen and soldiers.

Similar moments of "self-discovery" occur throughout the novels, and provide what could be called a first signification of identity: the encountering of myself, called "I," distinct from all others in the world, as continuous and unmergeable.

Immediately, however, a problem is raised for which the novels after *Night and Day* successively seek and offer solutions. Rachel's "vision of . . . herself" raises the question of who has that vision. It is not enough to say simply that the individual divides into a reflected and reflecting part. "I" is, for the most part, spoken as a received cipher for one being among others. The experience of self-discovery distinguishes the individual "I" from the faceless crowd that moves through all the novels, obliterating "I," sweeping people along *en masse.* This crowd is the background against which the experience of self-discovery stands out. To emerge from that background requires an effort, for it is easier to flow with the crowd, as Katherine Hilbery, the heroine of *Night and Day,* finds:

> She stood fascinated at the corner. The deep roar filled her ears; the changing tumult had the inexpressible fascination of varied life pouring ceaselessly with

a purpose which, as she looked, seemed to her, somehow, the normal purpose for which life was framed; its complete indifference to the individuals, whom it swallowed up and rolled onwards, filled her with at least a temporary exaltation.

The problem I have referred to above is that of discovering what inspires the effort to rouse an individual's "I" to emerge from the crowd. The question is put simply in "An Unwritten Novel," a sketch written in 1920 as Woolf was planning *Jacob's Room:* "When the self speaks to the self, who is speaking?" There is a distinction between the voice of the "self speaking to the self" and the "I" that is uttered in the shared world of relationships between one identity and another. The status of "I" as the defining word of identity is thus complex rather than simple. In what follows I will describe the novels' inquiry into the nature and status of identity, and into the possibility of a unitary, autonomous self.

"There is," says the narrator of *Jacob's Room,* "something absolute in us that despises qualification." In this novel that "it is no use trying to sum people up. One must follow hints, not exactly what is said, nor yet entirely what is done—" becomes almost a refrain. The narrative tone in *Jacob's Room* is inquisitive, uncertain; in its hesitancy can be seen a determination to inquire honestly into the human situation, a refusal to assume control and dictate a system into which life will be made to fit. That "life is but a procession of shadows," that we cannot know others (except as what Clarissa Dalloway will call "apparitions"), that there is no way of defining an individual—all this is affirmed. *Jacob's Room* sketches out the frame within which Woolf's investigations into the strange nature of human being take place:

> In any case life is but a procession of shadows, and God knows why it is that we embrace them so eagerly, and see them depart with such anguish, being shadows. And why, if this and much more than this is true, why are we yet surprised in the window corner by a sudden vision that the young man in the chair is of all things in the world the most real, the most solid, the best known to us—why indeed?—For the moment after we know nothing about him.
> Such is the manner of our seeing. Such the conditions of our love.

Such, it might be said, the conditions of her inquiry.

"Human reality cannot be finally defined by patterns of conduct," writes Sartre in *Being and Nothingness;* cannot, *Jacob's Room* suggests, be finally defined at all. The novel undercuts its own purpose by trying to create a unique character while at the same time admitting the impossibility of the project.

> But though all this may very well be true—so Jacob thought and spoke— so he crossed his legs—filled his pipe—sipped his whisky, and once looked at his pocket-book, rumpling his hair as he did so, there remains over something which can never be conveyed to a second person save by Jacob himself. Moreover, part of this is not Jacob but Richard Bonamy—the room; the

market carts; the hour; the very moment of history. Then consider the effect of sex— ... But something is always impelling one to hum vibrating, like the hawk moth, at the mouth of the cavern of mystery, endowing Jacob Flanders with all sorts of qualities he had not at all—

The individual is enmeshed in the influences, relationships and possibilities of the world, caught up in the movement through time and space, and so cannot be realized as one absolute entity. If there is a unique self to be identified—a "summing-up" of the person—it must be separated from its intervolvement with the world. However, such an operation may well lead to nothing.

At the beginning of *Mrs. Dalloway,* Clarissa, recently recovered from an illness, delighting in a fresh day and the hustle and bustle of the West End, is undisturbed by the thought of her death. She will not say of herself "I am this, I am that," preferring to see herself as a "mist" diffused among the familiar people and places of her life. "Did it matter then, she asked herself, walking towards Bond Street, did it matter that she must inevitably cease completely; all this must go on without her; did she resent it; or did it not become consoling to believe that death ended absolutely? but that somehow in the streets of London, on the ebb and flow of things, here, there, she survived." In this mood Clarissa is particularly susceptible to the fading away of individual identity that engulfment by the crowd threatens. Content to be part of the "ebb and flow of things," her identity ("her life, herself") begins thinning away, spreading out further and further, until eventually no sense of "I" as an individual identity remains to her.

The crowd has absorbed Clarissa so completely that she can no longer say "I" and feel that she utters *her own* identity: "She had the oddest sense of being herself invisible; unseen; unknown; there being no more marrying, no more having of children now, but only this astonishing and rather solemn progress with the rest of them, up Bond Street, this being Mrs. Dalloway; not even Clarissa any more; this being Mrs. Richard Dalloway." "I" is Mrs. Richard Dalloway, just one more fashionable woman shopping in the West End. The importance of names should be noted here as they will be seen to be significant in the question of identity. "Dalloway" is, of course, not "really" Clarissa's name but one imposed over her own by marriage; to be "not even Clarissa any more" means that the "I" she utters does not have, to *her,* the distinction of a unique individuality.

An interesting comment on the significance of names is provided by the scene in which Clarissa's old lover, Peter Walsh, just returned from India, is seen following a pretty young woman. Having just left Clarissa's house, where their meeting again after a long separation has aroused many painful memories for Peter, he fantasizes about this "ideal" girl he has glimpsed in the street:

> Straightening himself and stealthily fingering his pocket-knife he started after her to follow this woman, this excitement, which seemed even with its back turned to shed on him a light which connected them, which singled him out, as if the random uproar of the traffic had whispered through hollowed

hands his name, *not Peter, but his private name which he called himself in his own thoughts.* (my italics)

This unnamed name seems suggestive of an essence transcending mere identity; but here we are anticipating what must be more clearly explained. As a comment on this passage I will cite the following from Geoffrey Hartman's *Saving the Text:* ". . . for those who have a name may also seek a more authentic and defining one. The *other* name is usually kept secret precisely because it is sacred to the individual, or numinous (*nomen numen*): as if the concentrated soul of the person lodged in it." There will be more to say about names later, but for now it is enough to note their function of providing one of the bases for identity. Names may serve to fix an identity, but they may not reflect what a person feels is his or her "true" self.

In *Mrs. Dalloway* the simple "I," with which Rachel Vinrace was seen to lay claim to an individual identity, gives way to more complex notions. Clarissa is engaged in what may be seen as a search for her ownmost identity: her recollections of childhood and an unresolved early love affair often prevent her from having a sense of continuity in her being. Memories dislocate her sense of a single identity by irrupting into her present life, so that she "would not say of Peter, she would not say of herself, I am this, I am that."

When she returns home to discover that her husband, Richard, has been invited to lunch without her, Clarissa feels empty and lost: identity once more drains away, because she has not been included. To regain her sense of identity she detaches herself from the present and dips into the past, into her memories. As the sense of a rich relationship (with Sally Seton) and a moment of vision returns to her, the emptiness occasioned by her exclusion fills. She abruptly returns to the present, and "plunged into the very heart of the moment, transfixed it, there—the moment of this June morning on which was the pressure of all the other mornings." This circling of the moment with all the other moments of life gives her identity point and continuity. Memory thus plays a double role, both disturbing and restoring the individual's sense of identity; Clarissa is able to fill the moment and regain her sense of identity, of being someone in the world to whom things have happened; to whom people have spoken; someone who has caused both happiness and sadness. Her physical being also has a part to play in this gathering together of herself. To see her own body gives her some security; when she cannot see herself, the fading of identity that she experienced in Bond Street is quickened; she feels "invisible." On returning home, her image in a mirror joins with memory as she reassumes (what is here specifically called) her self:

> That was her self—pointed; dart-like; definite. That was her self when some effort, some call on her to be her self, drew the parts together, she alone knew how different, how incompatible and composed so for the world only into one centre, one diamond, one woman who sat in her drawing-room and made a meeting-point, a radiancy no doubt in some dull lives, a refuge for the lonely to come to, perhaps.

There is another "self," the "she" who "alone knew" that this assembly of elements is "composed so for the world only," and so "self" here is not unqiue, but a momentary resolution of scattered attributes that saves Clarissa from a moment of despair.

The constitution of identity here takes place under the form of a circle: the "I" at the center, named and founded in part on an image of the body, holds in tension a circumference of memories that pertain to that center; furthermore, memories involve relations with others.

Identity, then, is not a "thing," as Rachel Vinrace put it, but a flex of sensations and attributes that can be drawn together by an effort based on such a security-ensuring stimulus as the sight of one's own body in a mirror. Identity is made up of what Clarissa later in the novel calls "apparitions." In this instance it appears to be an accumulation of reflections unified by a name. When there are no acute stimuli, nor an available "base" for identity, it can slip, as it does for Clarissa in the crowded street and for Peter Walsh walking through London after his reunion with Clarissa, which arouses a welter of memories: "The strangeness of standing alone, alive, unknown, at half-past eleven in Trafalgar Square overcame him. What is it? Where am I? And why, after all, does one do it? he thought."

Thus far it is suggested that if identity is not to be the undifferentiated identity of the crowd, an effort must be made. Individual identity is, however, formed in a nexus of relationships and influences without which it cannot emerge from the background of the crowd. What initially stimulates the necessary effort is not clear, but we may say that there is a tension between the desire for autonomy, and the necessity, in forming identity, of both interrelationships with others, and the boundaries of space and time.

The part is a foundation on which Clarissa can rely for identity, but, we now know, it is possible for identity to be "composed so for the world only." Because "anybody could do it," and because she feels she must *act* a part as a hostess, Clarissa once again feels that a "true" or "real" identity, her *own* "I," eludes her:

> Every time she gave a party she had this feeling of being something not herself, and that every one was unreal in one way; much more real in another. It was, she thought, partly their clothes, partly being taken out of their ordinary ways, partly the background; it was possible to say things you couldn't say anyhow else, things that needed an effort; possible to go much deeper. But not for her; not yet anyhow.

Even this late in the novel the sense of incompleteness in Clarissa's identity is still very strong; the "I" that she speaks in welcoming her guests does not satisfy her. She is still uncertain of what, or who, "herself" is; she still will not say of herself that she is one thing or another, a virgin in a narrow bed, or a smart London hostess.

Clarissa cannot feel herself as a single identity because she feels herself "everywhere; not 'here, here, here': . . . but everywhere." Her "youthful theory" states what we have already seen to be the situation of identity: to know anyone

"one must seek out the people who completed them; even the places." All that appear in the world are "apparitions," but there is another "unseen" part of us that can survive even death, by attaching to other people, haunting other places.

> It ended in a transcendental theory which, with her horror of death, allowed her to believe, or say that she believed (for all her scepticism), that since our apparitions, the part of us which appears, are so momentary compared with the other, the unseen part of us, which spreads wide, the unseen might survive, be recovered somehow attached to this person or that, or even haunting certain places, after death. Perhaps—perhaps.

The problem of identity is intricately bound up with that of knowing others, and because relationships form such a constantly shifting and widening web of interconnections there is no way of isolating one identity. Clarissa suggests an "essence" that is somehow "truer" than the "apparitions" of it which are identities in the shared world. The novel does not attempt to analyze what this essence might be, but clearly the fact of death is significant in the experience that allows for its perception.

The double aspect of death as a completion and cutting off of being dominates Clarissa Dalloway's thoughts. On one level *Mrs. Dalloway* can be read as her coming to terms with her death. During the day of the novel Clarissa moves from the crowd's understanding of death (the supreme expression of which is war) to a grasping of the fact of her own death for herself. Death is the prime manifestation of the horizon of time in human being, and it is important in Woolf's thinking, as will become increasingly clear; eventually we must be concerned with her idea of temporality.

The news of a young man's suicide disturbs that identity "composed so for the world only" that Clarissa had assumed for her party. It is through others' deaths that our "experience" of death comes. The first time Clarissa thinks about her death she feels it does not really matter, as she is fixed on the present moment. "Everyone remembered," she thinks, and to set herself apart she plunges into "this, here, now, in front of her." Against the thought of death as absolute, ending her delight in the present moment, she sets her belief that she will survive on the "ebb and flow" of things, persist in the memories of those who know her. Later in the book, her "theory of life" recalls this belief, but for now her meditation springs from the loss of identity she suffers as she walks in the crowd up Bond Street.

That Clarissa is trying to recover an "image of white dawn in the country" reveals her more particular concern: the loss of time. Her quasi-mystical idea of death as transcending the limits of time is a turning away from the fact of death itself. The quotation from *Cymbeline,* that gently beats in Clarissa's mind throughout the book, and forms one of the links between her and Septimus, puts her thoughts under suspicion for the dirge operates under a double delusion: Guiderius and Arviragus not only believe wrongly that Imogen is dead, but also that she is the boy, Fidele.

Clarissa is further allied with Septimus by imagining herself as a mist. His death leads her to think of death itself; the finery of her party is stripped away; "one was alone." For the first time in the novel, there is a sense that Clarissa has reached some sort of plateau; the death seems to have led her to a transcendence of identities; she becomes simply "Clarissa." The final lines of the novel—"It is Clarissa, he said./For there she was"—endorse this sense (not *stated*) of completion, of unity.

—MARK HUSSEY, "Identity and Self," *The Singing of the Real World: The Philosophy of Virginia Woolf's Fiction* (Columbus: Ohio State University Press, 1986), pp. 21–29

HERBERT MARDER

The disparity between the tolerant Clarissa and the snobbish Mrs. Richard Dalloway has often been noticed. Again, Lytton Strachey was the first to detect "some discrepancy in Clarissa herself. He thinks she is disagreeable and limited [Woolf reported in her diary] but that I alternately laugh at her and cover her, very remarkably, with myself. ⟨Alex⟩ Zwerdling observes that she is "a laminated personality made up of layers that do not interpenetrate." These comments don't quite do justice to the effectiveness and coherence of the portrait. The narrator obeys a logic of her own, breaking up the narrative plane in a sense as the cubists broke up the visual plane. The lyrical receptiveness and the social rigidity fit together within a new space that curves back on itself. It is not a matter of explaining a "discrepancy" in the characterization but rather of recognizing that Woolf's assumptions about self and identity are different from those to which we are accustomed.

Her method is to hold two mutually exclusive views in mind at once and to believe in them both. The tension between different kinds of truth about Clarissa is matched by the narrator's ability to tolerate the contradiction, to proceed as if it were the most natural thing in the world. Such dual consciousness frees, rather than encumbers, the mind. Woolf knows that the self is transcendent and unbounded; she knows that it is socially determined; and she presents both of these truths with equal conviction. Thus she participates in the "modernist" assault on personality while at the same time respecting the boundaries of social realism.

Woolf defines identity in terms of overlapping visionary and social domains. On the visionary plane the self is open and luminous, a bit of mind-stuff within a flowing universal medium. Suspended like a cell in this plasma, the individual being knows other people, objects and ideas through direct experience, that is, by penetration and merging. The heroine of *Mrs. Dalloway* enjoys a transcendent consciousness in which, as Jean O. Love has suggested, all humans "take part and are at one, even while they experience illusions of separateness." But this mythic vision is constantly qualified by Woolf's social realism. Clarissa moves in fashionable society as if the other mythic world were non-existent. On the "sociological" plane the self is definite, impermeable and limited. Its attitudes are shaped by a precise combination of innate and acquired characteristics. It has no visionary powers, no knowledge of anything beyond the orbit of consciousness. Its sympathies are determined by narrow self-interest. So Clarissa, admiring the roses her husband has brought her, shrugs off the charge that she is spoilt, and admits that she feels nothing for distant victims of genocide who are being "maimed, frozen." "Hunted out of existence . . . she could feel nothing for the Albanians, or was it the Armenians? but she loved her roses." Such myopia is hard to reconcile with Clarissa's personal sensitivity, but it reflects Woolf's view of upper-class attitudes.

The split in this novel, then, belongs not merely to the main character, but to the narrator. It is not only Clarissa Dalloway who moves alternately in the oceanic sphere and in the drawing-room, but the narrator who assumes the equivalence of these domains. Let Clarissa be an illuminated spirit, says the creative intelligence. And it is so. Let Mrs. Dalloway be a narrow social dilettante. And it is equally so. Furthermore, although Woolf was often amused by ironic contrasts, the implications of her experiments in this novel were ultimately serious and far-reaching. For we can only conceive of "reality," she declared, as the resultant of disparate views, as a complementarity of open and closed selves. Realism, in the non-trivial sense, must be more than an arbitrary record either of material or psychological data. It must be a vision of the whole, which would embrace both the worldly Mrs. Dalloway and the free spirit who is her alter ego. The intention to be comprehensive in that sense formed Woolf's program for modern fiction, as a careful reading of her well-known essay on the subject will show.

"Modern Fiction" has been misread as a defense of the stream-of-consciousness novel, a manifesto of modernist aims. Its point of view is at once more conservative and more ambiguous than such labels suggest. James Naremore has pointed out that the essay's famous invitation to the reader—"examine for a moment an ordinary mind on an ordinary day"—is not a summary of Woolf's own position, but of James Joyce's, "an abstract of what she thinks Joyce's method tells us." Perhaps more precisely, her attitude is ambivalent, or deliberately evasive. At one point she appears to embrace the experimentalist position: "Life is not a series of gig-lamps symmetrically arranged; but a luminous halo, a semi-transparent envelope, surrounding us from the beginning of consciousness to the end." But then, by casual qualification, she distances herself again: "It is, at any rate, in some such fashion as this that we seek to define the quality which distinguishes the work of several young writers, among whom Mr. James Joyce is the most notable, from their predecessors." Here the cool judicial tone denies that she herself might be identified with these young writers (Joyce was her exact contemporary), while the persuasive tone of the preceding passage implies just the opposite.

Read as a whole, the essay is decidedly not a defense of any existing school of writers. Rather it seeks to suggest an alternative, a kind of metarealism, which will avoid the superficiality of the traditional realists and the narrowness of the avant garde. It is true that Woolf scolds the "materialists," Wells, Bennett, and Galsworthy, and prefers the younger writers who are interested in revealing "the dark places of psychology." Attention to the workings of "an ordinary mind on an ordinary day" does allow the writer a certain amount of spiritual freedom and deepens insight. But such an interest is too limiting to provide an effective guiding principle. The artistic challenge, as she sees it, cannot be met by swinging from a materialistic to an introspective extreme. It may be useful to chart unknown regions of the mind, as Joyce has done in the early chapters of *Ulysses,* but it is not sufficient to do so. Although Joyce's accounts of personal consciousness are admirable in their way, they are also one-sided. In comparison to *Youth* and *The Mayor of Casterbridge, Ulysses* must be judged a failure. Woolf suspects that Joyce's work suffers from "some limitation imposed by the method as well as by the mind. . . . Is it due to the method that we feel neither jovial nor magnanimous, but centered in a self which, in spite of its tremor of susceptibility, never embraces or creates what is outside itself and beyond?"

Freedom from the snares of "personality" or self-centeredness is a recurring theme in Woolf's writings. The plunge into the self leads us into dark places, and for that very reason the mind must constantly renew its traffic with the social realities "outside itself and beyond." As a corrective to the narrowness of *Ulysses* we are advised to open "*Tristram Shandy* or even *Pendennis* and be by them convinced that there are not only other aspects of life, but more important ones into the bargain." What counts here is not Woolf's judgment of *Ulysses,* which she subsequently modified, but her emphasis on the two-fold orientation of the novelist—facing inward and outward at the same time—her insistence that no matter how poetic a work is, or how much it departs from "reality," the writer must still "have one toe touching Liverpool." Several of Woolf's exemplary writers are strict realists—Thackeray, Hardy, Chekhov—and she attaches great importance to the faithful representation of social contexts. The whole essay is based on the assumption that such objective definition will continue to be as important in the art of the future as it has been in the past. The proper goal of modern fiction, as Woolf sees it, is to render a complete account of "life itself," that is, to create a perspective that will link spiritual and material realms, mystical unity and empirical diversity.

—HERBERT MARDER, "Split Perspective: Types of Incongruity in
Mrs. Dalloway," Papers on Language and Literature 22, No. 1
(Winter 1986): 59–62

PERRY MEISEL

With Virginia Woolf, we move to the middle ground—the switch or circuit—between Forster's taxonomic reflexive realism and Strachey's historiographical one. ⟨. . .⟩ it is worth nothing that Woolf is not only a literary corridor between Forster and Strachey, but also an exemplary—and reflexive—participant in Bloomsbury's collective sensibility by virtue of her outrageous borrowings (especially from *Howards End*) of phrases that become perhaps more familiar as tropes in her own prose ("rainbow bridge," "prose and passion"); even of organizing conceits such as Pointz Hall's doubling of Howards End in *Between the Acts* (1941). To call it borrowing or theft, however, is to maintain a sense of private property, literary or otherwise, that Bloomsbury itself rejects because it knows the notion is little more than an illusion and proper authority little more than a transpersonal function.

To speak of *Mrs. Dalloway* as we might wish—as the perfect whole it seems to be—is, of course, as critically problematic as it is to speak seriously of anything categorically autonomous. Like Pater and Forster, Woolf, too, submits the Arnoldean ideal of the proper to interrogation ⟨. . .⟩ The instance of music serves her, as it does Pater, as an especially clear example of the difference underlying all signification, and of the temporal or belated structure of its action. Like *Howards End, Mrs. Dalloway* is not an expression of the will to modernity, but a catalogue of the kinds of modernist ideals temporality or belatedness disallows, together with an enormously lucid account of the larger structure of modernism that produces such ideals symptomatically. The novel's own appearance of unity is therefore aligned with the customary ideal unities it presents in a number of registers (the pastoral nostalgia of Bourton, for example), chief among them the self. In perhaps the novel's most famous scene, Clarissa, (re)composing her selfhood before the mirror, thinks of herself as a "diamond." And yet—in a strategy like Forster's—the trope's identification elsewhere in the novel with precisely that public world to which it is opposed contaminates the privacy it otherwise signifies here. After all, "diamond" resonates with the novel's seemingly unrelated tropology of finance, empire, and the material resources of colonialism "where only spice winds blow," a tropology into whose range "diamond" may vibrate so as to make it signify a specific type of imperial wealth, and that suggests Clarissa's personal wholeness to be dependent in turn upon the stability of her husband's money. The identification of psychic and real economy is as exact as Forster's: the language of privacy and that of common or public mythologies are once again the same. Woolf's like figuration of Clarissa as now "disinterested" in Sally Seton resonates with the figure of Richard's apparently constrasting "deposit" of affection for her, both terms conjoining in the tropology of imperial riches, and setting off a series of familiar Bloomsbury puns such as Clarissa's desire to "repay" or "pay back" sentiments, the crowd's "unspent" emotions early in the novel, even the ironic "treasures" of Septimus's psychosis. "Signs," in short, "were interchanged." *Mrs. Dalloway* is little less than a textbook of the "shuffle" of "sunken meanings" in words, as Woolf herself presents it in "Craftsmanship" (1937), a strategic discourse of puns disguised (like Forster's, but unlike Joyce's overt ones) within the apparent semantic stability of common idioms.

Woolf's ambivalence about belief in the fiction of property, or, as she calls it in *Mrs. Dalloway*, "Proportion"—Farfrae's machine now in the unabashedly antiseptic garb of the doctors Holmes and Bradshaw—is evident in Clarissa's own ambivalence about her social standing and consequent double values ("being part of it" on the one hand, being "outside, looking on" on the other. It is even more evident in Woolf's (later) construction during the draftings of the novel of a "double" for Clarissa who flaunts Proportion with as much calculation as she cultivates it. Septimus, after all, is Clarissa's opposite, no longer shackled by the impossible desire for pure selfhood or "properness," since he gives in entirely to the public determinations that undermine any pure privacy in any case, allowing all Proportion to fall away. Clarissa instead represents just that citizenly contrast that produces ego over against the schizophrenia as displayed by Septimus himself. Hence both the advertising airplane and the motor-car early in the novel demonstrate not only the determinate reality of public languages in the world itself—now overtly a product of a political or ideological unconscious, a set of shared cultural presuppositions or representations—but also the ways in which such public symbols or languages send given spectators into distinct worlds of private thought. Like the various clocks that strike a few moments apart in relation to the central authority represented by Big Ben, the particularities that fashion privacy are each permutational instances of the dominant ideological arrangements of culture at large.

—PERRY MEISEL, "Deferred Action in *To the Lighthouse*," *The Myth of the Modern: A Study in British Literature and Criticism after 1850* (New Haven: Yale University Press, 1987), pp. 102–4

CRITICAL ESSAYS

Reuben Arthur Brower

SOMETHING CENTRAL
WHICH PERMEATED

It was something central which permeated ...   —*Mrs. Dalloway*

The best preparation for understanding *Mrs. Dalloway* is to read *The Tempest,* or *Cymbeline,* or, better still, *The Winter's Tale*. One might go further and say that in her singleness of vision and in her handling of words, Virginia Woolf has a Shakespearean imagination. If that sounds like nonsense—and it may—perhaps by the end of this chapter the reader will agree that it sounds 'so like sense, that it will do as well.'

Mrs. Dalloway has a story and some characters—by conventional standards, a fragmentary dramatic design—but the fragments of which the novel is composed would not seem related or particularly significant without another sort of connection. The dramatic sequences are connected through a single metaphorical nucleus, and the key metaphors are projected and sustained by a continuous web of subtly related minor metaphors and harmonizing imagery.

Once we have seen this design and the vision of experience it implies, we shall understand why *Mrs. Dalloway* take the form it does, why as a story it has properly no beginning or ending. It opens one morning with Clarissa Dalloway in the midst of preparing for a party; it closes in the early hours of the next morning with Clarissa very much involved in giving the party. The major event of her day is the return of Peter Walsh, the man she had almost married instead of Richard Dalloway, a successful M.P. Clarissa and Richard have a daughter, Elizabeth, who is temporarily attached to a religious fanatic, a woman with the Dickensian name of Miss Kilman. There is also in the novel another set of characters who at first seem to have no connection with Clarissa and her world: Septimus Smith, a veteran of the First World War, and his Italian wife, Rezia, a hatmaker by trade. Septimus, who is suffering from shell shock, is being treated—somewhat brutally—by a hearty M. D., Dr. Holmes. During the day of Clarissa's preparations, Septimus visits Sir William Bradshaw, an eminent psychiatrist, who recommends rather too firmly that

From *The Fields of Light: An Experiment in Critical Reading* (New York: Oxford University Press, 1951), pp. 123–37.

Septimus should be taken to a sanatorium. In the late afternoon, as Dr. Holmes comes to take him away, Septimus jumps from the balcony of his room and kills himself. That evening, Sir William Bradshaw reports the story of his death at Clarissa's party.

Readers of the novel will recognize this outline as more or less accurate, but they will want to add that the impression it gives is very remote from their remembered experience of *Mrs. Dalloway.* For the peculiar texture of Virginia Woolf's fiction has been lost. The ebb and flow of her phrasing and the frequent repetition of the same or similar expressions, through which her characteristic rhythmic and metaphorical designs are built up, have completely disappeared.

No one needs to be shown that the novel is full of odd echoes. The Shakespearean tag, 'Fear no more,' occurs some six or seven times; certain words turn up with surprising frequency in the various interior monologues: 'life,' 'feel,' 'suffer,' 'solemn,' 'moment,' and 'enjoy.' Less obvious, and more peculiar to Virginia Woolf is the recurrence in the individual monologues of expressions for similar visual or aural images. Some of these images—the aeroplane and the stopped motorcar are examples—connect separate dramatic sequences in a rather artificial way; but others, such as Big Ben's striking and the marine images, often connect similar qualities of experience and so function as symbolic metaphors. There are many repeated words, phrases, and sentences in the novel, besides those already quoted, which gradually become metaphorical: 'party,' 'Holmes and Bradshaw,' 'there she was,' 'plunge,' 'wave' and 'sea,' 'sewing,' 'building' and 'making it up,' 'Bourton,' et cetera. Almost innumerable continuities, major and minor, may be traced through the various recurrent expressions; but as compared with Shakespeare's practice in *The Tempest,* the continuities are less often built up through the use of explicit metaphors. The repeated word does not occur in a conventional metaphorical expression, and its metaphorical value is felt only after it has been met in a number of contexts. Virginia Woolf's most characteristic metaphors are purely symbolic.

I can indicate from the adjective 'solemn' how a recurrent expression acquires its special weight of meaning. By seeing how metaphor links with metaphor, the reader will also get a notion of the interconnectedness of the entire novel. The word appears on the first page of *Mrs. Dalloway:*

> How fresh, how calm, stiller than this of course, the air was in the early morning; like the flap of a wave; the kiss of a wave; chill and sharp and yet (for a girl of eighteen as she then was) solemn, feeling as she did, standing there at the open window, that something awful was about to happen...

It is echoed at once, on the next page, in the first account of Big Ben's striking (an important passage in relation to the whole novel):

> For having lived in Westminster—how many years now? over twenty,— one feels even in the midst of the traffic, or waking at night, Clarissa was

positive, a particular hush, or solemnity; an indescribable pause; a suspense (but that might be her heart, affected, they said, by influenza) before Big Ben strikes. There! Out it boomed. First a warning, musical; then the hour, irrevocable. The leaden circles dissolved in the air.

'Solemn,' which on our first reading of the opening page had only a vague local meaning of 'something awful about to happen,' is now connected with a more particularized terror, the fear of a suspense, of a pause in experience. Each time that 'solemn' is repeated in subsequent descriptions of Big Ben, it carries this additional meaning. The word recurs three times in the afternoon scene in which Clarissa looks across at an old woman in the next house:

> How extraordinary it was, strange, yes, touching, to see the old lady (they had been neighbors ever so many years) move away from the window, as if she were attached to that sound, that string. Gigantic as it was, it had something to do with her. Down, down, into the midst of ordinary things the finger fell making the moment solemn.

And a little further on:

> ... Big Ben ... laying down the law, so solemn, so just ... on the wake of that solemn stroke which lay flat like a bar of gold on the sea.

In the early morning scene near the end of the book, Clarissa goes to the window, again sees the old lady, and thinks, 'It will be a solemn sky ... it will be a dusky sky, turning away its cheek in beauty.' In all but the last passage there is some suggestion in the imagery of Big Ben's stroke coming down and marking an interruption in the process of life. By the end of the book we see the significance in the use of 'solemn' on the first page in a passage conveying a sharp sense of freshness and youth. The terror symbolized by Big Ben's 'pause' has a connection with early life, '... one's parents giving it into one's hands, this life, to be lived to the end.' The 'something awful ... about to happen' was associated with 'the flap of a wave, the kiss of a wave'; the 'solemnity' of life is a kind of 'sea-terror' (so Shakespeare might express it in *The Tempest*). Wave and water images recur in other 'solemn' passages: 'the wave,' 'the wake,' 'the leaden circles dissolved in the air.' So, through various associations, 'solemn' acquires symbolic values for the reader: some terror of entering the sea of experience and of living life and an inexplicable fear of a 'suspense' or interruption.

While following a single symbolic adjective in *Mrs. Dalloway*, we have seen that it was impossible to interpret one continuity apart from several others. Various expressions—'solemn,' 'wave,' 'Big Ben,' 'fear,' and 'pause'—kept leading us toward the key metaphor of the book. The metaphor that links the continuities and gives unity to the dramatic design of *Mrs. Dalloway* is not a single, easily describable analogy, but two complementary and extremely complex analogies which are gradually expressed through recurrent words and phrases and through the dramatic pattern of the various sequences. Though they are salient in the sequences of nearly all the main characters, they are best interpreted from Clarissa's, since her experience forms the center of attention for the reader.

One of the two metaphorical poles of the novel emerges in a passage that comes just after the first account of Big Ben's striking:

> Such fools we are, she thought, crossing Victoria Street. For Heaven only knows why one loves it so, how one sees it so, making it up, building it round one, tumbling it, creating it every moment afresh; but the veriest frumps, the most dejected of miseries sitting on doorsteps (drink their downfall) do the same; can't be dealt with, she felt positive, by Acts of Parliament for that very reason: they love life. In people's eyes, in the swing, tramp, and trudge; in the bellow and the uproar; the carriages, motor cars, omnibuses, vans, sandwich men shuffling and swinging; brass bands; barrel organs; in the triumph and the jingle and the strange high singing of some aeroplane overhead was what she loved; life; London; this moment of June.

The key phrase here is 'they love life,' and what is meant by 'life' and 'loving it' is indicated by the surrounding metaphors—'building it,' 'creating it every moment,' 'the swing, tramp, and trudge'—and also by the various images of sights, sounds, and actions.

'Life' as expressed in Mrs. Dalloway's morning walk (and in the walks of Peter and of her daughter Elizabeth) consists first in the doings of people and things and in the active perception of them. To meet Clarissa's approval, people 'must do something,' as she did in 'making a world' in her drawing room, in 'assembling' and 'knowing' all sorts of individuals, in running her house, and in giving 'her parties,' which were for her 'life.' But the perception, the savoring of these doings of oneself and of others is itself a creation. For Mrs. Dalloway, 'enjoying' and 'loving' is 'creating' and 'building up,' not passive enjoyment. Life is experienced in successively created 'moments'; the sense of succession, of process, is inseparable from Clarissa's feeling about life; it is implicit in her movement along the streets, 'this astonishing and rather solemn progress with the rest of them, up Bond Street.' She thinks of 'all this' as *going on* without her.' ('This' and 'all this' also become metaphors for life.) Later, in Elizabeth's experience of going up Fleet Street, all these metaphors are explicitly combined: 'this van; this life; this procession.' To live, then, is to enter into the process of action and active perception, to be absorbed in the successive moments: '. . . yet to her it was absolutely absorbing; all this.'

But the sense of being absorbed in the process is inseparable from a fear of being excluded, from the dread that the process may be interrupted. The progress is a 'solemn' one, the adjective suggesting (as elsewhere) the terror of 'plunging' into experience. The sense of being *in* experience is inseparable from the sense of being *outside* of it:

> She sliced like a knife through everything; at the same time was outside, looking on. She had a perpetual sense, as she watched the taxi cabs, of being

out, out, far out to sea and alone; she always had the feeling that it was very, very dangerous to live even one day.

Though the terror lies in having to go through with life, paradoxically the escape from terror lies in building up delight and sharing in the process:

> Even now, quite often if Richard had not been there reading the *Times*, so that she could crouch like a bird and gradually revive, send roaring up that immeasurable delight, rubbing stick to stick, one thing with another, she must have perished.

The central metaphor of Clarissa's narrative (and of the novel) is thus twofold: the exhilarated sense of being a part of the forward moving process and the recurrent fear of some break in this absorbing activity, which was symbolized by the 'suspense' before Big Ben strikes. We are to feel all sorts of experiences qualified as at once 'an absorbing progression' and 'a progression about to be interrupted.' Such in crudely schematic terms are the two analogies which make up the metaphorical nucleus of the novel. As my analysis has indicated, this complex metaphor is expressed through countless variant minor metaphors and images.

Both of the major aspects of the metaphor are intricately linked in the wonderful sewing scene in which Clarissa's old lover, Peter Walsh, returns to announce his plans for a second marriage:

> Quiet descended on her, calm, content, as her needle, drawing the silk smoothly to its gentle pause, collected the green folds together and attached them, very lightly, to the belt. So on a summer's day waves collect, overbalance, and fall; collect and fall; and the whole world seems to be saying 'That is all' more and more ponderously, until even the heart in the body which lies in the sun on the beach says too, That is all. Fear no more, says the heart. Fear no more, says the heart, committing its burden to some sea, which sighs collectively for all sorrows, and renews, begins, collects, lets fall. And the body alone listens to the passing bee; the wave breaking; the dog barking, far away barking and barking.

Through the wave simile the opening statement expands in a metaphorical bloom which expresses in little the essence of the novel. The quiet, calm, and content (Clarissa's absorption in what she is doing) and the rhythmic movement of the needle are the points in the immediate situation from which the two main meanings of the key metaphor grow. The comparison between sewing and wave movements draws in these further levels of meaning, thanks to the nice preparation of earlier scenes and the delicate adjustment of those that follow. There are the wave and sea images which have been appearing when Clarissa recalls the terror of early life or when she hears Big Ben's solemn stroke. Much later in the novel, there is Clarissa at her party in her 'silver-green mermaid's dress . . . lolloping on the waves.' Here, in the scene with Peter, as in the final party scene, the waves mainly symbolize

Clarissa's complete absorption in her life: 'That is all'—the phrase she had used twice while shopping and which had come back in her musings on 'the solemn progress up Bond Street.' There is for the heart at this moment nothing but the process, and the individual becomes a mere percipient body, intensely aware of the immediate sensation. But the moment has a dual value, as has been suggested by the oblique allusions to solemnity and terror ('waves,' 'ponderously,' 'That is all'). So the reader is perfectly prepared for the return of 'Fear no more,' which it is now clear suggests both freedom from fear and the fear of interruption, meanings which are dramatized in the scene that immediately follows.

Clarissa's quiet is rudely shaken by the sound of the front-door bell:

> 'Who can—what can,' asked Mrs. Dalloway (thinking it was outrageous to be interrupted at eleven o'clock on the morning of the day she was giving a party), hearing a step on the stairs. She heard a hand upon the door. She made to hide her dress, like a virgin protecting chastity, respecting privacy.

The nature of the interruption, the return of her former lover, Peter Walsh, and her gesture, 'like a virgin protecting chastity, respecting privacy,' point to another analogy in *Mrs. Dalloway,* which is simply a special aspect of the 'life' metaphor. We might call it the 'destroyer' theme. Peter's coming in temporarily destroys Clarissa's domesticity, even her marriage. As a lover Peter had allowed her no independence, and as a husband he would have been intolerable, leaving her no life of her own. Clarissa reasserts herself and her life by calling after him as he leaves, 'Remember my party to-night!' Peter is one of those who would cut her off from her way of living by making her into another person: he is one of the 'destroyers of the privacy of the soul.' Compulsion of this sort is a special form of the 'suspense' in life's exhilarating process. The 'suspense' may be fear itself, or the sense of time's passing, or death, or a failure in personal relationships, or, finally, the loss of independence which results from love or hatred or officiousness.

We shall now see to what a remarkable extent the central metaphor penetrates and organizes the novel. The dramatic sequences of the principal characters are all linked with Clarissa's through a shuttling pattern of verbal reminiscences. (Curious readers may amuse themselves by finding dozens more than can be cited here). Although 'life' is peculiarly the key figure in Clarissa's experience, it is important in that of other characters, including Septimus and Miss Kilman, who are unable to 'live' as Clarissa does.

We may begin with Peter Walsh, who as a lover has the role of one of the 'interrupters' and 'destroyers.' But in the two accounts of his walks through London, he shows much of Clarissa's eager experience of life. He sets off on his morning walk, speaking rhythmically her parting words, 'Remember my party, remember my party.' He then 'marches up Whitehall' as she has gone 'up Bond Street,' and he too 'makes up' life (his mild 'escapade with the girl'). During his evening walk, he expresses Clarissa's sense of enjoyment:

Really it took one's breath away, these moments . . . absorbing, mysterious, of infinite richness, this life.

Elizabeth also shares her mother's perceptiveness, and in her bus ride has an experience closely paralleling Clarissa's morning walk. As all three characters pass through the 'procession' of experience, they savor life as a series of exquisite moments, a sensation summed up by the motif of the scene in which Richard brings Clarissa the roses: 'Happiness is this.'

The crude parallel between the roles of Mrs. Dalloway and Septimus is obvious; the finer relations and how they are expressed may be best seen by tracing the links made through the 'life' metaphor. While Clarissa usually feels her inclusion *in* everything and only occasionally feels *outside,* Septimus is almost always 'alone' and unable to connect with the world about him. He had 'felt very little in the war,' and 'now that it was all over, truce signed, and the dead buried, he had, especially in the evening, these thunder-claps of fear. He could not feel.' Rezia, his wife, is his refuge from fear, though like Mrs. Dalloway she too has moments of panic when she cries, 'I am alone; I am alone!' But she is shown as having some of Mrs. Dalloway's gift for active enjoyment, and through her Septimus is for once able to recover his power of feeling and to enter into the real life around him. The moment comes near the end of his narrative, in the late afternoon, as he lies on a sofa while Rezia is making a hat. The writing in this scene shows wonderfully the way in which Virginia Woolf moves from one narrative plane to another via image and metpahor. (The parallel with Shakespeare is obvious.)

Immediately preceding the scene comes the episode of Elizabeth's bus ride, with 'this van; this life; this procession.' These metaphors are then echoed in a long description of cloud movements which cast changing lights on the moving buses; the transition to Septimus takes place as he watches the 'goings and comings' of the clouds. The movements and colors referred to and the verbal rhythm ('watching watery gold glow and fade') prepare us easily for the return of the wave and sea imagery of Clarissa's and Peter's monologues:

> Outside the trees dragged their leaves like nets through the depths of the air; the sound of water was in the room and through the waves came the voices of birds singing. Every power poured its treasures on his head, and his hand lay there on the back of the sofa, as he had seen his hand lie when he was bathing, floating, on the top of the waves, while far away on shore he heard dogs barking and barking far away. Fear no more, says the heart in the body; fear no more.

The last words anticipate the next phase of the scene. Septimus, watching Rezia sew a hat, temporarily loses himself in his interest in her activity: 'She built it up, first one thing, then another, she built it up, sewing.' (The 'building' is an echo of the 'life' metaphor, and the sewing is now symbolic.) Septimus begins to note actual objects around him, as Rezia gives him assurance that real things are real: 'There she was, perfectly natural, sewing.' The words, 'There she was' (also the concluding sentence of the novel) are an exact repetition of one of Peter's earlier remarks about Clarissa, where they signified her 'extraordinary gift, that woman's gift, of making a world wherever she happened to be.' Septimus' participation in life is interrupted, as was Clarissa's, by one of the compellers, Dr. Holmes. His suicide is a protest against having his life forcibly remade by others.

In the figure of Sir William Bradshaw we get an almost allegorical representation of a 'destroyer.' His talk of keeping a 'sense of proportion' and his tactful questions are a screen for his firm intention of getting patients to do what he thinks best. There is a close relation, we are told, between preaching proportion and being a converter, for Proportion has a sister, Conversion, who 'feasts on the wills of the weakly.' Clarissa also is pursued by a compeller of this less lovely type, the horrendous if pious spinster, Miss Kilman. She ruins Clarissa's enjoyment of life and is shown as having herself no capacity for delight (if we overlook her perverse fondness for chocolate éclairs!). In the mock-heroic tea-table scene she fails in her attempt to exert a negative influence over Elizabeth, who leaves to go to her mother's party. As Miss Kilman questions Elizabeth, the reader recalls that Mrs. Dalloway's parting words to Miss Kilman and her daughter had been those she had used to Peter: 'Remember my party!' Her words are symbolic of defiance.

Just after this episode the mysterious old lady makes the first of her two appearances, the value of which can now be seen. The old lady, Clarissa says, was 'merely being herself.' 'There was something solemn in it—but love and religion would destroy that, whatever it was, the privacy of the soul.' 'Solemn' connects this 'privacy' theme, symbolized by the old lady, with the attitudes expressed through the key metaphor of the novel, especially with the precarious and terrifying sense of enjoyment. To experience life, terror and all, we must be left alone.

All of the related analogies that make up the key metaphor are combined near the end of the novel, at the point when Bradshaw tells Clarissa of Septimus' death and when Clarissa, reflecting on its meaning, looks out of the window at the old lady going to bed. Bradshaw, a man 'capable of some indescribable crime—forcing your soul, that was it—,' momentarily ruins her party ('in the middle of my party, here's death, she thought . . .'). But Clarissa immediately recognizes that Septimus' death has a further meaning in relation to his life and hers. By killing himself Septimus had defied the men who make life intolerable, and though he had 'thrown it away,' he had not lost his independence of soul. This (in so far as we can define it) is 'the thing' he had preserved. By contrast Clarissa had sacrificed some of this purity. She had made compromises for the sake of social success, 'She had schemed; she had pilfered.' But she had not given in to Peter, and by marrying Richard she had been able to make a life of her own. The delight, though impure, remained. The old lady, in her second appearance as in her first, symbolizes the quiet maintenance of one's own life, which is the only counterbalance to the fear of 'interruption' whether by death or compulsion.

This scene shows in the highest degree the concentration of various dramatic relationships through a central metaphor. What we would emphasize here is Virginia Woolf's literary feat in achieving this result—literary in the primitive sense of Frost's pun, 'feat of words.' The unity of her design depends on the building up of symbolic metaphors through an exquisite management of verbal devices: through exact repetitions, reminiscent variations, the use of related eye and ear imagery, and the recurrence of similar phrase and sentence rhythms. The novel has as a result a unique closeness of structure which is only slightly dependent on story, though also supported by the time patterns which David Daiches has chosen to emphasize. What is most remarkable is the way in which so many different experiences have been perceived through a single metaphorical vision: the lives of Clarissa, Peter, Richard, Septimus, and Rezia as glimpsed at various periods, and of Elizabeth at the moment of growing up. Most of the characters are seen, too, in some relation to the persons who 'make life intolerable': Miss Kilman, Holmes, Bradshaw, and Peter in his role as lover. Experience, rich and various in its range, has struck the mind of the novelist at a single angle and been refracted with perfect consistency. The singleness in reception and expression, as evidenced in the metaphorical design, is what we mean by integrity of imagination in Virginia Woolf.

But there are certainly points in the novel at which this singleness of vision shows signs of strain. Philistine readers have observed that the men of the novel are not full-blooded or are barely 'men' at all—a type of criticism that could be applied with disastrous results to *Tom Jones,* or *Emma,* or *The Portrait of a Lady.* But the strain that is truly a sign of weakness appears in the relating of dramatic elements through the central metaphorical nucleus. That Peter is no man—whether we mean not lifelike or not masculine—is a relevant comment only because of the symbolic role in which he is sometimes cast. As a lover he stands in Clarissa's thoughts for one of the dark 'forcers of the soul'; but in much of his behavior he is described as a womanish sort of person who has little power to manage himself or to move others. In one rather embarrassing episode, Peter's half-imaginary pursuit of a young girl, Virginia Woolf is apparently attempting to present his passionate side. The lack of lively sensuous detail in this narrative contrasts very badly with the glowing particularity of Mrs. Dalloway's walk through Bond Street or with the vividness of Peter's impressions of a London evening, while by way of a poor compensation there is a good deal of generalized emotional language: 'vast philanthropy,' 'exquisite delight,' 'mournful tenderness,' 'laughing and delightful,' et cetera. Peter calls this 'making up' an 'exquisite amusement,' which is in this instance a painfully accurate label. The metaphor ceases to be an instrument through which experience is connected for us in a new relation and remains a simple declaration of a connection never made.

On occasion Virginia Woolf becomes so fascinated with this instrument that she elaborates the metaphor out of all proportion to its expressive value. (*The Waves* is a kind of metaphorical monster of this sort.) The purest and most interesting example of such elaboration in *Mrs. Dalloway* comes just after Peter's imaginary flirtation, the interlude of 'the solitary traveller.' The passage—which is not a dream, though it covers the time while Peter is sleeping—is an enlarged symbolic version of Peter's experience with the girl and in part an expression of his desire for a more satisfactory relationship with Clarissa. As various echoes show, it is, like the experience on the street, a grand example of 'making up,' a vision of the consolatory woman who gives the kind of understanding which Peter had attributed to the girl and which he had not found in Clarissa. It is in a picturesque sense a beautiful passage, but merely beautiful, a piece which could be detached with little loss. The detailed picture of the woman, the evening, the street, and the adorable landlady does not increase or enrich our knowledge of Peter or of anyone else in the book.

Perhaps the most obvious examples of metaphorical elaboration for its own sake are the super-literary, pseudo-Homeric similes which adorn various pages of *Mrs. Dalloway*. Whether they are in origin Proustian or eighteenth-century Bloomsbury, we could wish that they might be dropped. Here is a relatively short example from the scene following the sewing passage:

> 'Well, and what's happened to you?' she said. So before a battle begins, the horses paw the ground; toss their heads; the light shines on their flanks; their necks curve. So Peter Walsh and Clarissa, sitting side by side on the blue sofa, challenged each other. His powers chafed and tossed in him. He assembled from different quarters all sorts of things; praise; his career at Oxford; his marriage, which she knew nothing whatever about; how he had loved; and altogether done his job.

The contrast between such a literary pastiche and the wave-sewing simile shows us in part what is wrong. The particular sense images, 'paw,' 'toss,' 'light shines,' are not grounded on the dramatic and narrative level, since there is no preparation for this Homeric horseplay in the account of Clarissa's and Peter's talk and gestures. (By contrast the wave motion was anticipated through describing Clarissa's movements as she sewed.) So the reader is unprepared to take the further jump to the psychological levels of the metaphor. The efforts to show any similarity in Peter's internal 'chafings' and 'tossings' come too late. The metaphor is crudely explained; but it doesn't work. Such simulations—like Peter's escapade and the solitary traveler's vision—are verbally inert matter, sending no radiations through the reader's experience of the novel.

But what is vital in the writing of *Mrs. Dalloway* is both more nearly omnipresent and more unobtrusive. To say, as I did at the beginning of this chapter, that Virginia Woolf creates a Shakespearean pattern of metaphor tells us something, of course; but to see how she connects diverse moments of experience by playing on a single analogy, or on a single word, tells us much more. As Clarissa is thinking of the death of Septimus Smith, she says to herself: 'But this young man who had killed himself—had he plunged holding his treasure?' She has just recalled that he had 'plunged' by 'throwing himself from a window,' which in turn echoes his earlier agonies ('falling through the sea, down, down') and his actual death ('flung himself vigorously, violently down'). But Septimus' 'plunge' recalls experiences of a very different sort in Clarissa's social life:

> ... as she stood hesitating one moment on the threshold of her drawing-room, an exquisite suspense, such as might stay a diver before plunging while the sea darkens and brightens beneath him ...

'Darkens' suggests that 'plunge' has also a more fearful significance, as we saw on the first page of the novel:

> What a lark! What a plunge! For so it had always seemed to her, when, with a little squeak of the hinges, which she could hear now, she had burst open the French windows and plunged at Bourton into the open air. How fresh, how calm, stiller than this of course, the air was in the early morning; like the flap of a wave; the kiss of a wave; chill and sharp and yet (for a girl of eighteen as she then was) solemn, feeling as she did, standing there at the open window, that something awful was about to happen ...

Septimus' plunge from the window is linked with those earlier windows and 'the triumphs of youth' and thereby with the exhilarating and 'solemn' sense of delight in life's process (the 'treasure'). This twofold sense of life is constantly being expressed through the central metaphor of *Mrs. Dalloway*. The recurrence of a single word is a quiet indication of the subtlety and closeness of the structure which Virginia Woolf was 'building up' as she wrote this novel.

Geoffrey H. Hartman
VIRGINIA'S WEB

This goddess of the continuum is incapable of continuity.

—Valéry, on the Pythoness

Transitions may well be the hardest part of a writer's craft: Virginia Woolf shows that they are also the most imaginative. One remembers, from *Mrs. Dalloway,* the inscrutable motor car proceeding toward Piccadilly, and the way it serves to move the plot with it. Or, in the next episode, how the skywriting plane moves different minds, each guessing at the slogan being dispensed and then dispersed. The wind stealing the smoky letters before any guess is confirmed is the same that, fifteen years later, miscarries the players' words in *Between the Acts.* Suppose now that these letters or words or glimpses are divided by years, by some indefinite or immeasurable gap. We know that years pass, that words are spoken or spelled, and that cars reach their destination; yet the mystery lies in space itself, which the imaginative mind must fill, perhaps too quickly. The dominant issues in the study of Virginia Woolf have been her solipsism and her treatment of time and character; I propose to suspend these and to see her novels as mirrors held up primarily to the imagination.

Let us consider a fairly simple passage from *To the Lighthouse.* To look at it closely requires a concern, a prior interest: in our case, how the novelist goes from one thing to another. The context of the passage is as follows. Mr. Ramsey and his two children, Cam and James, are being ferried to the Lighthouse. The weather is calm, and it seems the boat will never get there; Cam and James, moreover, do not want it to get there, resenting the tyrannous will of their father. In the first section of the novel, with Mrs. Ramsey still alive, it is he who dampens the childish eagerness of James to go to the Lighthouse; and now (many years later) he insists on this outing as a commemorative act.

> The sails flapped over their heads. The water chuckled and slapped the sides of the boat, which drowsed motionless in the sun. Now and then the sails rippled with a little breeze in them, but the ripple ran over them and ceased.

From *Beyond Formalism: Literary Essays 1958–1970* (New Haven: Yale University Press, 1970), pp. 71–81, 84. First published in *Chicago Review* 14 (Spring 1961): 20–32.

The boat made no motion at all. Mr. Ramsey sat in the middle of the boat. He would be impatient in a moment, James thought, and Cam thought, looking at her father who sat in the middle of the boat between them (James steered; Cam sat alone in the bow) with his legs tightly curled. He hated hanging about.

The continuity is kept on the verbal as well as visual plane by echo and repetition (flapped, slapped, drowsed, them, them, boat, boat). This is an intensifying device any writer might use, but one is hardly aware with what skill the sentences lead inward, to that parenthesis and fine slowing-up that encompasses boat, man, and children. Mrs. Woolf's style is here at its best, and the continuities going from the freest to the stillest part of the scene (from the sail to the middle of the boat) do so with an almost humorous resistance. It is interesting to think that the rhythm should be generated by an avoidance; there is, in any case, a stop and go pattern to it, magnified perhaps by the subject of the passage. In terms of plot or subject we have a pause; in terms of the prose that describes it, a sustained if not augmented interest in continuity. As the description reaches the inside of the boat, and then the inside of the mind, the rhythm slows, and as the rhythm slows the continuity is made more obvious as if to counterpoint the pausing. This pattern, however, may be found elsewhere too and cannot be purely an intensifying or descriptive device. It may originate in the writer prior to the particular subject.

I am suggesting that continuity is a deeper matter here than craft or style. In his first important essay Valéry remarked that the extension of continuity by means of metaphor, language, or other means was the common gift of genius. His thesis implied two things: that there is "space" or apparent discontinuity, and that the genial inventor can project his mind into it. If we identify this ability to project (or better, interpolate) with imagination, then the crucial question is what this space may be. There can be only one answer which is not a gross generalization, and this is—anything. We are dealing, it must be remembered, with appearances, and there is nothing that may not succumb to blankness.[1] Art respects appearances so much that everything may become questionably blank, even the continuities firmly established by science. For though science has shown them to exist, it has not shown why they should exist so unapparently, and the formula that proves them also proves the coyness of nature.

To the Lighthouse begins with a sense of fullness and continuous life as we are led in and out of Mrs. Ramsey's mind. There are few apparent pauses to threaten the continuity of thought or existence. The dark space between the beams of the Lighthouse does, however, penetrate consciousness. "A shutter, like the leathern eyelid of a lizard, flickered over the intensity of his gaze and obscured the letter R. In that flash of darkness he heard people saying—he was a failure—that R was beyond him. He would never reach R. On to R, once more. R—" Mr. Ramsey's intellectual ambitions are described, and there are other fine sequences of the same kind.

These darker intervals, rare in the first part, consolidate as the encroaching and live darkness of the second part, which traces the gradual abandonment of the Ramsey house and its last minute rescue from oblivion. Then, in the last section of the novel, a horrid calm moves directly into the heart of the characters. The becalming of the boat is part of a larger sequence, in which all are involved with death, present as distance or the sea's calm or the absence of Mrs. Ramsey. Each person is compelled by a stilling glance, like the wedding guest by the Mariner. They must suffer the suspense, endure the calm, and ultimately resist it—its intimations of peace and of a happy death of the will.

Resistance is the major theme of this novel. The lighthouse itself is a monitory object, warning off, centered in hostile elements. Mr. Ramsey, an enemy of the sea that becalms his boat, is a stronger resister than Mrs. Ramsey, who lives toward the sea. Resistance is a matter of imagination which can either actively fill space or passively blend with it and die. Imagination could also die to itself and become pure will, as in the case of Mr. Ramsey, who wishes to cross the sea, or from Q to R, by force. He denies space and violates the privacy of others. Yet to keep imagination alive involves staying alive to space, to the horrid calms of Virginia Woolf's ocean.

The imagination itself neither acknowledges nor denies space: it lives in it and says to every question "Life, life, life," like Orlando's little bird or Blake's cricket.[2] Affirmation, not meaning, is basic to it, and the problem of meaning cannot even be faced without considering the necessity or fatality of some primary affirmation. Religious belief is such a primary act, but a special form of it. The founding of a fictional world is such a primary act. Fiction reveals something without which the mind could not be, or could not think. The mind needs a world, a substantialized Yes.

Yet every great artist rebels against this, and today his rebellion is conventional. By beginning to question the necessity of fiction, i.e., the inherently affirmative structure of imagination, he joins the philosopher who seeks a truth greater than that arbitrary Yes. The more Henry James seeks the definitive word, the more his mind shrinks from affirmation. It is, similarly, Mrs. Woolf's resistance, her continuous doubting of the continuity she is forced to posit, that we are interested in. At the end of *To the Lighthouse*, Lilly Briscoe's "It is finished," referring in turn to the reaching of the Lighthouse and to her picture, is deeply ironic. It recalls a suffrance greater than the object attained by this last term, by any term. Each artist resists his own vision.

This resistance, however, cannot take place except in the space of fiction and requires the creation of a work of art which is its own implicit critique. The reason that an artist's critique cannot be discursive, or purely so, is that it still involves an affirmation—the new work of art. It is therefore quite proper to put our question in strictly literary terms: What kind of novel does Mrs. Woolf write? And how does it criticize its origin in the affirmative impulse?

*   *   *

I shall try to define Virginia Woolf's novel as the product of a certain kind of prose and a certain kind of plot. This dyad should justify itself as we proceed, but what I say is experimental and may lead to some undue generalizing. The reason for omitting character should also appear: there is only one fully developed character in Mrs. Woolf's novels, and that is the completely expressive or androgynous mind.

Her concern for the novel is linked everywhere with that for prose style. She often remarks that prose, unlike poetry, is still in its infancy, and her first experimental novel, *Mrs. Dalloway,* matures it via the peregrinations of a woman's mind. It may be said with some truth that the novel is, for Virginia Woolf, simply the best form of presenting a completely expressive prose.

A Room of One's Own (1929) illustrates in slow motion how this mature prose came to be. Mrs. Woolf's "sociological essay" is about the future of fiction and woman's part in it. But we are not given a straight essay. She refuses to separate her thought from certain imaginary accidents of time and place and writes something akin to the French *récit.* Her mind, porous to the world even during thought, devises a prose similar to that of *To the Lighthouse,* which makes continuities out of distractions. It is as if a woman's mind were linked at its origin, like the novel itself, to romance; and one is quite happy with this natural picaresque, the author walking us and the world along on the back of her prose.

Still, prose in a novel is different from prose in some other form. Its function can be determined only within a particular structure, and a novel or story requires some finite series of events necessary to produce suspense and move the reader toward the resolving point. This raises the question of the relation of plot and prose.

In the modern novel there are at least two significant ways of making prose subsume the suspense previously offered by plot. One is to structure it as highly as the verse of the seventeenth-century classical drama in France, so that even the simplest conversation becomes dramatic. Henry James's prose has affinities to this. The other is to have the plot coincide with the special perspective of a character. Faulkner and many others (including James) may use this method, which creates a kind of mystery story, the mystery being the mind itself. Mrs. Woolf's prose has some affinities here, but it is not made to issue from a mind limited or peculiar enough to make us suspect the darkness it circles.

The curious fact is that neither the prose nor the plot of Mrs. Woolf's novels can explain the suspense we feel. Perhaps suspense is the wrong word, since we are not avid for what happens next but fascinated by how the something next will happen. To understand this let us take *Mrs. Dalloway.* Its plot is simple and realistic, as is always the case with Virginia Woolf (*Orlando* is only an apparent exception). The suspense or fascination cannot come from that source. Nor does it come, in isolation, from the rich prose woven by Clarissa's mind, since the plot often parts from her to present other people or views, yet our attention does not flag at those points. But if Mrs. Woolf goes at will beyond Clarissa's consciousness, it is on condition that some line of continuity be preserved. There are no jumps, no chapters; every transition is tied to what precedes or has been introduced. The first line of the novel, "Mrs. Dalloway said she would buy the flowers herself," pre- supposes some immediate prior fact already taken up in consciousness and is emblematic of the artist's mood throughout the novel. Our fascination is involved with this will to continuity, this free prose working under such strict conditions.

The plot, however, does play an important role. Clarissa waiting to cross the street, then crossing, is part of the plot; her thoughts while doing so effect many finer transitions. A tension is thus produced between the realistic plot and the expressive prose; the latter tends to veil or absorb the former, and the former suggests a more natural continuity, one less dependent on mind. We know that certain things happen in sequence, that a play will go on, that people fall in love or cross streets, that a day moves from dawn to dusk. The simpler continuity of the plot tempts the mind forward, as a relief from the essential prose, or as a resting place in something solid.

This tension between two types of continuity also makes the mind realize the artificial or arbitrary character of both. It is moved to conceive the void they bridge. A void is there, like the pauses or thoughts of death in Mrs. Dalloway. But the mind conceives it joyfully, rather than in terror, because of the constant opening up of new perspectives, and the realization through this of its connective power. The continuities we have labeled "plot" and "prose" are, moreover, not unrelated or without special value. I would now like to show that they stand to each other dialectically as major types of affirmation, the plot line coinciding mostly with what we call nature, and the prose line intimating something precarious but also perhaps greater—the "Nature that exists in works of mighty Poets." To do so I return to A Room of One's Own, in which Mrs. Woolf (or her persona) is thinking about women writers, and the last of her thought sequences suggests the structure of her novels in microcosm.

Mrs. Woolf looks from her window at London waking for the day's business in the fall of '28. She looks out, not in, allowing herself to be distracted. The city seems to be indifferent to her concerns, and she records the fact strongly:

> Nobody, it seemed, was reading Antony and Cleopatra ... Nobody cared a straw—and I do not blame them—for the future of fiction, the death of poetry or the development by the average woman of a prose style completely expressive of her mind. If opinions upon any of these matters had been chalked on the pavement, nobody would have stooped to read them ... Here came an errand-boy; here a woman with a dog on a lead.[3]

Something is wrong. Can a writer be so calm about indifference, especially when it threatens art? But Mrs. Woolf is hastening the end. Not her own, but the end of a civilization which had exalted one part of the soul at the expense of the rest. The twenties are reaching their close; the first world war is not forgotten; Proust, Bergson, and Freud have advertised human possessiveness and male arbitrariness, the subtlest workings-out of the patriarchal will. The bustle she welcomes has, at least, the arbitrariness of life rather than of the will: an errand boy here, a funeral there, business men, idlers, shoppers, each going his way.

But her thought does not stop at this point; she lets it found its dialectic. The mind, to begin with, accepts a life indifferent to itself. The affirmative movement is not overcome, though what Virginia Woolf affirms is life rather than her will. Yet she is less interested in life as such than in the life of the mind, which can only appear if thought is left as apparently free as the goings and comings beneath her window.

That this freedom may be an illusion does not matter. It is still a window to the truth and, in any case, lasts a short time. As Mrs. Woolf continues to look, the life disappears, and only the indifference remains: "There was a complete lull and suspension of traffic. Nothing came down the street; nobody passed. A single leaf detached itself from the plane tree at the end of the street, and in that pause and suspension fell." Her mind, however, will not accept this pause, this emptiness. The affirmative movement attaches itself the more strongly to the slightest sign. "Somehow it was like a signal falling, a signal pointing to a force in things which one had overlooked."

What the mind has overlooked seems at first to be nature, an impersonally and constantly active principle of life. This certainly has a presence in Mrs. Woolf's novels. It is much more important to her than the spice of illusionistic realism. In her wish for a purer affirmation, one which does not merely go toward the male will, she often has her characters go toward nature. Their direct relationships are diverted by a second one: "human beings not always in their relations to each other but in their relation to reality; and the sky too, and the trees or whatever it may be in themselves." No human being, she adds, should shut out the view.

Yet it becomes clear, as Mrs. Woolf continues, that the mind had also overlooked something in itself. The falling leaf reminds her, it is true, of a natural force—but in the artist. It is the artist, the person at the window, who affirms a world where there is none. She imagines that the signal points to "a river, which flowed past, invisibly round the corner, down the street, and took people and eddied them along." In *Mrs. Dalloway* the author's consciousness is precisely this: a stream of prose that moves people together and apart, entering at will this mind and that. Nature, as she now conceives it, is one in which the artist participates, so that Shakespeare, poetry, and the finding of a new prose style become once again vital issues.

The artist, at this point, is clearly a Prospero figure. She stages an illusion whose object is a marriage: the mind coming together outside of itself by means of the world or the stage. Nature and art conspire for this illusion or prothalamion; the river, we notice, is a natural and artificial image of rhythm and leads directly to the closing event. As if the river had eddied them together, a girl in patent leather boots and a young man in a maroon raincoat meet a taxi beneath Virginia Woolf's window and get in. "The sight was ordinary enough," she remarks; "what was strange was the rhythmical order with which my imagination had invested it."

Only now does she withdraw from the window, reflecting on the mind.

Because of her topic—the woman as writer—she had been thinking intensely of one sex as distinct from the other. But, seeing the couple, the mind felt as if after being divided it had come together again in a natural fusion. Perhaps, she goes on, a state of mind exists in which one could continue without effort, because nothing is required to be repressed and no resistance develops. Interpreting the event literally as well as analogically, she concludes that the fully functioning mind is androgynous.

There is much fantasy in this. What remains is a sustained act of thought, a dialectic that comprises certain distinct types of affirmation. *Dialectic* is not, at first glance, the right word, since all we see is an affirmative movement increasing in scope. There comes, however, a critical pause, a moment of discontinuity, in which the *negative* almost appears. "Nothing came down the street; nobody passed." Such "power failures" are not rare in Virginia Woolf and not always so lightly overcome. They assume a cosmic proportion in her last novel. Miss La Trobe, the illusionist, cannot sustain her country pageant. The wind is against her, life is against her, the rhythm breaks. She learns the depth of space between her and her creation; the vacuum, also, between it and the audience. "Miss La Trobe leant against the tree, paralyzed. Her power had left her. Beads of perspiration broke on her forehead. Illusion had failed. 'This is death,' she murmured, 'death.' " At this very moment, as in the scene beneath Virginia Woolf's window, nature seems to take over and reestablish the rhythm in an expressionistic passage revealing the complicity of art and nature: "Then, suddenly, as the illusion petered out, the cows took up the burden. One had lost her calf. In the very nick of time she lifted her great moon-eyed head and bellowed. All the great moon-eyed heads laid themselves back. From cow after cow came the same yearning bellow. . . . The cows annihilated the gap; bridged the distance; filled the emptiness and continued the emotion."

Between the Acts reveals the same voracious desire for continuity as *Mrs. Dalloway* and *To the Lighthouse,* yet in this last work the novelist has dropped all pretense as to the realism of her transitions. She is outrageously, sadly humorous. "Suddenly the cows stopped; lowered their heads, and began browsing. Simultaneously the audience lowered their heads and read their programmes." This is how she gets from the cows to the audience, with the result, of course, that one feels the space she bridges more intensely. Yet does not the whole novel turn on what is between the acts, on the interpolations of the novelist who continually saves the play for Miss La Trobe? As in the example from *A Room of One's Own*, it is finally irrelevant whether the continuities discovered by Mrs. Woolf are in nature or in the artist.

Our question as to the kind of novel Virginia Woolf writes can now be answered. There is a line of development which goes from the realism of *The Voyage Out* (1915) to the expressionism of *Between the Acts* (1941), and passes through the experimental period of 1925–31 containing *Mrs. Dalloway, To the Lighthouse, Orlando,* and *The Waves.*[4] Mrs. Woolf sought to catch the power of affirmation in its full extent, and her effort to do so includes this shuttling between realistic and expressionistic forms of style. She never abandoned realism entirely because it corresponds to an early phase of affirmation. It is realism of the simple and illusionistic kind which guides our powers of belief toward the world we see, when we see it most freely. We can call this world nature, understanding by that a continuous yet relatively impersonal principle of life, even when (as in the bustle beneath Virginia Woolf's window) it assumes a more human shape. The next phase, more complex, raises the problem of "interpolation." The falling leaf is a signal from Nature, but it points to the artist who sees or affirms a nature persisting through the negative moment. Art, therefore, becomes interpolation rather than mimesis. Though Mrs. Woolf retains a realistic plot, everything of importance tends to happen between the acts, between each finite or external sign. *Mrs. Dalloway* and *To the Lighthouse* are distinguished by this indefinite expansion of the interval, of the mind-space, for example, between the beams of the lighthouse. The realistic plot is sustained by an expressionistic continuity. ⟨. . .⟩

Virginia Woolf's use of a realistic plot and an expressionistic continuity seems to me as deep a solution to the structural problems of prose fiction as that found in *Ulysses*. Though the form cannot be said to originate with her, she gave it a conscious and personal perfection, and it remains a vital compromise with the demands of realism. She learned, of course, a great deal from (and against) Joyce, and to mention her in that company is itself a judgment. Her weakness, bound up with her virtues, lies less in any formal conception than in her subject, which is almost too specialized for the novel. I suspect that it is her subject, not her form, which is poetic, for she deals always with a part of the mind closest to the affirmative impulse. We do not find in her great scenes, passionate and fatal interviews with the characters restricted to and revolving around each other. For however complex her characters may be, they are caught up essentially in one problem and are variations of the "separatist" or "unifier" type. The one lives by doubting, and the other by affirming, the illusion of a divine or childhood nature. Poetry gives us this nature more vividly than Virginia Woolf, but it is she who makes us aware of its daily necessity and deception.

NOTES

[1] For a strictly philosophical account, see Hegel's *Phenomenology of Mind* (1807), introduction and opening section on "Sense-Certainty"; Heidegger's *What Is Metaphysics* (1929); and Sartre's *L'Imaginaire* (1940).

[2] *Orlando*, chap. 6; *Auguries of Innocence:* "A Riddle or the Cricket's Cry/Is to Doubt a Fit Reply."

[3] The thought-sequence from which I quote in this section is found in the last chapter (6) of *A Room of One's Own*.

[4] I am probably unfair in omitting *Jacob's Room* (1922) from the experimental novels. The link between imagination and interpolation is gropingly acknowledged: "But something is always impelling one to hum vibrating, like the hawk moth, at the mouth of the cavern of mystery, endowing Jacob Flanders with all sorts of qualities he had not at all—for though, certainly, he sat talking to Bonamy, half of what he said was too dull to repeat; much unintelligible (about unknown people and Parliament); what remains is mostly a matter of guesswork. Yet over him we hang vibrating."

Blanche H. Gelfant

LOVE AND CONVERSION IN
MRS. DALLOWAY

While Virginia Woolf's technique as a novelist has been studied in close detail, her themes have usually been defined broadly in general terms. Time and personality have been considered the main underlying themes of her fiction. In *Mrs. Dalloway*, time and personality are related to a more specific issue, the conflict between love and conversion. I should like to discuss this relatively unexplored conflict by beginning with the more familiar problem of Mrs. Dalloway's personality.

Early in the novel *Mrs. Dalloway*, Clarissa Dalloway has a private searching moment when she examines her image in the mirror. There she sees a face distinctively "pointed; dartlike; definite"—the familiar face, composed and tense, that her mirror has reflected "many million times."[1] This clearly focused image represents a unified and static self, the person she can produce whenever she needs a recognizable social mask. But she knows that her social image conceals "incompatible" aspects of her personality which could be refracted into divergent and contradictory images. Each of the other characters sees only one of these incompatible aspects and takes this to be her total personality. Thus, as the novel progresses, the early static image in the mirror gives way to a series of shifting and contradictory views of Mrs. Dalloway; and her identity expands to encompass all the divergent images while remaining unencompassed by them. The other characters' fragmentary glimpses of Mrs. Dalloway exist side by side, each contradicted but uncancelled by the others, all of them together suggesting the total incompatible aspects of her personality of which only she is aware. The special way that each character has of seeing Mrs. Dalloway reflects an incompatibility in points of view. While one character can see her significance, another sees her triviality; while one sees her generosity, another sees her selfishness; while one reacts to her life-giving force, another responds to her parasitism. Thus, her personality begins to emerge as a relative quality, determined by who observes her rather than by what she is.

From *Criticism* 8, No. 3 (Summer 1966): 299–45.

Like the characters in the novel, literary critics who have discussed Clarissa Dalloway over the years have also had different points of view. To them too she has presented many faces. While to one critic she has seemed "a successfully realized" and "fully rounded character,"[2] to another she has remained "obstinately insubstantial," not a woman, but a "fairy . . . from adult folklore . . . a belle dame sans merci."[3] Another critic has found her "convincing" though elusive,[4] in contrast to one who thought her a "sharply clear figure."[5] Still another considered her "unhappy," having "missed her moment" in life and made the "wrong choice."[6] I wish to suggest here that her choice was inevitable for her, and right. Some critics have concluded that "almost everyone loves Mrs. Dalloway," although she is "cool, snobbish, and superficial in social relationships."[7] Virginia Woolf did not love her (as she did, for example, Mrs. Ramsey in *To the Lighthouse*); in fact, she rather disliked her for being "too stiff, too glittering and tinselly."[8]

Thus Mrs. Dalloway has remained an evasive heroine, but this very quality of her personality makes her remarkably contemporary. For in *Mrs. Dalloway,* as in much of our modern fiction, personality has lost the fixed quality of an absolute and has become elusive, evasive, strangely fluid.[9] Unknowable in itself, personality comes to be reflected only obliquely, through the distorting and kaleidoscopic glimpses of unrelated observers. But the images caught by these observers seldom coincide, not only because of their multiple viewpoints, but also because of the character's multiple, and sometimes contradictory, roles. In the contemporary novel, a hero's identity is often relative to the part he is playing as well as to his audience. He becomes like a masquerader who no longer knows his true identity because he is always wearing different masks and wandering through a hall of distorting mirrors. As he loses touch with his own reality, he turns into one of the faceless protagonists of modern fiction who find in the mirror either a vague and blurred image or the apparitional face of a stranger.

Clarissa Dalloway, however, never experiences this loss of identity—despite the ambiguities of her personality and the various images reflected to her by others. Whenever she wishes, she can summon to the mirror her dependable and familiar image, her pointed, dartlike face. For she remains certain of a fundamental identity beneath all her masks. This is the identity she reveals in the novel by her decisions, not the trivial decisions of the day—which book to select for an invalid friend, how to arrange her flowers, whom to invite to her party—but by her fundamental decisions with regard to the alternatives of love and conversion. The polarity of love and conversion in the novel gives Mrs. Dalloway the opportunity for the moral choices by which she creates herself. Also this polarity provides the novel with an underlying structure and its specific theme.

Love and conversion are Virginia Woolf's terms for antithetical life-attitudes: the creative and the coercive. In the novel, love implies an attitude of allowance; letting others be; recognizing in them an inviolable private self. A character who experiences love has a sense of wonder at life, for he sees that it offers him the possibilities of both solitude and society. He is free to be himself, and yet he can come together with others in a close but unstultifying relationship. Love inspires creativity. The exponent of love wishes to express the beauty of his vision of life as it allows the one and the many to come together. Conversion, on the other hand, is a destructive force, always indicating coercion. It is symbolized in the novel as an iron Goddess whose worshippers identify themselves by their desire for power. The followers of conversion seek out people they can dominate, the weak, or sick, or disenfranchised. They "swoop" upon their victims, always concealing their true motives under a charitable guise. They appear as the helpers, the philanthropists, scientists, or evangelicalists, who know what is good for others. Their true natures cannot be concealed from Mrs. Dalloway: she has the unique ability to see through the charitable gesture to its tyrannical meaning. Indeed her principal and coherent action, the action, that like her party preparations, gives unity to the novel, is to expose and condemn the various forms of conversion. Her basic opposition to the coercive will is an absolute quality of her personality. As she stands intransigent in her resistance to conversion, she becomes more than the sum of her multiple roles, and more than the sum of responses to her. She becomes her unique and individual self. Viewed against this perspective of the theme of love and conversion, Mrs. Dalloway's personality takes on special significance; and the meaning of the novel, so often considered tenuous or elusive,[10] emerges in a rather new and important light.

Love and conversion are dramatized by a double apposition of characters: in the main plot, Peter Walsh, Miss Kilman, and Lady Bruton are set against Mrs. Dalloway; in the sub-plot, Dr. Holmes and Sir William Bradshaw are apposed to Septimus Smith. The conflict in the sub-plot, which ends in violence and death, intensifies the more tenebrous apposition involving Clarissa. This double polarity of characters creates a structure for the novel as important thematically as the careful structuring of time and place.[11] The narrative progresses through a series of revealing encounters between the exponents of love and those of conversion. Some encounters juxtapose present and past; Clarissa as she now is recalls the girl of eighteen as she made her first discovery of conversion and her early affirmation of love. Some encounters show the clash between reality and delusion. The most terrible of these are Septimus' hallucinatory meetings with the brute conversion bearing down on him with nostrils aflame.

Clarissa's party, the climax of the action, unites both plots as it gathers together the double set of characters. The party is Clarissa's creation, her equivalent to a work of art, such as the painting Lily Briscoe finishes in *To the Lighthouse* or the drama Miss La Trobe stages in *Between the Acts*. The party brings to life Mrs. Dalloway's vision of the irrefragable possibilities for free and easy mingling. The exponents of conversion are present at her party, but deprived of the opportunity, and even the will, to exercise power. As the party momentarily banishes differences between the strong and the weak, the "dominators" and their victims, it becomes Clarissa's symbolic victory over the forces of conversion. Here, in this configuration of people that she has created and maintained for the evening, she establishes her presence and shows the full weight of her personality. Her party is for her an existential *act* by which she deliberately evokes and expresses the identity she has chosen to call her own. Her evening thus reveals the meaning of her day, for it shows that Mrs. Dalloway's "dallying" had a purposeful purposelessness which suited her private and essentially rebellious view of life.

For secretly, beneath the veneer of her conventional middle-class manners, Mrs. Dalloway lives as a rebel and existentialist before her time. Outwardly, her life is one of propriety and order; her gestures seem gentle and conservative. But inwardly, she is carried away by overwhelming emotions: she hates, she fears, she achieves ecstasy, and she rebels. She most clearly asserts this unsubdued and unsuspected private aspect of her personality when she identifies herself with Septimus Smith. She feels a tremendous empathy with this mad poet whom she has never seen because he had chosen death in defiance of authority. This act, she felt, had created even as it had destroyed him, and only by acts of volition, those seemingly passive (like her own) and those violent, did one achieve and assert his identity. Like the existentialist, Clarissa gives precedence to being over essence. She does not believe in God, and she looks upon death as a finality that makes life both absurd, in the existentialist sense, and precious. Death gives each moment an incandescence that the thought of eternity would have dimmed for her. Like many contemporary characters, Clarissa exalts the moment and seeks within it an "illumination," which she imagines to be like "a flame burning in a crocus."

Preoccupied as she is with time and death and the apocalyptic vision, she withdraws into the private world of herself, and her rebelliousness finds implicit expression in her refusal to conform to prescribed social roles. Through excuses of ignorance, ineptness, frailty, or disinterest, she keeps herself apart from social institutions. She does not participate in politics, religion, philanthropy, or social reform. Despite her sociability, she lives, essentially, a life of her own, as detached and singular in its way as the pathologically isolated life of her counterpart, Septimus Smith. She expresses her detachment in a way at once different from and yet similar to that of the modern disengaged characters of beat literature. She gives parties—quiet, staid affairs, but purposeful only in their purposelessness. Parties are her gestures toward art, for they create what she considers to be a free and self-contained configuration of people that is beautiful. Thus Mrs. Dalloway's day represents a search for values. Like most of Virginia Woolf's protagonists, Clarissa seeks the meaning of life (while her "double" becomes progressively convinced that life is meaningless). By sifting through her memories, by taking an imaginative leap into the lives of others, by questioning her own image in the mirror, and above all, by exposing and condemning conversion, she tries to arrive at a hierarchy of moral values and to define a code to live by.

The key term in her code—decency—has for her the same special meaning later given to it by Hemingway and Sartre. If the world lacks divine meaning, and if the confrontation of death reveals this meaninglessness (for Mrs. Dalloway, with her weakened heart, is in her own way confronting death), then the individual must create order and value by his deliberate choice to behave decently. Death has preoccupied Mrs. Dalloway; as she mused in her secluded attic room, she has even mystically anticipated a final dissolution of self,[12] perhaps out of a hidden suicidal impulse, acted out for her in the novel by her surrogate, Septimus. But she has also had the traumatic experience of seeing death strike fortuitously and without meaning. That her own sister should have been "killed by a fallen tree," a "girl . . . on the verge of life, the most gifted of them," seemed to her an act devoid of meaning.[13] Such an accident could not be considered part of a divine plan, whether benevolent, malicious, or inscrutable; it could be only a revelation of the lack of ulterior meaning in life and the absence of an ulterior being. If this was so, then the meaning of life must be created, so she thought, by one's own decisions. Like the existentialist, Mrs. Dalloway creates herself from moment to moment—this explains in part the "fluidity" of her personality—but underlying all decisions of the moment is her will to live decently. Her desire for decency is her response to what she considers to be a moral void, a world in which man is no longer sustained by traditional religion, but is instead threatened by the indifference of a scientifically oriented world.[14] When she read Huxley and Tyndall, as Peter Walsh remembers she did, then "possibly she said to herself, As we are a doomed race, chained to a sinking ship . . . let us, at any rate, do our part . . . be as decent as we possibly can" (p. 117).

How to behave decently is one of the questions raised by Mrs. Dalloway and the novel to which she gives her name. Decency seems to us to demand some kind of allegiance, a loyalty to a personal commitment. But to what cause can a woman of her time, class, and frame of mind commit herself? For Mrs. Dalloway, decency comes to mean not action, but a state of being. She expresses choice and commitment through *non*-activity, and unlike all the characters who surround her, she does not *do* anything. Indeed, she achieves her reality and justification by not doing—by not joining committees and playing the social game (as does Hugh Whitbread), by not seeking religion (Miss Kilman), by not serving science (Dr. Holmes, Sir William), by not supporting social causes (Lady Bruton), and by not pursuing personal passions (Peter Walsh). Yet as she lives by her self-created code of non-action, she achieves a presence that overshadows that of the purposeful and dominating characters about her. The novel, titled after her, becomes focused about her presence, beginning with her name and ending with her appearance:

> It is Clarissa, he said.
> For there she was.

Thus by a special kind of inactivity, which is her expression of social defiance, she achieves a sense of self-identity that many contemporary characters lack and seek to find in frenetic activities, sexual adventures, social and political involvements, and in movement, sheer desperate wandering, sometimes throughout the world. Mrs. Dalloway, however, finds gratification in the present moment and the immediate place. She has the capacity to project upon an ordinary London scene her excited sense of life, so that she sees even in the abject drunks a quality of "being" that is to her the ecstatic fact of life—that people *are,* that in being, in letting be, they know and love life:

> Such fools we are, she thought, crossing Victoria Street. For Heaven only knows why one loves it [life] so, how one sees it so, making it up, building it round one, tumbling it, creating it every moment afresh; but the veriest frumps, the most dejected of miseries sitting on doorsteps (drink their downfall) do the same; can't be dealt with, she felt positive, by Acts of Parliament for that very reason: they love life. In people's eyes, in the swing, tramp, and trudge; in the bellow and the uproar; the carriages, motor cars, omnibuses, vans, sandwich men shuffling and swinging; brass bands; barrel organs; in the triumph and the jingle and the strange high singing of some aeroplane overhead was what she loved; life; London; this moment of June (p. 5).

So Mrs. Dalloway finds in the city streets "that divine vitality" she loved. Her quiet stroll to the flower shop is an inward adventure in a day made adventuresome by the quality of her own sensibility. Her morning walk makes her feel ecstatically alive and fulfilled, and free—for she is under no compulsion to change or manipulate the scene about her. Her response to life is aesthetic, and unlike Lady Bruton, Miss Kilman, Peter Walsh, or Sir William Bradshaw, she is content to let the frump stand and the drunkard lie, feeling they share with her, in their own ways, an elated sense of life. She begins her day with this heightened, almost febrile, emotion that she tries to express that evening through her party.

Mrs. Dalloway's exaltation of the ordinary scene is related to her double sense of time: she is aware always of the present passing hours, intoned by Big Ben, and of the past, the self-creating years that live on now as memory. This simultaneous past can be evoked for her by sensations as delicate as the whiff of fresh air or the sound of a squeaking hinge.[15] She associates the past with a specific place—Bourton: the seashore, the family dinner table, the terrace—and with parents, relatives, and friends, particularly, Peter Walsh and Sally Seton. Though this past holds painful memories, such as the death of her sister and the end of her affair with Peter, she returns to it because it holds also the secret of her identity. She differs, then, from the many dislocated characters of modern fiction who must flee from and exorcise the past, in their quest for identity, rejecting parents and childhood scenes as destructive elements. The formative acts of Mrs. Dalloway's past are her rejection of Peter Walsh in favor of Dalloway, and her friendship with Sally Seton; both were creative acts, for they defined the alternatives of love and conversion which are to become her moral guides. Peter Walsh, in his demanding passion, first revealed to her man's hidden will to dominate, and Sally Seton revealed the possibility of "disinterested love." As Clarissa saw how Peter could not tolerate either Sally's idiosyncrasies or her own conventionalities, she understood his drive to "maul" and "maltreat" people until he had shaped them to his own desires. Thus

Peter became the first personification of conversion and the first of her "enemies"—for Clarissa realized that "it was enemies one wanted, not friends" (p. 266). Enemies forced her to rally to herself, to achieve definition and point, to mobilize her inner energies and become who she was. Peter Walsh prepares the way for an assemblage of enemies that is to include Miss Kilman, Lady Bruton, Dr. Holmes, and Sir William Bradshaw. All of these people have a disguised will to dominate and control; all worship conversion, the iron Goddess, "who loving to impress, to impose, adoring her own features stamped on the face of the populace . . . feasts most subtly on the human will" (pp. 151–52).

The most blatant example of conversion is the eminent physician and "priest of science," Sir William Bradshaw. For his wife and patients he set a standard, his standard, of normality, and if they did not conform to it, he threatened confinement. Fifteen years ago his wife had "gone under" and submitted her will to his: "there had been no scene, no snap; only the slow sinking, water-logged, of her will into his" (p. 152). Now he presents Septimus with his standard of "proportion" as the cure for his madness. But while he appears in the guise of the healer, with "love, duty, self sacrifice" as his ostensible motives, his real drive is for power. If the sick or helpless refused his version of normality, then, "He swooped; he devoured. He shut people up" (p. 154). That evening at her party, Mrs. Dalloway recognizes Sir William as the quintessential enemy, the disciple of conversion; but all during the day she has been weighing love and conversion, and she has found beneath the spurious masks of charity, passion, or religion, the same cruel will to dominate.

What else, she thinks, is Miss Kilman's relationship to young Elizabeth Dalloway than the expression of a desire to convert? Miss Kilman's possessive desire for Clarissa's daughter is presented as almost comically excruciating: "She was about to split asunder, she felt. The agony was so terrific. If she could grasp her, if she could clasp her, if she could make her hers absolutely and forever and then die; that was all she wanted" (pp. 199–200). Any possible homosexual implication in her passion for Elizabeth would have horrified Miss Kilman, for her disguise for conversion was spiritual love. Her pressing emotions, however, are hatred, frustration, embarrassment, and greed. Unable to devour the girl, she gorges on sticky chocolate éclairs. But she cannot enjoy even her gluttony, for she is uncomfortable and awkward wherever she is because she always feels herself frustrated in her desire to dominate. Even her religion, or especially her religion, makes her ugly and potentially cruel, so thinks Mrs. Dalloway: "religious ecstacy made people callous,"—and she adds "(so did causes)."[16]

The main exponent of social causes is Lady Bruton. Her great cause, one of many in the novel,[17] is a "project for emigrating young people of both sexes" to Canada. This project has become the focus of her life, giving her "pent egotism" a form of release. Through emigration she will assume, she dreams, a position of leadership like that her forebearers held, the commanders and generals whose lust for power she has in her blood. Like Miss Kilman (both women have names that belie their good intentions), Lady Bruton stuffs herself at lunch, until bloated and drowsy, she falls into a sleepy fantasy of domination that leaves her content: "Power was hers, position, income" (p. 169). While Clarissa earlier held the drunkard on the street inviolate, Lady Bruton never asks whether the "young people" want to be moved to Canada, for her philanthropy, like Miss Kilman's religion and Sir William's science, is the sublimation of her strong egocentric will for power.

Peter Walsh represents another disguise of conversion. His dominating will takes the form of passion. As a young man in Bourton, his love for Clarissa threatened the privacy she held inviolate. He insisted that she change herself to conform to his image of the ideal woman; he wanted to absorb her personality into his. Thinking back on Bourton, Clarissa unites the present with the past, for she still believes that "in marriage a little licence, a little independence there must be between people living together day in day out in the same house; which Richard gave her, and she him.... But with Peter everything had to be shared; everything gone into" (p. 10). In Peter's dominating love, Clarissa found the first clue to the tyranny hidden behind the masks of the Goddess conversion, and she realized also that conversion destroyed, no matter what its benevolent guise. Peter said he loved her, but he could not let her *be:* his passion was a fire that consumed as it embraced. Richard, on the other hand, offered love that was protective but unconsuming, and that allowed her the solitude and freedom to be herself. Thus her early choice between the two young men is a distinction between love and conversion. Although she occasionally regrets the decision, thinking that with Peter she would have had a more intense and exciting life, she has found in her marriage that balance of solitude and society that she absolutely needs:

> ... there is a dignity in people; a solitude; even between husband and wife a gulf; and that one must respect, thought Clarissa, ... for one would not part with it oneself, or take it, against his will, from one's husband, without losing one's independence, one's self-respect—something, after all, priceless (p. 181).

The symbol that expresses for Mrs. Dalloway the balanced relationship between self and others is the window (later a central symbol in *To the Lighthouse*). The window reveals people to each other but also keeps them separate. Through her window, Mrs. Dalloway can see the old lady in the house across the way as she goes through her preparations for the evening, privately and undisturbed. For Clarissa, this ordinary sight is reassuring, and indeed, beautiful:

> ... she watched out of the window the old lady opposite climbing upstairs. Let her climb upstairs if she wanted to; let her stop; then let her, as Clarissa had often seen her, gain her bedroom, part her curtains, and disappear again into the background. Somehow one respected that—that old woman looking out of the window, quite unconscious that she was being watched. There was something solemn in it—but love [passion] and religion would destroy that, whatever it was, the privacy of the soul (pp. 191–92).

At one point in the novel, Septimus Smith cries out that for him too "beauty was behind a pane of glass." But to him the glass represents total withdrawal, a barrier that shuts him away from society and keeps in his pain.[18] Solitude without society is madness. Septimus cannot share experience; he has lost the ability to relate to others except in a way that victimizes him. He feels himself either totally isolated or under coercion. His pathological withdrawal, first symptomized by a strange numbness at his friend's sudden death, has continued into his marriage. Shut in upon himself, he experiences horror at the sheer emptiness of life. To live in dread as he does must mean, he thinks, that he is guilty of unspeakable crimes, and guilt haunts him in the form of hallucination. Hallucination takes him out of a terrifying reality to an even more ominous world filled with unseen voices and figures of the dead. When he finally confesses his utter helplessness and turns to others for support, he encounters the iron Goddess conversion. She appears to him under the masks of the Doctors Holmes and Bradshaw, those "repulsive brutes, with blood-red nostrils" who threaten to lock him up if he does not submit to them. In reaction to the forces that Septimus feels to be coercing him—Holmes and Bradshaw telling him what he "*must*" do—he calls forth the one strength left to him in his weakness. He has the freedom of utter detachment: "now that he was quite alone, condemned, deserted, as those who are about to die are alone, there was a luxury in it, an isolation full of sublimity; a freedom which the attached can never know" (p. 140). His sense of freedom is delusory, but it gives him the courage for defiance. At the expense of his life, he keeps himself inviolate—his suicide assures that he will never be converted to Sir William's standard of "proportion."[19]

Septimus Smith's sense of inviolability, though symptomatic of his paranoia, makes him Mrs. Dalloway's dark complement. He represents her possible destiny were she to lose her tenuously free contact with other people which gives her a hold on sanity. For like Septimus, she feels herself threatened, and she too experiences panic at the fact of being alive. Unlike him, though, she has the support of money, maids, position, and her husband; but her strongest support is really her own illuminated vision of life. This vision represents her moral victory over the neurasthenic fears and death-impulses that have threatened her during the day. She has already felt the pull of death so strongly that when she hears of Septimus' suicide she imaginatively re-experiences the horror of his impalement. Hidden beneath her heightened ecstatic sense of life is the threat of panic: "there was the terror; the overwhelming incapacity, one's parents giving it into one's hands, this life, to be lived to the end, to be walked with serenely; there was in the depths of her heart an awful fear" (p. 281).

In a sense, Mrs. Dalloway's party saves her from Septimus' fate (originally Virginia Woolf had intended her to die). Her party expresses her affirmation of life and creativity, even as it forces her to face the knowledge of death: "In the middle of my party, here's death, she thought" (p. 279). At this confrontation, she achieves more than a reconciliation to the fact of death: she comes to view it as the ultimate form of man's defiance. "Death was defiance," she thought, and secretly she applauds

Septimus' suicide because she surmises that it had preserved the integrity of his inviolable self. When once again the old lady appears in the window across the way, Mrs. Dalloway feels a rush of affirmation and love; and she reasserts the value of her party as a creative gesture. Her desire "to combine, to create" is her tacit acknowledgment of the darkness of life, and her victory over it. This darkness is not merely the threat of death: it is the possibility for total isolation in the solitude of madness, or for the brutality of power. As her party serves "to kindle and illuminate," it expresses her answer to the powers of darkness. Her party has taken the individual out of the possible panic of isolation while it has at the same time rendered powerless the "dominators and tyrants" who serve the Goddess conversion. At her party, she has momentarily vanquished the arch-enemy, Sir William Bradshaw, a man capable of that "indescribable outrage," "forcing your soul."

No one sees the parties in the same light as she. To Peter Walsh, who cannot conceive of an unegocentric or gratuitous act, they seem attempts at social climbing, directed towards her husband's advancement. To Lady Bruton, with her ideal of military command, they seem idle and vain. To her husband, they seem undue taxations of her strenth. To Miss Kilman, sin. But her party nevertheless establishes her in juxtaposition to the others and elicits their secret if begrudged admiration. For it shows her to be truly untyrannical; and while it also reveals her as trivial, snobbish and dependent, she can transcend her faults to become a definitive central figure. Having recognized and rejected the multifaces of power and coercion, she has achieved, through a mature and comprehending acceptance of self and others, her moral victory. Disinterested, in the best sense of the word, she is not a force. She is merely and above all herself; and her single "gift," to which she can give only inadequate expression through the party, is her respect for the privacy of the human soul.

Another point should be made about Mrs. Dalloway's defiance of conversion. Throughout the novel, conversion has been personified to her by the various characters she encounters; she has resisted the pressures of these characters and remained intransigent against them. But she seems to have a deep unconscious need to resist that far exceeds the threat they posed to her, for after all, she has managed to keep herself inviolate and to maintain into middle-age her own identity. Yet she seems under great emotional strain, and the intensity of her inner experience, so much at odds with her outer life, suggests that she is struggling against conversion not only in man and his institutions, but in life itself. To her, time, personality, and death come to be in themselves coercive forces, and she accepts the challenge to resist them also as the test of her self-identity. She wishes to resist the passage of time by retaining all experience within a single present moment. She refuses to relinquish her unique and individual personality to death, for she hates the thought of cessation and finality. She tries to keep her personality inviolate, protected from all the potential infringements of other people; yet she wishes to merge herself in the endless and continuous stream of humanity just as she loses herself in the moving London crowds.

In her resistance to the idea of interference and finality, Mrs. Dalloway projects Virginia Woolf's life-long interest as a novelist in the "idea of some continuous stream." Mrs. Woolf's poetic vision of life as a continuous stream is the vision of a kind of absolute freedom. Such a vision must come into conflict with reality, the reality of interference and finality which it seeks to reject. This conflict is reflected in the novel by a disturbing tension that often seems inconsistent with its lyrical mode. Despite its surface fluidity, the novel shows Virginia Woolf's struggle to reconcile the difficult antinomies of life: the one (solitude) and the man (society); the moment that is now, and the stream of time that sweeps away the present; sanity and insanity (that make Mrs. Dalloway and Septimus two sides of one person); the human impulse to create and the human desire to destroy; life and death. Against these antinomies, she has set the artistic will; and the tension within the novel may be attributed to an underlying resistance of the will to the terms of reality.

The form of the novel attempts to transmute the everyday realities of life into a metaphorical equivalent of the sea. The sea was Virginia Woolf's primal symbol of fluid continuity, and she tried to create an impression of life as being as flowing, as timeless, as continuous, as the sea. As *Mrs. Dalloway* flows in one uninterrupted stream from first word to last, aesthetic form mimetically simulates the theme of continuity. The stream-of-consciousness technique makes past and present continuous in the character's mind. The poetic language of the novel achieves a compression and ambiguity suited to its organic view of life; and symbolism weights a seemingly insignificant object or gesture with ramified meanings from other times and other contexts. Thus the surface of the novel suggests the movement of the sea, constantly flowing; and like the sea, it contains beneath its surface the dimension of depth.

On the surface, Mrs. Dalloway knew that she must stand intransigent against the iron Goddess conversion; but she did not realize that her wish never to coerce nor to be coerced implied a deep submerged longing for an impossible state of pure, disengaged existence. She wished to *be*—she wished never to clutch at life by dominating others, but to let life lift and carry her in its stream, just as the London crowds bore her along, just as her own viable memories made life a continuous and rushing flow. To maintain herself within such a flowing continuity, she gave up much: passion, religion, social commitment, the rewards of engagement in a cause. But was there some other way to defy the Goddess conversion than to reject through madness, death, or sheer intransigence of will, the seductions of power? This is the question Mrs. Dalloway raises by her unwillingness to perform an institutionalized act lest it turn out to be a hidden gesture of coercion. It is a question pertinent to our own age with its great institutionalized pressures for conformity. If we knew the answer to this question we would know how Mrs. Dalloway might have spent her day in some other way than in the desultory preparations for a party. And if Virginia Woolf could have conceived another answer, she might have solved some of the inherent aesthetic problems of the novel: that middle-class Mrs. Dalloway does not always seem an appropriate character to reflect and to reflect upon the theme of rebellion; that her creative "gesture," the party, does not convincingly fulfill, in fact, almost nullifies, its purpose;[20] that the rendition of an action through non-activity tends to be unconvincing or merely unmoving; and that the lyrical mode of the novel may not produce the overtones most suitable to its matrix of ideas.[21]

Yet despite these difficulties, the novel comes to life as an ambitious, serious, and beautifully written work. And it is interesting to think that it has become transformed by the passage of time in a manner that Virginia Woolf might have appreciated. For its technical aspects, once so startlingly new, now belong within the tradition of the modern novel, and its unusual experimental design seems to the contemporary reader familiar and appropriate. Certain implications of its theme, however, emerge in a newer light against the existentialism of our day. *Mrs. Dalloway* dramatizes most clearly Virginia Woolf's theme of rebellion, and this theme makes it particularly relevant to us. As our literature reflects concern over the individual's sense of loss of identity, Mrs. Dalloway's pointed, dartlike image asserts the possibility of maintaining one's self through an intransigent will placed in the gratuitous and ungrasping service of love. *Mrs. Dalloway* contains the hope that man's creative will is stronger than his destructive instincts—and this is the hope of our times.

NOTES

[1] Virginia Woolf, *Mrs. Dalloway* (New York: Harcourt, Brace and Company, 1925), p. 55. All subsequent references to *Mrs. Dalloway* are to this edition.

[2] Joan Bennett, *Virginia Woolf: Her Art as a Novelist* (New York: Harcourt, Brace and Company, 1945), p. 43.

[3] Aileen Pippett, *The Moth and the Star: A Biography of Virginia Woolf* (Boston: Little, Brown and Company, 1953), p. 200.

[4] J. K. Johnstone, *The Bloomsbury Group: A Study of E. M. Forster, Lytton Strachey, Virginia Woolf and Their Circle* (London: Secker and Warburg, 1954), p. 339.

[5] Dorothy Brewster, *Virginia Woolf's London* (New York: New York University Press, 1960), p. 48.

[6] Bernard Blackstone, *Virginia Woolf* (London: Longmans, Green and Company, 1952), pp. 26 and 35.

[7] Frederick Karl and Marvin Magalener, *A Reader's Guide to Great Twentieth Century English Novels* (New York: Noonday Press, 1959), p. 134.

[8] Joan Bennett thinks that Mrs. Dalloway's personality is sketched in the novel "with full sympathy," op. cit., p. 79. One of the first readers of the novel, Virginia Woolf's friend and fellow writer, Lytton Strachey, thought that Clarissa was "disagreeable and limited" and that Mrs. Woolf herself was ambivalent toward her protagonist, "alternately" laughing at her and identifying with her. See *A Writer's Diary: Being Extracts from the Diary of Virginia Woolf,* ed. Leonard Woolf (New York: Harcourt, Brace and Company, 1954), p. 77. See also p. 60.

[9] This view of the "fluidity" of personality appears also in contemporary "existential psychotherapy." See, for example, Carl R. Rogers, *On Becoming a Person: A Therapist's View of Psychotherapy* (Boston: Houghton Mifflin, 1961): " . . . a person is a fluid process, not a fixed and static entity; a flowing river of change, not a block of solid material, a continually changing constellation of potentialities, not a fixed quantity of traits" (p. 124). Virginia Woolf herself might have written these words, and used these metaphors (perhaps "sea" rather than "river") in her diary; and her critics emphasize the fundamental importance to her art of the concept of character as fluid and hence elusive.

[10] David Daiches finds "the real theme" of *Mrs. Dalloway* to be "the dissolution of experience into tenuous insights." See David Daiches, *Virginia Woolf* (Norfolk, Conn.: New Directions, 1942), p. 78. Aileen Pippett could not decide what kind of a work *Mrs. Dalloway* was: "Is this a love story? A ghost story? A parable of despair defeated . . . of life perpetually renewing itself?" Op. cit., p. 206.

11 See David Daiches, *The Novel and the Modern World* (Chicago: University of Chicago Press, 1960), pp. 202–12. (Published originally 1939.)

12 Earlier Mrs. Dalloway had imagined the possibility of a life after death, in which one's personal identity is gone, but one's influence upon other people becomes a form of impersonalized—or *depersonalized*—immortality (p. 12). A concept of life continuing after death in such a way—so that the personal form of being as we know it in life has turned to non-being, but the being continues after death in the new form of influences and effects upon others—is hypothesized in Jean-Paul Sartre's *Being and Nothingness: An Essay on Phenomenological Ontology* (New York: Philosophical Library, 1956), tr. Hazel Barnes. Virginia Woolf dramatized this view of death in *To the Lighthouse,* where Mrs. Ramsey's presence persists to influence her family and friends; and in *The Waves,* where Percival remains alive in the consciousness of his friends—that is, indeed, the only life he has in the novel.

13 Virginia Woolf's younger brother, Thoby Stephen, also a young person of great promise, died suddenly on a holiday abroad.

14 See David Daiches' discussion of the breakdown of tradition in the modern world and its effect on the writer's search for values in *The Novel and the Modern World.*

15 The theme of the simultaneity of all time is introduced by the street woman's mumbled rendition of an ancient love song (pp. 122–24). The beggar woman becomes, metaphorically, a "rusty pump" which brings burbling to the surface a timeless stream that had like love, of which she sings, flowed "millions of years ago" and would flow on forever, taking to an interminable future "the passing generations" in the streets.

16 In its generous and permissive attitude toward Elizabeth, the Dalloway family exemplifies love; the coercive potentialities in family life are dramatized in *To the Lighthouse* and in the early part of *The Years.* The children in *To the Lighthouse* make a pact to resist to death their father's tyranny. Delia in *The Years* dreams of her mother's death as a release from an oppressive and suffocating force. These children seem projections of Virginia Woolf's own ambiguous feelings toward her father, whom she admired but feared because she felt his life absorbed hers, and only his death had liberated her. Long after his death she wrote in her dairy: "Father's birthday. He would have been 96 … like other people one has known: but *mercifully* was not. His life would have entirely ended mine. What would have happened? No writing, no books—inconceivable."

17 Hugh Whitbread has his modest causes: "improvement in public shelters," "protection of owls," help to distressed servant girls, and improvement of parks (p. 156). Lady Bradshaw's causes are "child welfare, the after-care of the epileptic," and preserving the history of decaying churches through photography (p. 143). Not to be outdone, Sir William "toil[s] to raise funds, propagate reforms [and] initiate institutions" (p. 152).

18 See an interesting and pertinent letter, "The Poetry of Madness," in *The New York Review of Books,* II: 11 (July 9, 1964), 20–21, written in response to a review of *The Three Christs of Ypsilanti.* Here the anonymous writer, drawing upon her own emotions and use of language while institutionalized for mental illness, comments on the psychotic's "multifaceted use of language." She refers particularly to a mental patient's remark: "I lived behind a glass of pane" (quoted in an article in *Harper's* magazine). Her interpretation of the linguistic "reverberations" of the psychotic's statement applies entirely to Septimus' phrasing; and the rest of the letter, dealing mainly with the delusions of the "Three Christs," illuminates Septimus' expression of his grand and terrible delusions.

19 On Virginia Woolf's own hostility to doctors, intensified to paranoiac fear in her illness, see Leonard Woolf, *Beginning Again: An Autobiography of the Years 1911–1918* (London: Hogarth Press, 1964), pp. 80, 164 et passim.

20 Toward parties, Virginia Woolf had ambivalent reactions: she felt the many "mad parties" she herself attended sapped her time and energy. But she used the party again as a unifying climactic device in *The Years* (and the party provides the occasion for character revelation in her short story, "The New Dress"). In *To the Lighthouse,* the dinner party has a unifying effect and serves as Mrs. Ramsey's creative victory over the dark forces that like the sea surround the house and family. See *To the Lighthouse* (New York: Harcourt, Brace and World, Inc., 1927), pp. 146ff.

21 In her diary, Virginia Woolf had written: "In this book I have almost too many ideas. I want to give life and death …; I want to criticise the social system, and to show it at work, at its most intense" (p. 56).

Lee R. Edwards

WAR AND ROSES: THE POLITICS OF *MRS. DALLOWAY*

Two figures dominate Virginia Woolf's fourth novel: Clarissa Dalloway and Septimus Smith. The one buys flowers and gives parties; the second returns from war, goes mad, and dies. This relation—of the perfect hostess and the shell-shocked soldier—is obviously not fortuitous. Indeed, the multiple connections and disjunctions which sustain these figures in a complex, interconnected web have been noticed by virtually everyone who has ever written—or thought—about the book. Clarissa lives. Septimus commits suicide. But life and death are not transacted in a vacuum. To see the characters embedded in a social structure containing possibilities for both limitation and liberation is to discover the beginnings of a new analysis, both feminist and social, not just of *Mrs. Dalloway,* but of all the works of Virginia Woolf.

By way of beginning, let me note that Virginia Woolf, Clarissa Dalloway, and I share two common characteristics: our sex and, in the broadest sense, our class. Shaping and defining us, our status as middle-class women has traditionally served to keep us out of what convention has established as the center of power, that masculine world which we have tended to encircle like so many electrons around a nucleus, in an outmoded diagram. Distrusting this status, we distrust ourselves and the vision of the world that grows out of our condition. Seeing ourselves as insignificant, inconsequential, unimportant outside of the sphere of home, family, and friends, we see our world as both small and trivial. We dislike ourselves because, like Clarissa Dalloway, we fear that we are "spoilt."[1] Like Jane Eyre surveying the world from the top of Thornfield's battlements we are, at best, defensive.

The wish to escape from what we perceive as our social prison, as well as from the confines which our own minds have built around us, has usually taken one of several, by now quite predictable forms. Since our class and sex appeared to us

From *The Authority of Experience: Essays in Feminist Criticism,* ed. Arlyn Diamond and Lee R. Edwards (Amherst: University of Massachusetts Press, 1977), pp. 161–77.

as prison walls, we developed new constructs in terms which would allow us to deny or to transcend these limitations and chose—or discovered, after the fact, that we had chosen—to avoid the traps customarily set for us by adopting the strategies of the other sex. Accepting, that is, the world our fathers and brothers created, we accepted as well their evaluation of the relatively greater import of this world in comparison with our own. Agreeing that the public sphere is haloed with grandeur, we sought to move into it, believing also that no vacuum would be created behind us as we abandoned our old places. Alternatively, we rejected the role of bourgeois man just as passionately as we rejected that assigned to his feminine counterpart and tried to reconstitute ourselves as something entirely new under the sun, as radicals of some new order.

I am not now interested in quarrelling with either of these modes of adaptation or even in evaluating the tactics such strategies call into being. What is to the point, however, is to see that in *Mrs. Dalloway,* as well as in several of her other novels and essays, Virginia Woolf is offering yet another choice. This alternative is arrived at by means of a serious, implicitly political investigation of the strengths and failures of middle-class society. Her perspective, located firmly within that society, is yet original enough to move in a direction that such investigations seldom take. But our distrust of what is middle-class, in combination with our distrust of what is set out or perceived as traditionally feminine, has obscured this subject from us and has prevented critics in general from treating it.

Inventing Septimus Smith and setting him out as both match and foil for Mrs. Dalloway, Virginia Woolf was trying, I believe, to focus our attention on the primacy of her concern not simply with the topics of individual isolation and interaction commonly counted as her subjects, but with a larger framework depicting and examining modes of social organization. In and of themselves, the book suggests, the forms that society chooses to honor, value, and perpetuate tend to foster solitude, fragmentation, abstraction, rigidity, and death on the one side, or communion, harmony, spontaneity, and life on the other. Wars and parties, shell-shock and roses, authority and individuality, death and life, "manly" and "feminine" are counters, metaphors, or symbols, but also, Virginia Woolf suggests, the literal facts resulting from a society's choice of particular forms. Thus, in *Mrs. Dalloway,* wars, madness, the love of suffering and pain, adherence to an abstract, hierarchical, authoritarian set of values and means of organisation are linked to death, and frequently, if not exclusively, to a particular notion of masculinity; conversely, parties, roses, joy, and the celebration of the spontaneity and variability of life are tied to and embodied in various female figures. The politics of *Mrs. Dalloway* are such that life is possible only when roses, parties, and joy triumph over war, authority, and death. Clarissa's celebrations—ephemeral and compromised though they may be—are a paradigm of sanity, a medium through which energy can flow in a world which is otherwise cruel, judgmental, and frozen.

The problem with the brief schematization I have just presented is not simply the usual one of demonstrating that the proposed reading is supported by the text, although that necessity must, of course, be faced. The real difficulties, however, are embedded in both the nature and the implications of the stated propositions and account, I think, for the appeal that Virginia Woolf's novels make to close reading, technical analyses, a linking of value purely and solely to what we can comfortably call individual consciousness. For who could seriously entertain these theories on other grounds? If it seems certain that we all condemn war and hope for some alternative, it seems equally certain that most of us are not predisposed to take seriously the notion that giving parties and celebrating life provide viable social or political alternatives. The idea that they might seems at best either stupid or naive and, at worst, so blind to the conditions and possibilities of all but the most privileged lives as to reveal not simply a moral lapse but a total moral blindness. Recommending the politics of joy seems either a piece of cynicism or an attempt at outright fraud.

Furthermore, our whole notion of the meaning of politics, the standard defi- nition of the word, is in terms of precisely those qualities Virginia Woolf denounces or is at least skeptical about: the organisations of government, management, fac- tions, intrigue, parties whose conventions are most unfestive. To talk easily of politics and with assurance of being understood, you have to accept the assigned meaning of the word. If you don't, you leave yourself unprotected, vulnerable to the charge that you fail to comprehend the meaning of the word at the center of your discussion. Thus, Virginia Woolf is not generally regarded as a political—or indeed even a social—novelist.

But if politics has to do with government, and government has to do with the systems or policies by which a political unit is operated, and society is a political unit which is, if not the entire state, at least one of its aspects, then isn't any discussion political which considers and evaluates the systems or policies by which society operates? The problem really has to do with where one locates systems, how one defines policies, and what, of course, one imagines society to be. For Virginia Woolf, politics in both a general and an institutional sense has first to do with people conceived of as individual entities rather than corporate masses. The values by which people live, the order in which they consent to arrange these values, determine the shape of social as well as institutional structures.

The gap that she points to, the chasm that her writings both indicate and indict, is the one that opens up between human and humane values on one side and systems, bureaucracy, Acts of Parliament on the other. She identifies that con- striction in our notion of politics which makes it difficult to bridge this gap: we think too much of abstractions, not enough of single cases; we assume, too quickly and with much too little evidence, that all people are, at base, alike and can thus be "handled" most "efficiently" by appeals to generalities; we think of politics and government at an increasing distance from individuals, human values, ethical, emotional, even sensuous considerations. Therefore, she suggests, all revolutions have always been betrayed because, at a certain point, the makers of the revolution came to have more regard for the system they installed then they did for the less tangible beliefs initially responsible for installing that system. The solution is not simply to make another revolution, but to change the bases on which revolutions are made, not merely to shift the power balance within society so that those who make war no longer have power, but to imagine a society in which the having of power is no longer paramount.

The adjustment of vision and of imagination required by these premises is, however, of such magnitude that the call for such measures in the novels of Virginia Woolf has been, for the most part, overlooked. Even those who concede that she might, perhaps, think of herself as a social novelist tend to fall into two more or less dismissive categories. The first finds her vision bound by snobbishness or psychic narrowness; the second sees her characters as embodiments of transcendent archetypes, thus undervaluing the worldly reality Woolf is at such pains to establish.[2] The author herself seems to indicate her awareness of this situation and of its genesis in the following passage from her essay, "Women and Fiction" (1929):

> For a novel, after all, is a statement about a thousand different objects—human, natural, divine; it is an attempt to relate them to each other. In every novel of merit these different objects are held in place by the force of the writer's vision. But they have another order also, which is the order imposed upon them by convention. And as men are the arbiters of that convention, as they have established an order of values in life, so too, since fiction is largely based on life, these values prevail there also to a very great extent.
>
> It is probable, however, that both in life and in art the values of a woman are not the values of a man. Thus, when a woman comes to write a novel, she will find that she is perpetually wishing to alter the established values—to make serious what appears insignificant to a man, and trivial what is to him important. And for that, of course, she will be criticized; for the critic of the opposite sex will be genuinely puzzled and surprised by an attempt to alter the current scale of values, and will see in it not merely a difference of view, but a view that is weak, or trivial, or sentimental because it differs from his own.[3]

The paradox inherent in the critical treatment generally accorded Mrs. Dalloway is implicit in the general analysis Virginia Woolf provided in her essay. The greatness of the book has been acknowledged, while its scope has been largely ignored or overlooked by critics of both sexes, for conventions, the conventions of power and, if you like, of men, govern women, too. We would feel—or at least believe that we would feel—something amiss if critical consensus gave top honors to King Lear, while resolutely insisting that its greatness lay in its fidelity to the details of royal succession in the Dark Ages; but no such check has operated on the assessment that Virginia Woolf wrote her novels in "the subjective mode . . . the only mode especially designed for temperaments immersed in their own sensibility, obsessed with its movements and vacillations, fascinated by its instability"[4] and that "despite its grounding in social and political life, then, *Mrs. Dalloway* is designed as the fictional biography of a single character."[5]

But the values and visions of a woman may not be those of a man. And the subject of *Mrs. Dalloway* is not the same as its technique. There is a world in the work as well as a self, and the world is one which, recovering from one war, obsessed with the memory and the horror of it, is even yet hurtling blindly onward toward the next. The seeds of war make the roots of that society and are nourished by its tears. In these circumstances war comes as a disaster, certainly, but not as a surprise. In the middle of post-War London, on a beautiful day in June, five years after hostilities have ended, Peter Walsh encounters soldiers marching. There is no reason for the presence of this vision in the book, no reason for the entire network of references to war which includes in experience, memory, or association almost every character in the novel from Lady Bexborough and Clarissa's Uncle William at the beginning to old Miss Parry at the end, and certainly no reason for the particular rendering of the character and the dilemma of Septimus Smith unless we see and acknowledge that these visions, references, and characters constitute a significant portion of anything we might wish to call the subject of the book. Thus, when Peter Walsh finds his way through the city blocked, he looks up to see, out of the infinite things an author might have created as impediments to individual progress, specifically "boys in uniform, carrying guns," who "marched with their eyes ahead of them, marched, their arms stiff, and on their faces an expression like the letters of a legend written round the base of a statue praising duty, gratitude, fidelity, love of England" (p. 76). Watching the small procession as it passes out of view, Peter Walsh meditates on what he sees:

> [T]hey did not look robust. They were weedy for the most part, boys of sixteen.... Now they wore on them unmixed with sensual pleasure or daily preoccupations the solemnity of the wreath which they had fetched from Finsbury Pavement to the empty tomb....
>
> [O]n they marched, ... as if one will worked legs and arms uniformly, and life, with its varieties, its irreticences, had been laid under a pavement of monuments and wreaths and drugged into a stiff yet staring corpse by discipline. (Pp. 76–77)

Important in itself, this meditation on the metamorphosis that sixteen-year-old boys undergo when they become imprisoned in the carapace of armor gains additional significance in the context of a web of references interweaving war, mechanism, and human beings who have shifted their allegiance to some set of monumental abstractions. Thus, for example, the long grey car which appears in the book prior to the soldiers is important not simply because it provides a convenient way for Virginia Woolf to move through time and space. It is important precisely because, unlike a conventional plot, the device *is* arbitrary, is not connected with human motivation, makes individuals feel, for the most part, insignificant, makes them feel that because the car is powerful whoever rides in it must be powerful as well. The explosion of the motor provokes thoughts of "the voice of authority" and of the hymns of "the spirit of religion . . . abroad with her eyes bandaged tight and her lips gaping wide" (p. 20). The spirit of this religion is connected with Churches, with organizations, with a Westminster containing buildings and memorials—the Cathedral and the Tomb of the Unknown Warrior—with prayers and ritual, the Reverend Whittaker and Miss Kilman; it is in direct contrast to the Westminster inhabited by the almost offhandedly spiritual Mrs. Dalloway, who returns home, like "a Goddess, having acquitted herself honourably in the field of battle" (pp. 43–44) to improvise transitory celebrations, whose powers and forms must always be freshly generated. Unlike Mrs. Dalloway, the human agency responsible for the agitation the car produces will not be known until Judgment Day, but the emotion created proceeds without such knowledge or attachment: "for in all the hat shops and tailors' shops strangers looked at each other and thought of the dead; of the flag; of Empire" (p. 25). Impressive mechanism divorced from specific individuals quickly becomes associated with figures embodying the power of the state—the Queen, the Prince of Wales, the Prime Minister, and finally, significantly, Sir William Bradshaw. The association, in turn, provokes a community of response which leads, finally, to action: "In a public house in a back street a Colonial insulted the House of Windsor which led to words, broken beer glasses, and a general shindy . . ." (pp. 25–26). Even Moll Pratt, who "would have tossed the price of a pot of beer—a bunch of roses—into St. James's Street out of sheer light-heartedness and con-tempt of poverty" (p. 27) is prevented from doing so by her regard for a constable, another symbol of the state's authority. The car moves along a route that goes from a dissociation of personality and power, to reverence for power in the abstract, to fighting and damming up of life. While the particular instances here are trivial, the scale can all too easily enlarge, the consequences become more sinister in-deed, as happens in the case of Septimus Smith and the doctors, Holmes and Bradshaw.

When Peter Walsh looked at the soldiers, he saw them first as boys, then as corpses, and finally as artifacts, statues who had renounced life in order to achieve "at length a marble stare. But the stare Peter Walsh did not want for himself in the least . . ." (p. 77). Septimus Smith, too, might have preferred to retain his capacity to blink and cry. But nobody asked him and, in any event, nobody cared what his preference was. There was a war, and the war needed men. "Septimus was one of the first to volunteer. He went to France to save an England which consisted almost entirely of Shakespeare's plays and Miss Isabel Pole in a green dress walking in a square" (p. 130). The experience of war, however, smashed this vision; the reassembled pieces made hideous patterns. In addition, those who had sent Septimus to war had always been suspicious of that early dream. Culture made Mr. Brewer, Septimus' employer, as nervous as it later makes Dr. Holmes and Dr. Bradshaw. Imagination was not healthy. Miss Pole was not fit company for a rising young clerk. Exercise was what was needed, porridge more to the point. And "in the trenches the change which Mr. Brewer desired when he advised football was produced instantly; [Septimus] developed manliness . . ." (p. 130). Now only the birds talk Greek. The Classic world, the world of culture and, more importantly, the world which had served Septimus by giving his imagination form died in the War and can now exert itself only as part of the paraphernalia of madness.

How odd that what a man is should not be sufficient to define him as a man, and that "manliness" should be seen as a quality to be learned. We do not, after all, have to teach a horse to be horsely or a rose to be a rose. How odd, too, that for so long we have not noticed, much less condemned, this oddness. But these observations are merely parenthetical. What is most interesting in *Mrs. Dalloway* is to see the lesson Septimus learned when he became a man: he must not feel. Thus, when his best friend, Evans, "was killed, just before the Armistice, in Italy, Septimus, far from showing any emotion or recognising that here was the end of a friendship, congratulated himself upon feeling very little and very reasonably. The War had taught him. It was sublime. He had gone through the whole show . . . and was bound to survive. He was right there" (pp. 130–131).

Surviving, unfortunately, killed him; for Septimus was finally unable to turn himself into a statue by a simple exercise of will. He told himself he could not feel. He wished himself into insensibility. "He would shut his eyes; he would see no more" (p. 32). He lied. He did feel

> himself drawing towards life, the sun growing hotter. . . . The trees waved, brandished. We welcome, the world seemed to say; we accept; we create. Beauty, the world seemed to say. . . . To watch a leaf quivering in the rush of air was an exquisite joy. Up in the sky swallows swooping, swerving, flinging themselves in and out, round and round, yet always with perfect control as if elastics held them; and the flies rising and falling; and the sun spotting now this leaf, now that, in mockery, dazzling it with soft gold in pure good temper; and now and again some chime . . . tinkling divinely on the grass stalks—all of this, calm and reasonable as it was, made out of ordinary things as it was, was the truth now; beauty, that was the truth now. Beauty was everywhere. (Pp. 104–105)

Of the person who can entertain these perceptions, it is simply silly—or mad—to say he cannot feel. Septimus dies because the War has acted on him, as the possessor of such feelings and responses, trapping him between anguish and guilt and giving him no way out except through his own death. He feels anguish because of the discrepancy between his feeling that the natural world is beautiful, the human world corrupt, and guilt because despite the discrepancy the feeling for the goodness and the beauty of life persists. He feels anguish because he thinks he cannot feel, guilt because he wishes not to feel, and both because he cannot admit what, in fact, he does feel. He feels anguish because he cannot love and guilt because, in not loving, he has deserted the fallen, betrayed his love and betrayed, as well, an ideal of humanity which values love. Yet he feels equally tormented because he has, indeed, loved Evans and because this love violates the standards of manliness which the War and the trenches have taught him to honor. If he truly did not feel anything when Evans died, then he would not need to punish himself for this lack of feeling: the ability even to imagine the need for such punishment would be beyond his capacities. He feels anger because he has fallen and been deserted by those from whom he had hoped for help—the government, the doctors, his wife—anguish because, since he is also a deserter, he can, in justice, expect no better treatment, and guilt because he feels anguish at being unable to live in a cold, just world.

Trying to deny his feelings by trivializing them, he thinks of himself and Evans as two dogs romping in front of the fire. His feelings, however, refuse to be denied and avenge themselves by making him see dogs turning into men, giving him a vision of a world where such trivialization, such denial need not occur but making that vision appear, in the terms of this world, a grotesque one. He wishes to "escape . . . to Italy" (p. 139), the place where Evans died and was betrayed, where Rezia was married and betrayed, so he can live through these experiences again without betrayal. This wish is both literally and psychologically impossible; therefore, it is mad. Septimus' madness, then, is not so much the result of his misperceptions as it is of his inability to reconcile the conflicting—but accurate—information he perceives. What is worst, of course, is the failure of those around him to admit that they, too, are implicated in producing these contradictions and that what they ask of Septimus is either the impossible denial of their existence or, failing that, his death. Even Rezia must bear a portion of this burden, for in wishing to see herself as "the English gentleman's good wife" she would force Septimus to be "an English gentleman," a version of Hugh Whitbread. Because Septimus can only fleetingly provoke in Rezia the awareness that this vision is hollow at its core, Rezia persists in wishing that Septimus could manage to be simultaneously the good soldier and the loving, philoprogenitive husband. So she, too, contributes to the depth of the chasm at his feet.

There is a terrible logic behind Septimus' suicide. There is logic as well in the mental colloquy that precedes it, in Septimus' final statement, and in Dr. Holmes's response. Septimus is sitting on the window sill, feeling once again that, on the one hand life is good, nature beneficent, and on the other that the human world makes life horrible, desires death in general, his own death in particular. In flinging himself "vigorously, violently down on to Mrs. Filmer's area railings" (p. 226), Septimus believes he is taking the only action possible to him, escaping from his double bind by giving Holmes what he wants without also betraying his own vision of the possibilities of life.

Septimus is, in very large measure, correct in thinking that Holmes and Bradshaw desire his death. Ostensibly purveying cures, the doctors are themselves part of what has caused Septimus' disease, part of the machinery of destruction whose unacknowledged presence Septimus perceives but cannot conquer. Critics have often noted that the portraits of the two doctors—and particularly of Dr.

Bradshaw—constitute an oddity in the entire canon of Virginia Woolf's fiction. Nowhere else can one find characters rendered so simply in a single dimension, so deprived of any inner life or light which might act to save them from total villainy. In *Mrs. Dalloway*, even Hugh Whitbread, Miss Kilman, and Lady Bruton, flawed though each of them is, emerge out of shadows and highlights which serve to endow them with a certain measure of human dignity and to generate, on the part of reader and observer, some measure of fellow feeling which the characterization of Holmes and Bradshaw totally denies to them. This observation is true, but hardly, I think, as puzzling as is sometimes made out. Remembering that Septimus' madness is caused by his inability to find a way in which he can both respond to war and continue to live, and remembering, too, that the authority which bolsters the state in its martial appeal has sheltered Sir William Bradshaw as well, we can see that the reduction of Holmes and Bradshaw to counters symbolizing Proportion and Conversion, the deities they worship, is neither accidental nor a flaw in Virginia Woolf's technique. Both Holmes and Bradshaw are rendered crudely, emerge harshly and without shadows because Virginia Woolf wishes us to see them literally as vampires who feast "most subtly on the human will" (p. 152). They have done to themselves, she suggests, what they wish to do to Septimus. The thinness with which they are characterized corresponds to the thinness of their existence.

To be a soldier, a man must be persuaded or, if necessary, compelled to surrender his self. He must leave home, put on a uniform, forget that those he kills are individuals like himself, and, hearing only the assigned tune must march in the assigned rhythm to his predetermined and bloody destination. No one would do this, the book suggests, if there were no social imperatives sanctioning both means and goals, diverting attention from the real issues and consequences by appeals to what, in *Three Guineas,* Virginia Woolf would call "unreal loyalties." Holmes and Bradshaw embody these sanctions and imperatives. In a supposedly peaceful society theirs is the cause that makes war not simply possible but inevitable. They leave one no choice, no room to maneuver. One must, like Lady Bradshaw, succumb "to the craving which lit her husband's eye so oilily for dominion, for power..." (p. 152), give up one's claim to a personal vision and so die to oneself; or, if one refuses, one must simply die and be condemned by the system which has caused one's death in the language expressive of the system's categories. "'The coward!' cried Dr. Holmes," (p. 226) as Septimus leapt out the window. Virginia Woolf is using Holmes and Bradshaw to show in fictional terms the linkage she treats more abstractly in *Three Guineas,* a network that ties all forms of oppression to each other, that has at its roots a love of power, an egotistic craving to stamp the world out according to the pattern that exists in one's own head or, failing that capacity, simply to stamp out the other patterns in the world.

Virginia Woolf is not denying Septimus' madness by showing it as provoked by what society calls sanity. Nor is she offering a simple-minded or romantic endorsement of suicide as a solution to the problems posed by Septimus' dilemma. She is, however, suggesting that for one trapped as Septimus is, unable to find either a form which can adequately contain feelings or a mode of action to extend them, pressured by a society which covertly demands denial of both feeling and the necessity for feeling at the same time as it will not allow the admission that this denial has taken place, then death in order to preserve the integrity of feeling may be preferable to a life which offers no such possibility. Death is not, in these circumstances, a solution, but a statement that—for the dead one—solution was impossible. A solution, however, would be the discovery of a mode of being which enhances feeling and which develops a mode of action or a plot which can harmonize feelings by accepting their fluidity and multiplicity rather than by attempting to endorse some and banish others.

In *Mrs. Dalloway,* Virginia Woolf provides such a solution, such an action, such a plot most clearly through the figure of Clarissa herself and the parties she creates. Defined throughout the book by her love of life, by her capacity to preserve this attitude in the face of war, death, sickness, age, and the limiting demands of her own personal ego, Clarissa sees her parties as a prism, a medium through which the lives of others may pass unobstructed and be combined:

> [W]hat did it mean to her, this thing she called life?... Here was So-and-so in South Kensington; some one up in Bayswater; and somebody else, say, in Mayfair. And she felt quite continuously a sense of their existence; and she felt what a waste; and she felt what a pity; and she felt if only they could be brought together; so she did it. And it was an offering; to combine, to create; but to whom?
>
> An offering for the sake of offering, perhaps. Anyhow, it was her gift.... that one day should follow another... it was enough. (Pp. 184–185)

This delight in diversity, "in people's eyes, in the swing, tramp, and trudge; in the bellow and the uproar: the carriages, motor cars, omnibuses, vans, sandwich men shuffling and swinging; brass bands; barrel organs; ... London; this moment of June" (p. 5) marks the separation between Clarissa and what she represents, and what Holmes and Bradshaw are and stand for in the book. Where Bradshaw proposed to deal with Septimus' suicide through legislating "some provision in the Bill" (p. 279), Clarissa contends that "the veriest frumps, the most dejected of miseries sitting on doorsteps ... can't be dealt with ... by Acts of Parliament ..." (p. 5). They love life, too, she says; they must, therefore, be allowed to live it as they feel it and not as some external agency would interpret it for them.

Virginia Woolf validates Clarissa's view throughout the novel by pointing particularly to women who appear not as fully developed characters, but as images embodying Clarissa's sense of how people, in fact, proceed through the universe. Thus we see Moll Pratt wishing to toss roses; Rezia Warren Smith building up a world out of odds and ends, appearing triumphant as "a flowering tree" (p. 224) invisible to those "judges ... who mixed the vision and the sideboard" (p. 225); and old Mrs. Dempster, touching, but indomitable: "Roses, she thought sardonically. All trash, m'dear. For really, what with eating, drinking, and mating, the bad days and good, life had been no mere matter of roses, and what was more, let me tell you, Carrie Dempster had no wish to change her lot with any woman's in Kentish Town! But, she implored, pity. Pity, for the loss of roses" (p. 40). Most notably and vividly, of course, we see the old woman standing in the street opposite the Regent's Park Tube station, singing with a "voice of no age or sex, the voice of an ancient spring spouting from the earth; which issued . . . from a tall quivering shape, like a funnel, like a rusty pump, like a wind-beaten tree for ever barren of leaves which lets the wind run up and down its branches singing . . . and rocks and creaks and moans in the eternal breeze" (p. 122). This figure, humanity pushed as far as possible toward the eternal and the disembodied, sings of a love which is impersonal—as Clarissa's was for Sally Seton, as Septimus' might have been for Evans could either of them have acknowledged the bond that lay between them. It is unmarred by the self-regard and possessiveness that makes Peter Walsh, for example, wish to stamp all women with the indelible imprint of his own private vision of them and so flaws his passion for Daisy and, earlier, for Clarissa; that rots Miss Kilman's feelings for Elizabeth as well, and is, indeed, responsible for much of Clarissa's general hostility toward passion.

These presences, these brief glimpses of lives lived, these particularly pointed references to love are not invoked in aid of some feeble statement asserting the innate superiority of women over men, any more than Septimus' suicide was used to assert the virtues of insanity. Indeed, in order to prevent this sort of overly simple reading, Virginia Woolf is at pains to show Richard Dalloway bringing roses to Clarissa and including Ellie Henderson in the world of Clarissa's parties, Peter Walsh inventing the world which he inhabits and inventing the shape and values of "compassion, comprehension, absolution" (p. 86) which console the solitary traveller at the end of his ride, and Miss Kilman, Lady Bruton, Rezia, and even Clarissa participating in the rigid universe ruled by Proportion and Conversion, bolstered by egotism and by spiritual "contraction" marked by churches and by letters to the *Times*. On the other hand, one must also notice that neither Peter Walsh nor Richard Dalloway is, judged by the standards of society, quite "manly" or "successful," that Miss Kilman is as she is because the War took away her work, and society, declaring her ugly, also declared her outcast, that Lady Bruton's obsession with emigration is not quite in proportion and that she herself cannot finally produce—or even draft—the necessary note to the newspaper, that no man can fully understand why Clarissa gives her parties or what they mean.

If Virginia Woolf would not imprison the world in a code of feminism lest she be guilty of a crime on the order of Holmes's or Bradshaw's, she can, nevertheless, not ignore the presence of certain tendencies in the world she anatomizes. Not much interested in first causes, she never snarls herself in arguments about sex as an inevitable determinant of action. Her focus, instead, is always on the social, on the ways in which individuals respond to the roles assigned them by the world, and on the nature and significance of the roles themselves. Freedom in her books is measured by the degree to which individuals can manipulate their socially assigned and defined roles. Clarissa and Sally Seton survive in Mrs. Richard Dalloway and Lady Rosseter. The guests refrain from laughing at the Prime Minister not because his political function makes him awesome, but instead because he is "so ordinary. You might have stood him behind a counter and bought biscuits.... And to be fair, as he went his rounds... he did it very well" (p. 261). Conquering hatred of the idea of Miss Kilman by recognizing that Miss Kilman is both more and less than simply an idea, Clarissa inspires us to "be as decent as we possibly can" and do "good for the sake of goodness" (p. 118) even though our ethical notions are inevitably primitive and the world full of seemingly incomprehensible disasters. Finally, in those situations where a choice must be made, we can endorse the heart rather than the brain, choose roses and not war. Such freedom, Virginia Woolf suggests, is more easily available to women precisely because they have less power in society and therefore less of a vested interest in either society or power.

Having reached these conclusions I can, even now, feel an inward churning of those emotions which the novel raised in me when I first read it, and flung the book away with expressions of dismay. Had we—women, that is—come so far, I asked, merely to be confronted with a vision of woman as goddess, an endorsement, however complex or ambiguous, of our sex as maintainers of some ineffable "life," a vision of the world which suggested hostess as an honorable profession? Hadn't women been goddesses and hostesses long enough? Wasn't that the problem? How could Clarissa's life bring pressure to bear against harsher realities not included in a vision which, like Peter Walsh's saw civilization as a collection of "butlers, chow dogs; girls in their security" (p. 82) and of people assembled from London's better addresses? Clarissa's query that because "she loved her roses (didn't that help the Armenians?)" (p. 182) seemed frivolous, even shocking. Obviously, the answer would be negative, if such response did not dignify the question beyond its worth.

Suppose, however, we alter slightly the terms of Clarissa's interrogation, asking now not specifically about roses, but instead about what, in general, might help those like the Armenians "hunted out of existence, maimed, frozen, the victims of cruelty and injustice" (p. 182). The usual answers are: money, letters, and other signs of support to institutions which aim to aid the downtrodden and marshall the opinions of others in their favor; expressions of hostility toward those individuals or institutions which seem to be responsible for the conditions we deplore; in the last resort, some violent act which would heave out the agents of repression and make way for new agencies closer to our hearts' desires and, with any luck, closer to those of the Armenians as well.

Versions of this plan have been at work for as long as history has recorded the deeds of human beings. To some extent, one can only suppose that they have worked, that we are all in some sense better off for the various social, intellectual, and technological revolutions that bloodily accompanied our progress from the cave. Perhaps such motion really does require blood to feed it. And yet, if the study of economics is a dismal science, so too is the study of politics, filled with quarrels about the definition of progress, leading only to the conclusion that war follows war and revolution, revolution. Is it not possible, which is to say initially, simply conceivable, to find another way? Could we create an alternative motion and set of social patterns based neither on systems nor on power but deriving instead more directly from individuals, from a notion that people are quite various and variable and that therefore we must learn to live leaving the ideas of others alone, learn to live with their solitude and our own as well? Imagining such a notion could we adhere to it so that Clarissa's parties might extend themselves beyond the boundaries of a single house, a single evening, a small number of involved participants? Could we learn to value joy as much as we now treasure suffering and learn, as Virginia Woolf suggests in *Three Guineas,* that when the mulberry tree makes us dance around it too fast the only thing to do is sit down and laugh? Could we see that the perfect hostess has a history and a heritage both honorable and, at least potentially, political? And if we could do any or all of these things, would it matter? Would the Armenians be helped?

Maybe.

I wish I could be more positive, but the difficulty of an easier affirmation is again pointed to by Virginia Woolf when she shows us Clarissa standing at her party "drenched in fire" (p. 255), knowing Septimus is dead and knowing, too, that nothing she has done has been sufficient to prevent this death or the War which preceded it, or to change Bradshaw into someone who would not force one's soul. Faced with such knowledge it is easy to give up, difficult to have any faith in the efficacy of individual belief or action, simpler to die or to work for a cause or to locate reality somewhere else than one's own life. And yet we can say with certainty that the known routes of Religion or Love or War do not seem to have done the hypothetical Armenians much lasting good either. These ways have been tried repeatedly, while the way of the hostess has been confined to the private house. Perhaps we should open the door and let her out rather than deny that she ever existed or that we, men and women alike, might have anything to learn from her. Surely a society having at its center a "figure, made of sky and branches ... risen from the troubled sea ... as a shape might be sucked up out of the waves to shower down from her magnificent hands compassion, comprehension, absolution" (p. 86), a woman "lolloping on the waves and braiding her tresses ... , having that gift still; to be; to exist; ... her severity, her prudery, her woodenness ... all warmed through now, ... as if she wished the whole world well" (pp. 264–265) might be more pleasant to live in than one organized around "all the exalted statues ... the black, the spectacular images of ... soldiers" (p. 77). Virginia Woolf is suggesting that we damn ourselves if, in constructing a view of the world we deny a connection between politics and feelings or values, and so create a politics lacking both beauty and joy. She may be right.

NOTES

[1] Virginia Woolf, *Mrs. Dalloway* (New York: Harcourt, 1925), p. 182. All references are to this edition. Further references will be made parenthetically within the text.

[2] See, for example, Margaret Blanchard, "Socialization in *Mrs. Dalloway,*" *College English,* 34, No. 2 (1972), 287–305; O. P. Sharma, "Feminism as Aesthetic Vision: A Study of Virginia Woolf's *Mrs. Dalloway,*" *Women's Studies,* 3, No. 1 (1975), 61–74; Jean Alexander, *The Venture of Form in the Novels of Virginia Woolf* (New York and London: Kennikat, 1974), pp. 85–104; Avrom Fleishman, *Virginia Woolf: A Critical Reading* (Baltimore and London: Johns Hopkins Univ. Press, 1975), 69–95.

[3] In *Granite and Rainbow: Essays* (London: Hogarth, 1958), p. 81.

[4] William Troy, "The Novel of Sensibility," *Literary Opinion in America,* ed. Morton Dauwen Zabel (New York: Harper, 1937), pp. 324–337, reprinted in *Virginia Woolf: A Collection of Critical Essays,* ed. Claire Sprague (Englewood Cliffs, N.J.: Prentice-Hall, 1971), p. 27.

[5] Fleishman, p. 80.

Daniel Albright

PERSONALITY AND IMPERSONALITY IN VIRGINIA WOOLF

Who am I? What am I? What is life? These are the incessant questions that form and disperse throughout Virginia Woolf's work, questions as evanescent, helpless, and stubborn as the characters who pose them. The nineteenth century prepares us for many of the characteristic forms of the twentieth, but not, I think, for this tumult, this agony of identity, these dubious characters merging into each other or splitting like amoebas, whose only joy is self-assertion, whose only lament is that there is no one here to lament. When reading her novels we feel that her world's dynamics are impossible, exaggerated: one cannot say that her characters develop, for when they are moving it is with dizzy speed, swirling into the wind and the waves; when they are still they are struck dead still, grounded, sunk. Age, face, body, even sex—the usual marks by which the reader can sort out the actors in a novel—are as unstable as coat and dress; Orlando, fluctuant, transsexual, three hundred years old, wholly outrageous, is only an exaggeration of the liberties which Virginia Woolf's characters habitually take. Well might these invisible voices cry Who am I? out of the dazzling foreground of *Mrs. Dalloway* or *To the Lighthouse* or *The Waves;* and one must inquire carefully to learn what form a response might take, to learn what sort of outline, delimitation, or uniqueness is proper to these British names who seem to implore us from the text to help them. It is possible that humanity will not turn out to be quite so abject as it seems; for the chameleon's agony, the rage of Caliban, the very indefiniteness of character itself, may prove a secret witness to the impalpable triumphs of the human imagination.

Virginia Woolf attempts in several places the rudiments of a theory of personality, and if this theory is hesitant, partial, even contradictory, it may only be an example of one of her strengths as writer, empiricism. She admires Roger Fry in her biography for his fecundity of theories, always testing them against facts, always letting facts spawn new theories, so that the theories themselves have the

From *Personality and Impersonality: Lawrence, Woolf, and Mann* (Chicago: University of Chicago Press, 1978), pp. 96–100, 130–36, 143–44, 195–97.

spontaneous vivid patterns that any tentative crystallization of the real ought to have; and her own theories occur principally in novels, are themselves art. These theories of human development are to a large extent epistemological, just as her realism as novelist is primarily ocular, perceptual, like the realism of those nineteenth-century impressionists who regarded their paintings as the finest representation of retinal truth. Her fullest statement about the origin of human personality occurs in a passage which is perhaps her single most impressive achievement, surely her most painful, the final soliloquy of *The Waves:*

> Then a wood-pigeon flew out of the trees. And being in love for the first time, I made a phrase—a poem about a wood-pigeon—a single phrase, for a hole had been knocked in my mind, one of those sudden transparences through which one sees everything. Then more bread and butter and more flies droning round the nursery ceiling on which quivered islands of light, ruffled, opalescent, while the pointed fingers of the lustre dripped blue pools on the corner of the mantelpiece. Day after day as we sat at tea we observed these sights.[1]
>
> But we were all different. The wax—the virginal wax that coats the spine melted in different patches for each of us. The growl of the boot-boy making love to the tweeny among the gooseberry bushes; the clothes blown out hard on the line; the dead man in the gutter; the apple tree, stark in the moonlight; the rat swarming with maggots; the lustre dripping blue—our white wax was streaked and stained by each of these differently. Louis was disgusted by the nature of human flesh; Rhoda by our cruelty; Susan could not share; Neville wanted order; Jinny love; and so on. We suffered terribly as we became separate bodies.[2]

In the beginning there is neither body nor mind, only a nerve and its waxy insulation. This myth of the origin of the self is the culmination of a set of images that had been growing in Virginia Woolf's mind since the beginning of her career as a writer of fiction: in the early story "Kew Gardens" she speaks of heavy waxen bodies, candles whose flames are their voices. The use of wax as an image which defines the relation of the self to the environment makes certain obvious assumptions: we are born without features, without individuation, just lumps, passive, waiting for impression, quiet, dumb, incompetent. This passivity seems identical to that of the helpless mind menaced by perception that appears in an essay of 1919:

> The mind receives a myriad impressions—trivial, fantastic, evanescent, or engraved with the sharpness of steel. From all sides they come, an incessant shower of innumerable atoms; and as they fall, as they shape themselves into the life of Monday or Tuesday, the accent falls differently from of old.[3]

The wax is surrounded by a storm of sharp points; but somehow, miraculously, the needles score the wax into a precise pattern—a nose, a face, articulate limbs—as if a magnet were guiding the iron filings into a predictable form. The wax, then, is perhaps not purely passive, no simple three-dimensional analogue of Locke's *tabula rasa;* there is something inside, and the substance, the form of this core is the basis of identity, although not the determinant of it. The six characters of *The Waves* are identical, Bernard implies, at birth; but different experiences—and experience is always red-hot—destroy different patches of our insulation, leave us mottled, figured, articulated, regrettably human. The quick is half-enclosed, half-revealed; the sense of touch, quickened, leaves Louis permanently disgusted by flesh but permanently susceptible to it, for the waxy sheath, once violated, cannot be repaired: perfume, paprika, the sun, hot water are all dangerous and inevitable, make us increasingly battered, sodden, until the core itself begins to fail with age. It seems from Bernard's monologue that most perception is revulsion, that one person differs from another chiefly in shifting permutations of exposure and disgust; as Bernard remarks of his own sensory awakening, which occurred in a hot bath when he was very young, "Sometimes indeed, when I pass a cottage with a light in the window when a child has been born, I could implore them not to squeeze the sponge over that new body." So San Sebastian pleads that others not be martyred; it would seem that one is best advised to be left a fetus in a womb, a blanket, a bed, a glass jar filled with alcohol, anywhere unmolested and safe.

In Virginia Woolf all such feelings are half-truths to be debated. Sometimes we wish to be closed; other times we wish to be open. The nerve inside the spinal sheath is for the most part tranquil; when agitated it has but one desire, an extremely powerful one: it requires the existence of an external world. It is this urgency that makes womb an impossible climate, that drives us toward self-actualization; one can confirm one's own existence only through that which one most dreads, sensation. Bernard himself is far from immune from this feeling: he speaks often of the lovely palpability, objectivity, of things in themselves, seen unclogged, uncontaminated, with newborn eyes, and *The Waves* ends joyously in the confirmation of existence of things in themselves, cup, knife, fork, that are not Bernard, and *I,* who am Bernard, "worn out with all this rubbing of my nose along the surface of things." The compelling appetite for a real world is again a very ancient theme in Virginia Woolf; in "The Mark on the Wall," for example, she speaks of awakening from nightmare, the terrifying dark of the mind shut in itself, and "worshipping reality, worshipping the impersonal world which is a proof of some existence other than ours. That is what one wants to be sure of . . ."[4] But of course at best our relation to an objective world is love and hate commingled; our evolution is a process of maiming and abrasion; but we can be shocked, if only for a moment, out of bad dreams.

Sometimes perception can be a source of delight, although if it is intense enough it is a scary delight; when Bernard sees the woodpigeon, when a pigeon-shaped hole is knocked out of his waxy insulation, letting in the radical light, he feels a kind of exultation. But to explain this rapture we must, perhaps, look beyond the model of wax and spinal nerve. There is another class of myth of the origin of personality in Virginia Woolf's writing, never stated as explicitly as the previous one, but at least as important: the model of skull and eye.

> But when the door shuts on us, all that vanishes. The shell-like covering which our souls have excreted to house themselves, to make for themselves a shape distinct from others, is broken, and there is left of all these wrinkles and roughness a central oyster of perceptiveness, an enormous eye.[5]

The whole brain, the whole inside of the body, is, according to this essay, written at the same time as *The Waves*, equivalent to an eye; and in her essay on Walter Sickert one of the speakers mentions South American insects in which the eye is so developed that they are all eye: "Were we once insects like that, too . . . all eye? . . . Ages ago we left the forest and went into the world, and the eye shrivelled and the heart grew, and the liver and the intestines and the tongue and the hands and the feet."[6] This myth of human evolution, which is equivalent to a myth of the birth of mind, has its epistemological ramifications. Here the quick interior does not recoil from perception—the eye has instead a desperate need to see; and the mind's concepts, its abstract knowledge of the outer world, are metaphorically identical to retinal images. Openness not experience, the melting of the wax sheath, is in this class of myth a felicitous event, the enriching of the mind's eye with perception, the populating of the internal kingdom. In this manner the two classes of myth are diametrically opposed in value, even though their forms are so similar; I would attribute this disparity to Virginia Woolf's basic hatred of sexuality, the sexual body, about which Quentin Bell has recently enlightened us—the myth of the waxy spine is fundamentally a myth of touch—as opposed to her fascination with the act of vision. The eye that constitutes the whole self is not at all passive or reticent; it changes form, shuts its lids, clouds itself with tears, hallucinates and storms; the eye has all the possibilities for aperture and closure, the stippledness of personality, of the wax around the spine.

⟨. . .⟩ the visionary, the open seeker for the open universe, must be the enemy of the body; and what this entails for the sane visionary is a somewhat bizarre phenomenon of characterization, the fissure of the body into two bodies. Perhaps the first character to announce that she has two bodies is Katharine Hilbery in *Night and Day:*

> [A]ll the time she was in fancy looking up through a telescope at white shadow-cleft disks which were other worlds, until she felt herself possessed of two bodies, one walking by the river with Denham, the other concentrated to a silver globe aloft in the fine blue space above the scum of vapours that was covering the visible world. . . . There was no reason, she assured herself, for this feeling of happiness; she was not free; she was not alone; she was still bound to earth by a million fibres; every step took her nearer home.[7]

One body is airy geometrical form, as globular and felicitous as the eye itself, billowing on the incorporeal sky; the other body is mere obtuse flesh, a participant in life rather than the vertiginous spectator. The relation between the two bodies is complex; in this passage it seems that the globe is almost a metaphor for the brain itself, floating isolated and detached, possessing two methods of perception, the direct vivid eye, and the blunt connections of the other senses which must travel thousands of miles up through the "million fibres" of the body's nerves, as if, were Ralph to brush her elbow, the globe humming through the stratosphere would be eventually informed of the rash deed by some botched, weak, and intermittent telegraphy. But the body that is the globe, the real body of which the reddish flesh is only a simian replica, also can manifest itself on earth as an ideal body complete with arms and legs, astral, luminous; in this same passage Ralph looks at the happy Katharine, and sees her "not so much a real person, as the very woman he dreamt of" (p. 301). In later novels this kind of rapture, in which sexual joy is refined out of the organic entirely, in which the stale body bubbles away into a creature made of light, is much more developed: the young Clarissa Dalloway, at the height of her infatuation for Sally Seton, sees her lover resolve out of pink gauze into luminous fuzz, sublime out of the strictures of gravity: "She *seemed* anyhow, all light, glowing, like some bird or air ball that has flown in, attached itself for a moment to a bramble." By the time of *Orlando* this process of the replacement of one body by another is so well understood by the narrator that she can present Orlando's two bodies contending for Orlando's spirit, as if a human being were by nature a Siamese twin:

> For Love, to which we may now return, has two faces; one white, the other black; two bodies; one smooth, the other hairy. It has two hands, two feet, two tails, two, indeed, of every member and each one is the exact opposite of the other. Yet, so strictly are they joined together that you cannot separate them. In this case, Orlando's love began her flight towards him with her white face turned, and her smooth and lovely body outwards. Nearer and nearer she came wafting before her airs of pure delight. All of a sudden (at the sight of the Archduchess presumably) she wheeled about, turned the other way round; showed herself black, hairy, brutish; and it was Lust the vulture, not Love, the Bird of Paradise that flopped, foully and disgustingly, upon his shoulders.[8]

This memorable passage, which is incidentally the source of Quentin Bell's celebrated description of Virginia Woolf's childhood molestation by her half-brother, shows how far the doctrine of the two bodies has evolved from 1919 to 1928. In *Night and Day* Katharine spends most of her time in her habitual physical body, tending her parents, reading prosaically, doing the common chores of the rich; and there is only occasionally the emergence of the other body, the exaltation that accompanies young love, meditations upon the stars, the solution of mathematical problems. Orlando, however, lives in a world that is close to perpetual fantasy, and finds this rare intrusion of the corporeal, the lower body, most distressing. Orlando may have learned how to survive in a body that is nearly pure ectoplasm, the most quicksilver and obliging body ever seen, given to sudden fits of sexual reversal; yet even in Arcadia there is a second, excrementitious body congruent to one's romantic body hair by hair and toe by toe which asserts itself at the least twinge of low sexual arousal, asserts itself in all its hideous opacity.

These tendencies pushed a little too far result in Septimus Smith. It is he who hates the physical body most intensely of any character in Virginia Woolf; and it is he who is the final proof of the impossibility of openness as a way of life. No character elsewhere is ever so devastated by the dilation of the pupil, the loss of the boundary between the *I* and the *not-I;* it is as if a hole had been cut in his skull, by the ancient operation of trephination mentioned in *Between the Acts,* and the light poured in steadily, uncontrollably. Like most insane characters, he is driven raving by his own transparency, his body so hopelessly transpierced by the sun, and he therefore attempts to close himself utterly, shelter his head from the light. Thus he is brought back to his hateful body, his dog's body, his paranoid self-revulsion; he is isolated from humanity and is hunted down like a dog by "Human Nature," a pack of doctors; and delirium is his only escape. He oscillates wildly between the closed state and the open, neither of which offers any relief, only a change from one sort of pain to its equally intense opposite. Half the time he declares that nothing has meaning, half the time that everything has meaning; these statements are equally sinister, equally insane. For the insane character, the pellucid meaning inherent in the universe—which Septimus wishes to declare a new religion—is not a pleasant immanence of exterior order, but something thrilling, peculiar:

> There is a God. (He noted such revelations on the backs of envelopes.) Change the world. No one kills from hatred. Make it known (he wrote it down). He waited. He listened. A sparrow perched on the railing opposite chirped Septimus, Septimus, four of five times over and went on, drawing its notes out, to sing freshly and piercingly in Greek words how there is no crime and, joined by another sparrow, they sang in voices prolonged and piercing in Greek words, from trees in the meadow of life beyond a river where the dead walk, how there is no death.[9]

Here is an earlier, more concise version of this theme from the short story "An Unwritten Novel," in which the narrator decides to attribute insanity to an unknown woman sitting across from him in a railroad carriage:

> . . . everything has meaning—placards leaning against doorways—names above shop-windows—red fruit in baskets—women's heads in the hairdresser's—all say "Minnie Marsh!" But here's a jerk. "Eggs are cheaper!" That's what always happens! I was heading her over the waterfall, straight for madness.[10]

This, then, is what everything means if everything has meaning: the whole world utters your name. It is not accusation, but acknowledgment, worship; it is Berkeley's universe paying homage to the mind that informs it, sustains it. We see that the theory of identity of Jacob Flanders and Mrs. Dalloway—that the configurations of the world are a set of cues and indexes toward a single personality—has its demonic extremes: the universe can become the thin penetrating reflex of a single mind. While Septimus can feel ecstasy that all things can resolve themselves into the uniform melody of his name, the liquid justice of his soul, nevertheless the inspiration of this upheaval, this revolt against the established order of things is hatred of the body, revulsion against the physical.

> She threw herself from a window, which, however, was not high enough from the ground to cause her serious harm. It was here too that she lay in bed, listening to the birds singing in Greek and imagining that King Edward VII lurked in the azaleas using the foulest possible language.[11]

This is Quentin Bell's account of Virginia Woolf's breakdown in 1904 following the death of her father; it suggests that even while the wondrous birds sing Greek, the obscene muttering of the body forms a counter-refrain of its own; and in Quentin Bell's description of another episode, in 1913, we learn that she felt her belly, mouth, and excretion tainted, monstrous.

Septimus finds sexuality unbearable, renounces copulation, declares that emotions do not exist, only various forms of lust; indeed there is every reason to believe that in heaven there is neither lust nor emotions, only the one brain, the labyrinth of whose cortex enfolds garden and town, sun and sky. For Septimus the body is forever depraved and deranged, just as Rachel Vinrace in *The Voyage Out,* in the insanity of her final illness, imagines her body growing until her knees are mountains, her toes wholly separated from her body, her mind flitting discarnate around the corners of her sickroom. In Septimus this alienation from his body takes the form of treating his body as a mechanical instrument, as if he were in fact a little man inside his skull, manipulating muscles, staring through the windows of his eyes; he hears his wife sobbing like a "piston thumping," for she must be considered a machine, and makes a deliberate, false gesture, in order to pretend an emotion he does not feel:

> His wife was crying, and he felt nothing; only each time she sobbed in this profound, this silent, this hopeless way, he descended another step into the pit.
>
> At last, with a melodramatic gesture which he assumed mechanically and with complete consciousness of its insincerity, he dropped his head on his hands. (*Mrs. Dalloway,* p. 136)

This would impress anyone acquainted with the writings of the psychiatrist R. D. Laing as a state identical to what he calls the adoption of a false-self system; indeed much of the progress of Septimus' insanity seems quite similar to our contemporary notions of schizophrenia. Septimus has in effect willed the loss of his identity at the moment when he repudiates the natural ease of his body; and so in *Mrs. Dalloway,* for almost the first time in Virginia Woolf's fiction, we begin to suspect that the physical body, the humble lower self, has its uses, even its advantages, over the rarefied ecstasies of the higher body. Septimus has expunged every trace of human sympathy; indeed he is occasionally disturbed that he cannot feel, is numb even over the death of his beloved, Evans; Septimus at his most transcendent is all brain:

> But what was the scientific explanation (for one must be scientific above all things)? Why could he see through bodies, see into the future, when dogs will become men? It was the heat wave presumably, operating upon a brain made sensitive by eons of evolution. Scientifically speaking, the flesh was melted off the world. His body was macerated until only the nerve fibres were left. It was spread like a veil upon a rock.
>
> He lay back in his chair, exhausted but upheld. He lay resting, waiting, before he again interpreted, with effort, with agony, to mankind. He lay very high, on the back of the world. The earth thrilled beneath him. Red flowers grew through his flesh; their stiff leaves rustled by his head. (Pp. 102–3)

Virginia Woolf occasionally discusses the condition of the world without flesh, the skeleton of things. There is a fascinating passage near the end of *Jacob's Room,* in which night falls, a breath of exterior wind blows off the flesh of Flanders; but there, as here, what remains when the world is unclothed is not rattling articulation of bone but a network of nerves, as if the absolute core of the body or the world were the optic nerve and the minute reticulation of the tactile nerves, tendrils which creep out of the skin and curl themselves around distant objects; it is the brain's skeleton, the eye's skeleton, the body grown so huge and porous that flowers grow, birds fly, through its interstices. Like Blake, Septimus can see nothing that is not human; so drenched is the world in Septimus' massive single humanity that dogs turn into men as they approach him, a tree vibrates in exact empathy with his spine, he can see another world extending into the depths of printed wallpaper, find Evans inside a painted screen, for his field of existence is interchangeably flat or round, past or present, simply himself.

The brain, unable to bear the lusts of the body, retaliates by annihilating the whole physical world. Sometimes in Virginia Woolf's writing it seems that every act of the eye is a minute aggression against the solidity of the real, against the inductility, the illiteracy, of the body, against death. The great hope of opening one's eye and pores to their uttermost is that the world, once translated entire into the brain, will conform to one's personal requirements; but instead the world imposes on the open psyche an image of its own fragmentation, tumult; it is the whale swallowed by Jonah. It is much safer to live in the intransigencies of the physical, to admit the otherness of the Other; and even Septimus is willing to attempt at last to rid his eye of hallucination, to return to a kind of sanity. It is an unusual perceptual experiment for Septimus: he opens his eyes just slightly, for sanity is clearly a middle condition, neither fully open nor fully closed:

> He began, very cautiously, to open his eyes, to see whether a gramophone was really there. But real things—real things were too exciting. He must be

cautious. He would not go mad. First he looked at the fashion papers on the lower shelf, then, gradually at the gramophone with the green trumpet. Nothing could be more exact. And so, gathering courage, he looked at the sideboard; the plate of bananas; the engraving of Queen Victoria and the Prince Consort; at the mantelpiece, with the jar of roses. None of these things moved. All were still; all were real. (*Mrs. Dalloway*, p. 215)

The sane world has an amazing inertia; instead of the fluctuance and the lability of hallucination, everything stays still—his wife's face is surprisingly undeformed, just normal; he can achieve real communication, make a little joke; it is, like all things real, very exciting. This passage has in it the seed of all of Virginia Woolf's later retreat from the figured ebullition of the novels of the 1920s; to present the expansive, molten consciousness is a perhaps considerable achievement, she seems to feel, but the vision of reality which it entails is finally wrong. The excitement, the intensity, of Septimus' solipsism is at last somewhat factitious; the brilliance of the external, of plain English is more compelling. Septimus insane is, in effect, unsatisfying; Virginia Woolf wondered even when she was writing *Mrs. Dalloway* if the novel would not be better without him. Since Septimus represents the autonomy of the eye, the brain evolved to the end point of the human, Virginia Woolf's repudiation of him suggests the possibility for a new accommodation with the finitude of the physical world. The body is not always merely apish; it is in *Mrs. Dalloway* the seat of human sympathy, human community. Poised against Septimus' cerebral rapture is Clarissa Dalloway's party:

> "What does the brain matter," said Lady Rosseter, getting up, "compared with the heart?"
> "I will come," said Peter, but he sat on for a moment. What is this terror? what is this ecstasy? he thought to himself. What is it that fills me with extraordinary excitement?
> It is Clarissa, he said.
> For there she was. (P. 296)

The brain is only one organ, just as Septimus exists in a sense for Clarissa's sake, to define one of her problems, and if the brain hypertrophies it leads to a falsification of the self and the world. Clarissa's body, in its physiological totality, is a remarkably full, empathic structure; when she hears of Septimus' death, she feels the rusty spikes pierce her body. Septimus' mode of death is a parody of the openness of his nervous system during his life; but it seems that his life and death signify as much for Clarissa as for himself, her body's intuition, her body's telepathy. The life of the eye and the brain, with its sham fascination, its illusory triumph over the perceived world, seems increasingly insipid next to real human interaction; and two subsequent novels, *To the Lighthouse* and *The Waves*, will be needed in the attempt to mediate between the eye's blandishments and the substantial demands of friends and lovers. The weariness of Septimus' model of himself as a brain stretched out on a rock, with fibers connecting it to all creation, can be observed in an analogous passage from a story which remained unpublished in Virginia Woolf's lifetime, "Together and Apart," in which a vapid middle-aged woman encounters a man who succeeds for an instant in twitching the extinct nerve of her real passion:

> Fibres of her were floated capriciously this way and that, like the tentacles of a sea anemone, now thrilled, now snubbed, and her brain, miles away, cool and distant, up in the air, received messages which it would sum up in time.[12]

The nerve fibers do not link the brain to the world so much as hold it at a distance; and in this manner the overextended brain becomes mushy, languid, incompetent. ⟨. . .⟩

Virginia Woolf, like D. H. Lawrence, wrote her first novel considerably under Wilde's enchantment. Mrs. Dalloway, the threadbare Mrs. Dalloway of *The Voyage Out,* looks at the receding shore as the *Euphrosyne* sails out toward South America, and exclaims, "It's so like Whistler!" suggesting, for the first time in Virginia Woolf's fiction, the ceaseless effort of nature to accommodate itself to the painterly eye; but the true Wildean quality of the novel is not in smart talk but in the character of the intellectual, St. John Hirst. Here he is, shortly after Rachel's party arrives in South America:

> Hirst, who had been eating and drinking without interruption, now lit a cigarette, and observed, "Oh, but we're all agreed by this time that nature's a mistake. She's either very ugly, appallingly uncomfortable, or absolutely terrifying. I don't know which alarms me most—a cow or a tree. I once met a cow in a field by night. The creature looked at me. I assure you it turned my hair grey. It's a disgrace that the animals should be allowed to go at large."[13]

He has all the opinions of Wilde, and the cadence of his voice has the friable softness associated with decadence in the popular imagination; but, even though the human race is evolving in his cerebral direction, he is an unlovely character, a deformed neurasthenic, timorous, an intellectual bully, hostile to the human affection of Terence and Rachel. Hirst seems in fact a textbook case of early twentieth-century opinion and prejudice about decadence, and there is some evidence that Stratchey's circle at Cambridge embodied every excess here described; as soon as he delivers his little speech about cows, the scholar Hughling Elliot immediately hears its ultimate source, asks him, "Wasn't it Wilde who discovered the fact that nature makes no allowance for hip-bones?" (p. 122). He is a parody homosexual, like his mentor; at one point he claims that what he abhors most of all is the female breast; and he attributes massive insensitivity, lack of tactile feeling, to heterosexuals generally. More significantly, Terence opines, with full authority, that Hirst has lived in a mirror, in the manner of Tennyson's Lady of Shalott, or perhaps Dorian Gray:

"You see, Miss Vinrace, you must make allowances for Hirst. He's lived all his life in front of a looking-glass, in a beautiful panelled room, hung with Japanese prints and lovely old chairs and tables, just one splash of colour, you know, in the right place,—between the windows I think it is,—and there he sits hour after hour with his toes on the fender, talking about philosophy and God and his liver and his heart and the hearts of his friends." (P. 156)

This is the aesthetic life; one insulates oneself with cunning beauty, perhaps with some velvet to muffle sound, becomes wrapped in exquisite involution, aesthetic safety. But Virginia Woolf has presented this refuge through a sufficiently unattractive character that the reader does not find the aesthetic life seductive; Hirst is not only ugly, but desperately unhappy, nearly lunatic from self-consciousness. He is a damned academic, *a professor maudit* in the distinguished lineage of Casaubon, forever eunuch and alien, and indeed the novel ends with his brain tortured by the apparitions of the living and the dead, equally black, indistinguishable.

⟨. . .⟩ The characters about whom ⟨Woolf⟩ writes are undefined, some would even say unreal; but she has, in *Mrs. Dalloway*, in *Orlando*, in *Flush*, in *Between the Acts*, extended as significantly as any writer of the twentieth century the boundaries of the human character. We know from her diary that at times she thought herself as fuzzy and ill-defined as any of the characters; she worries that her multitude of styles do not cohere, even says at one point, "I'm 20 people";[14] yet surely a novelist can well afford to be even more than twenty people, for much of what seems to be inchoateness is simply the twisted form which human sympathy takes in the twentieth century.

One of her most profound inquiries into the nature of literary characterization is found in her paper of 1924, "Mr. Bennett and Mrs. Brown." She confesses that the characters of books are typically derived from idle musing about someone unknown to the novelist whom he sees by chance, for instance in a railroad car; from an old lady sitting across the carriage one can infer an occupation, a past, a family, a situation which necessitates a trip; and this mass of nacreous inference is the raw material of a novel. This situation is borrowed exactly from the early short story, "An Unwritten Novel," and it will appear again in *The Waves,* when Bernard meditates about a man in a railway carriage whom he calls Walter J. Trumble. It is not enough for a novelist, in the standard English fashion, to make Mrs. Brown into a "character," to "bring out her oddities and mannerism; her buttons and wrinkles,"[15] nor is it enough to describe with the unwearying superficial eye of Arnold Bennett her clothes and probable class; the novelist must attend to something deeper, the old lady in herself. "Mrs. Brown is eternal, Mrs. Brown is human nature":[16]

You should insist that she is an old lady of unlimited capacity and infinite variety; capable of appearing in any place; wearing any dress; saying anything and doing heaven knows what. But the things she says and the things she does and her eyes and her nose and her speech and her silence have an overwhelming fascination, for she is, of course, the spirit we live by, life itself.[17]

This is the doctrine of the rigid core of identity, like Mrs. Ramsay's wedge, or, more precisely, the paleolithic hag of *Mrs. Dalloway;* but it is also a firm reminder that the literary artist is dealing with something inviolable and objective which he must respect. The object of his fidelity, however, is not outside himself; it is not strictly the old lady; instead it is his vision of the old lady, about whom he in fact knows nothing. This is Virginia Woolf's solution to a major paradox of modern fiction: on one hand, characterization is a form of reference to the human exterior; on the other hand, there is nothing in the novel which refers to anything but the equable and impalpable personality of the novelist. For Virginia Woolf, stray passersby give her the clues by which she can split off and project various aspects of herself. This is true, she says, even of such a master of typed and quirky characters as Dickens:

> above all some gigantic and dominating figure, so stuffed and swollen with life that he does not exist singly and solitarily, but seems to need for his own realization a host of others, to call into existence the severed parts that complete him.[18]

But the more of oneself that is farced into any given character, the less sternly outlined and defined that character becomes. At times Mrs. Woolf could find this indefiniteness relaxing; a certain loss of the rigors of identity can cause tranquillity; and once she stated, in her essay "On Being Ill," that self-multiplicity is in fact the highest human joy: heaven.

> Heaven-making must be left to the imagination of the poets. Without their help we can but trifle—imagine Pepys in Heaven, adumbrate little interviews with celebrated people on tufts of thyme, soon fall into gossip about such of our friends as have stayed in Hell, or, worse still, revert again to earth and choose, since there is no harm in choosing, to live over and over, now as man, now as woman, as sea-captain, or court lady, as Emperor or farmer's wife, in splendid cities and on remote moors, at the time of Pericles or Arthur, Charlemagne or George the Fourth—to live and live till we have lived out those embryo lives which attend about us in early youth until 'I' suppressed them. But 'I' shall not, if wishing can alter it, usurp Heaven too, and condemn us, who have played our parts here as William or Alice, to remain William or Alice for ever. Left to ourselves we speculate thus carnally.[19]

What a pleasure, to be man or woman, knight or country maid; it is the disquieting carnal joy of *Orlando*. It is personality swollen and conglomerated into paradise. Who am I?—the cry comes from the sickbed; from the British Museum; from the undulation of land and sea. I am everybody; I am Virginia Woolf.

NOTES

[1] *The Waves*, in *Jacob's Room & The Waves* (New York: Harvest, 1950, 1959), p. 343.

[2] Ibid., p. 344.

[3] *Collected Essays II* (New York: Harcourt Brace and World, 1967), p. 106.

[4] *A Haunted House and Other Short Stories* (New York: Harvest, 1949), p. 45.

[5] *Collected Essays IV* (New York: Harcourt Brace and World, 1967), p. 156.

[6] *Collected Essays II*, pp. 234–35.

[7] *Night and Day* (New York: Harvest, 1948), pp. 300–301. Subsequent references occur in the text.

[8] *Orlando* (New York: Harvest, 1956), pp. 117–18.

[9] *Mrs. Dalloway* (New York: Harvest, 1953), p. 35. Subsequent references occur in the text.

[10] *A Haunted House and Other Short Stories*, p. 14.

[11] Quentin Bell, *Virginia Woolf: A Biography* (New York: Harcourt Brace Jovanovich, 1972), I, p. 90.

[12] *A Haunted House and Other Short Stories*, pp. 139–40.

[13] *The Voyage Out* (New York: Harvest, 1948), p. 121. Subsequent references occur in the text.

[14] *A Writer's Diary* (New York: Harcourt Brace, 1954), p. 33.

[15] *Collected Essays I* (New York: Harcourt Brace and World, 1967), p. 325.

[16] Ibid., p. 330.

[17] Ibid., pp. 336–37.

[18] Ibid., p. 193.

[19] *Collected Essays IV*, p. 199.

John G. Hessler

MORAL ACCOUNTABILITY
IN *MRS. DALLOWAY*

Any account of the ethical stance of *Mrs. Dalloway* must begin with the suicide of Septimus Warren Smith and with the series of rationalizations by which Clarissa Dalloway comes to construe that suicide not only as an affirmation of Septimus' right-to-be but as a ratification of her own continuing life as well. Lucio Ruotolo, in his book, *Six Existential Heroes,*[1] argues that Mrs. Dalloway's affirmation is an act of great imaginative generosity and he sees her as a model, a sort of exemplary life, pointing to modern men a way out of the existential dilemma. I would caution against this hagiographic impulse. The temptation to annex great writers to our own needs is always strong, but when we succumb to that temptation neither the writers nor our needs are ever fairly served. While Ruotolo, touching on Kierkegaard and Heidegger among others, dovetails modern philosophy with Virginia Woolf's artistic intuitions in important and illuminating ways, he loses sight of Mrs. Dalloway's real greatness when he tries to make her a saint for the modern condition.

Mrs. Dalloway belongs to a tradition that extends as far back at least as Moll Flanders and that includes such distinguished characters as Emma Woodhouse, Catherine Earnshaw, and Dorothea Brooke along the way. Like Moll and the others, Mrs. Dalloway is enmeshed in a world determined by money and class and must struggle for a self-definition that in part accepts and in part defies those determinants. From Moll to Mrs. Dalloway, then, we can trace the career of the mercantile world view; what we see is the bourgeois mind encountering its own fatal limitations. For Moll, an early version of the bourgeois mind's confidence in itself, the world seems limitless and open to conquest; she exults in her freedom and power. For Clarissa Dalloway, however, the world has shrunk and become brittle; she senses confinement and impasse, and her struggle for self-definition borders on hysteria and suicide. The history of the bourgeois mind is, then, a history of diminishment, of encounter with dark ambiguities, and of dismay.

From *Renascence* 30, No. 3 (Spring 1978): 126–36.

Matthew Arnold recorded the discovery in "Dover Beach" as a change in the moral landscape. In that poem he speaks of the world which once seemed "like a land of dreams, / So various, so beautiful, so new," and which now is revealed to have "neither joy, nor love, nor light, / Nor certitude, nor peace, nor help for pain." And the prospect has become a "darkling plain" punctuated with "alarms of struggle and flight." *Mrs. Dalloway,* set in Arnold's world of blighted possibility, is great not because it offers any solution to the existential dilemma, but because it shows how real the dilemma is, because, with clarity and surgical brilliance, it exposes the equivocations and self-deceptions beneath which bourgeois culture fights for its precarious balance. Mrs. Dalloway is not a heroine who transcends the limitations of her environment, but an all too pathetic product of social forces she has not recognized.

The scrutiny of literature for ethical instruction is a loaded undertaking; it can, imperceptibly, become a formula for self-congratulation. E. D. Hirsch is right to apply strictures against too free a rein for the ethical impulse.[2] A literary work, as he shows, is in a way neutral; it awaits the reader's engagement. But, while we may hope for ideal, objective, self-skeptical readers, intent on identifying the text as it is, at some point we must accept the validity of self-reflexiveness, the question of the text's relevance. Critical evaluation is an historical act; it must recognize the contingency not only of the work being scrutinized but of the scrutinizing activity itself. Although a work of art—take Keats's Urn—exists first as palpable object and then as record of a particular historical reality, beyond this dual existence it remains to "tease us out of thought," to invite us, that is, to moral speculation.

Lionel Trilling proposed the study of literature because it enables the individual to see through his culture, "to stand beyond it in an autonomy of perception and judgment."[3] Trilling's intention is clearly ethical. His proposition rests on the most venerable of assumptions: that man is a moral agent, responsible for his choices, and that right action is a chief end of life. We engage literature because by it we can examine our conscience, begin to appreciate the ambiguities that shadow our own first premises, and learn to lead wiser, more humane lives.

Behind Trilling's formulation lies the notion that engagement with a literary work is a dialectic. Two visions of the world confront each other, the reader's and that represented in the fictive work. From this confrontation a third term emerges, the reader's new perception of the world as altered by his encounter with the imagined world. The reader's perception may differ little from his earlier one, or it may differ radically, depending on the relative strength of his own previous way of understanding the world as compared with the persuasive power of the fictive world. But only when he is scrupulously watchful of the delicate balance between his own integrity and the integrity of the worlds he encounters, and when, in that spirit of watchfulness, he assumes an attitude of imaginative openness, a commitment to be changed by his experience, can the reader benefit, in Trilling's sense, from the exercise. If every person is responsible for the shape the world takes as a result of what he chooses to believe and do, if he is responsible for all that ramifies from what he has assumed about the world, he would do well to acquaint himself with as many of those ramifications as he can, so that he not perpetrate in ignorance something that knowingly he would never do. Clearly, insight is the key to an ethical life in any world where men and women must act and where yet they have imperfect knowledge.

We question Mrs. Dalloway, then, for her lack of insight. She appears to have led her entire life in ignorance of complacent denial of the normative role—for the possibilities of human intercourse in a given society—played by the structure of material relations prevailing *in* that society. Despite the subtlety and fine tune of her sensibilities, despite even the generosity of her intentions, because she acts without regard to the definitions imposed on her by the position she has accepted in the economic structure of her society, she continually compromises herself. Further, despite the brilliance of Virginia Woolf's verbal gifts and the acuteness of her perceptions, to the extent that her narrative invites the reader to condone Mrs. Dalloway's view of the world, her narrator must be faulted as complacent as well. Any assessment of the fictive world of *Mrs. Dalloway* must lead the reader to deep reservations about the middle-class, capitalist world of which the text is both artifact and exponent.

The extent of these allegations should be clarified. It would be unjust to conclude, on the basis of any document produced by her, that Virginia Woolf was bound in a one-to-one correspondence with the omniscient narrator she created in that document. In her life both before and after the writing of *Mrs. Dalloway,* she may well have been appalled by the economic and social inequality undermining her society and have suffered unmeasurable personal anguish at her failure to connect satisfactorily with people all around her, from some of whom she may have been alienated by the distinctions of money and class. Such facts cannot be verified one way or the other. I do conclude that the omniscient narrator of *Mrs. Dalloway* is not appalled by the social and economic inequalities of the society he describes, that if he recognizes economic factors at all he does not think them important as constitutive of social reality, and that he identifies unreservedly with Mrs. Dalloway's conduct. I base these conclusions on the striking absence of self-irony in the verbal intensities with which the narrator details Mrs. Dalloway's mental life. While it is false to assume that the perceptions and mental processes of Virginia Woolf's narrator are self-identical with those of Virginia Woolf, we cannot help noting how totally she is absorbed in the detailing of that exquisite, interior life.

Clarissa Dalloway prides herself on her awareness of, and respect for, the right of other human beings to their own private experience of the world, the right not to have their souls "forced." But what does her awareness amount to? Reverence for the integrity of the "other," respect of its right-to-be, while a noble rule of conduct, is, like most moral imperatives, open to a wide range of inter-pretations. For Clarissa it is merely a strategy of escape; her asseveration of everyone else's freedom masks her own urgent need to deny the structure of material relations that obtains in her world. If one talks loudly enough and at sufficient length about his refusal to force somebody's soul, he may succeed in diverting his own attention as well as that of his listeners from the very real ways in which he is forcing that person's body. But if one assents to an economic structure whose basis is the exploitation of human labor and the aggrandizement of natural resource, if he profits by his position in that economic structure, then the mode of his relationship to those at whose expense he profits is, plainly and simply, that of exploiter to exploited. It is the idlest, and most criminally mistaken, of pretenses to think that exploiter can transcend this primary connection with the exploited and achieve some other connection which might be more gratifying to his moral sense. What nobility of feeling is there, for instance, in a person's refusal to tamper with the souls of those who dwell in his tenements when in fact it is their poverty and labor that support him in his mansion? One can only exploit that which he considers an extension of his own ego, a mechanism for the satisfaction of his wants, not an "other" human being with inalienable rights of his own. One cannot deny a person his personhood on the one hand and pretend that he assures it on the other.

There is no operative recognition, in *Mrs. Dalloway*, that the world really exists "out there," historical, changing, its shape dependent on the way human beings relate to it. The world in its otherness has been reduced to a construct inside the fantasist's mind, changing as the kaleidoscope changes. There is no reference point but the individual mind; the public, the political are invalidated. What else can Mrs. Dalloway's notion of private experience mean? The world, after all, the one that actually exists "out there," is only what is at any given time congruent in the experience of everyone. It assembles itself continually from the intersections of individual experience. "The world" is just that which is sharable; it exists only as social mediation produces it. To the extent, then, that a person's experience is private, he does not really participate in the world. To say that a person has a right to his private experience has no meaning; everyone has private experience inevitably. What a person has a right to is shared experience, participation in a common world. To take refuge in private experience is to abandon that encounter of individual worlds from which alone the new world, the shared world, can emerge. To adopt such a mode of behavior is to act as if life were a purely mental phenomenon, as if human beings were disembodied consciousnesses whose experience, private with a vengeance, were without common foundation in a material world. Such a pretense ignores the fact that human beings are biological organisms, breathing the same air, relying for continued subsistence on the same sources of food, inhabiting the same finite planet, in short, that all human experience resides in a limited body of the material resource. This is the dead end to which capitalism and the bourgeois mind come: because what is shared, what the actual vectors of relation are, has become too painful to entertain, social reality must be denied altogether.

Stream-of-consciousness as technique becomes the formal equivalent of the retreat into private experience, of the decision to settle for solipsism, and represents not so much a failure of confidence in the possibility of social reality as a failure of nerve, an unwillingness to face the deepening contradictions in the shape social reality takes in a capitalist world. By exploring the effects of alienation on the isolated mind, by absorbing oneself in the mechanisms of the interior life, one can avoid confronting the causes of alienation altogether. Solipsism accepts these prearranged boundaries as absolute: we will not consider what brought on this alienation; we will only dwell on its effect, delineate it as a feeling. But in making this pact, it surrenders the world, which is a defeat of enormous proportions. The stream-of-consciousness novel is not non-dramatic; the focus of attention has simply shifted. What is being dramatized is now no longer the fabric of social reality, but the workings of the isolated, self-conscious mind, frightened fugitive in a hostile world. By creating the impression of rapid, unsorted sensations flickering across a receptive mind, stream-of-consciousness narrative excuses itself from the charge of sorting or valuation, suggesting instead that there is no accountability in the experiencer for a world whose shape is at once exotic and arbitrary. Though the tone of Clarissa Dalloway's inner monologue is gay, the gaiety seems a trifle forced as if verging on hysteria. After all, for a mind reinforced by nothing but its own will, admitting no relation to the world but the false one of detached observer, the hysteria is real enough:

> Such fools we are, she thought, crossing Victoria Street. For Heaven only knows why one loves it so, how one sees it so, making it up, building it round one, tumbling it, creating it every moment afresh; but the veriest frumps, the most dejected of miseries sitting on doorsteps (drink their downfall) do the same; can't be deal with, she felt positive, by Acts of Parliament for that very reason: they love life. In people's eyes, in the swing, tramp, and trudge; in the bellow and the uproar; the carriages, motor cars, omnibuses, vans, sandwich men shuffling and swinging; brass bands; barrel organs; in the triumph and the jingle and the strange high singing of some aeroplane overhead was what she loved; life; London; this moment of June.[4]

The world becomes at once arbitrary and inevitable. Clearly the kaleidoscope is the generating metaphor implicit in this passage. The incidence of old women drunk on doorsteps cannot be lessened by any affirmative action because, in a jolly sort of way, old women on doorsteps love life and like being drunk. Here, as elsewhere, Clarissa follows the creed of the solipsist, refusing to question the order of things, to probe beneath the surface, to seek causes. It requires less commitment simply to observe the phenomenal world and stop comfortably at the stage of wonder. She prefers to pretend that there is no such thing as history, that her actions have not defined her as one particular person, that her ordering of her life on certain principles has not confirmed those principles and contributed, for better or worse, to their maintenance:

> She would not say of anyone in the world now that they were this or were that. She felt very young; at the same time unspeakably aged. She sliced like

a knife through everything at the same time was outside, looking on. She had a perpetual sense, as she watched the taxicabs, of being out, out, far out to sea and alone; she always had the feeling that it was very, very dangerous to live even one day. Not that she thought herself clever, or much out of the ordinary. How she had got through life on the few twigs of knowledge Fraulein Daniels gave them she could not think. She knew nothing; no language, no history; she scarcely read a book now, except memoirs in bed; and yet to her it was absolutely absorbing; all this; the cabs passing; and she would not say of Peter, she would not say of herself, I am this, I am that. (10–11)

For Clarissa, the best life is the unexamined life. Her pose of ignorance is a pose of simplicity, a claim to be regarded as an innocent, but it has its calculated economy nevertheless. In the childlike world of make-believe she can be everything and nothing at once. Knowing no history, she must be excused from history's some-times stern accounting. Might her conduct have social repercussions? Might some advantage she enjoys be, for instance, the virtual reason that certain old women in the meaner streets of town sit drunk on doorsteps? Examined, life has an unpleasant way of pinning people down, of assigning social cause to social effect. Once the whispers of self-doubt start to circulate, their reverberation builds to a deafening roar. Escape, to a mind so threatened, presents itself in suppression: never let those whispers sound at all.

At the two most critical moments of her day, when Doris Kilman lures away Elizabeth, and when the news of the suicide of Septimus Warren Smith intrudes in insidious whispers at her party, Clarissa attempts, with sham success, this sup-pression, averting by a mental trick any confrontation with the experiences of Kilman or Smith, whose worlds call into question her own. Rather than submit to the collisions which would inevitably reshape her world, she screens herself by interposing an artificial third term, the product of her own protean fancy. Threatened by Kilman, and again by Smith, she shifts her attention from them to the old woman she can see moving in the bedroom across the street, and whose observable presence she invokes in a sort of ecstatic meditation. Unable to bear the reality of her connections with Kilman and Smith, she fantasizes a connection with the old woman across the street. In this connection, ungoverned by reality, her own charmed prescriptions—for beauty, wonder, and above all inscrutable mystery—can prevail. Refusing responsibility as a participant in a particular historical reality, she creates a fantasy world where the mode of experience is not participation at all but merely detached observation. In this fantasy the "other" is not historical, the encounter with it not at all conditioned by material factors; it is instead mystical, eternal, ineffable, unchanging. Good bourgeoise that she is, Clarissa predicates her interior economy on preserving intact the serenity of her surface. The hysteria which flutters disconcertingly beneath her calm is simply the barometer of her fear, fear not so much that her isolation is inevitable but that it is something she persists in perversely and unnecessarily. Her economy does not permit her to consider a salutary break in that serenity; it only allows, with obsessive disregard of the cost, for intensified fortification of the surface.

I want to examine now the passages in question to demonstrate in detail how Clarissa's fantasy of connectedness functions. The first of these passages occurs on Doris Kilman's leaving the house with Clarissa's daughter Elizabeth, their destination the Army and Navy stores. Encountering them on the landing as they pass, Clarissa withdraws again into her room, extremely agitated:

> Love in religion! thought Clarissa, going back into the drawing-room, tingling all over. How detestable, how detestable they are!... The cruelest things in the world, she thought, seeing them clumsy, hot, domineering, hypocritical, eavesdropping, jealous, infinitely cruel and unscrupulous, dressed in a mackintosh coat, on the landing; love and religion. Had she ever tried to convert anyone herself? Did she not wish everybody merely to be themselves? And she watched out of the window the old lady opposite climbing upstairs. Let her climb upstairs if she wanted to; let her stop; then let her, as Clarissa had often seen her, gain her bedroom, part her curtains, and disappear again into the background. Somehow one respected that— that old woman looking out of the window, quite unconscious that she was being watched. There was something solemn in it—but love and religion would destroy that whatever it was, the privacy of the soul. The odious Kilman would destroy it. (140)

Doris Kilman sweats, is not beautiful, and wears a mackintosh; her grandfather had kept "an oil and colour shop in Kensington" (145). She is, in short, lower class; or, to borrow Forster's witty formulation for Leonard Bast in *Howards End,* she stands "at the extreme verge of gentility."[5] Moreover, she is a vulgar activist, who attends meetings, her knowledge of modern history is "thorough in the extreme" (139), and she reads books which foster the scurrilous opinion that the English are not "invariably right" (144). If Clarissa admitted that Doris Kilman were a creature conditioned by her personal history, by her experience of class, then she might also be forced to recognize that she herself has been conditioned by class. Because Clarissa cannot see herself as Doris Kilman sees her, because she cannot entertain Kilman's real "otherness," she simply puts her out of mind altogether, dismissing her contentiousness as vulgar and pretending that her own hushed and reverent observation of the old woman across the way establishes a mode of relationship with other human beings superior to that offered by Kilman's everywhere. I quote from a point further on in Clarissa's musings:

> Big Ben struck the half-hour.
> How extraordinary it was, strange, yes, touching to see the old lady (they had been neighbours ever so many years) move away from the window, as

if she were attached to that sound, that string. Gigantic as it was, it had something to do with her. Down, down, into the midst of ordinary things the finger fell, making the moment solemn. She was forced, so Clarissa imagined, by that sound, to move, to go—but where? Clarissa tried to follow her as she turned and disappeared, and could still just see her white cap moving at the back of the bedroom. She was still there, moving about at the other end of the room. Why creeds and prayers and mackintoshes? when, thought Clarissa, that's the miracle, that's the mystery; that old lady, she meant, whom she could see going from chest of drawers to dressing-table. She could still see her. And the supreme mystery which Kilman might say she had solved, or Peter might say he had solved, but Clarissa didn't believe either of them had the ghost of an idea of solving, was simply this: here was one room; there another. Did religion solve that, or love? (141)

Significantly, as the syntax of her argument reveals, Clarissa's thought patterns move in such a way that unfounded assertions come to stand for proof. "Why creeds and prayers and mackintoshes?" she asks, as if the very obviousness of her rhetorical question dismissed creeds and prayers as ludicrous, uncalled-for phenomena. But the question is not rhetorical at all; we might answer, "Why? because people's experiences differ and no consensus can emerge without formulation of the differences and contention between their respective claims." Clarissa's last point—that here is one room, there another, and that no amount of contention will solve that—is too glib to be the triumphant dismissal of all argument that it purports to be. Rooms here and rooms there are not preordained inevitabilities of an unchanging reality. If there is a drawing-room here, with discreet and sumptuous appointments, that drawing room is not without its reasons, or its costs. And if there is a bedroom there, with chest of drawers and dressing-table of questionable design, that too is not without its historical and material causes. All the talk about the irreducible integrity of rooms is obfuscation. The important point about the old woman across the street, which Clarissa misses, is that she has her own particular life, a life that is not a momentary blossom in Clarissa's mind called into being without antecedent cause, but real and "other." She is not merely a puppet responding magically to the chords of Big Ben for Clarissa's distraction and delight. If Clarissa chooses to indulge that sort of fantasy, administering it to herself as an anodyne when pained by some intrusion from the real, she in fact practices a sort of elevated voyeurism. If the connection were real rather than fantastic, if the old woman were aware of the role Clarissa had designed for her, she might well take exception to it. But one of the convenient features of Clarissa's "connections" is that they do not consult the object connected with.

In the second of the crucial passages, when the suicide is announced, Clarissa's recourse to her fantasy world occurs according to pattern. It is only more remarkable for the enormity of the contradiction which it this time manages to dismiss. Lady Bradshaw comes up to Clarissa and whispers that what Sir William is whispering to Mr. Dalloway across the room is that some young man, a Septimus Warren Smith, has just killed himself. Again extremely agitated, Clarissa quits the party and retires to her room. There she makes several partial gestures of embrace, several attempts to comprehend the meaning of the occurrence. She reflects that the doctors who hounded Septimus and tried to force his soul are monsters and that they are responsible for his death. She does not reflect that these same doctors, monsters though they be, are welcome and honored guests at her party. She reflects that she herself might commit suicide were she not cushioned by material and psychic comforts:

> Then (she had felt it only this morning) there was the terror; the overwhelming incapacity, one's parents giving it into one's hands, this life, to be lived to the end, to be walked with serenely; there was in the depths of her heart an awful fear. Even now, quite often if Richard had not been there reading the *Times,* so that she could crouch like a bird and gradually revive, send roaring up that immeasurable delight, rubbing stick to stick, one thing with another, she must have perished. (204)

She does not reflect that the very securities that solid Richard can offer her are securities he has at his disposal because of the role he executes in an exploitive society. She concludes instead, with self-congratulation that is touching only because it is so blind, that she has suffered too, that "It was her punishment to see sink and disappear here a man, there a woman, in this profound darkness, and she forced to stand here in her evening dress" (205). Here again she conceives of experience not as participation in a shared reality but as detached observation of a nightmare. She suggests, absolving herself of responsibility, that roles are arbitrarily and externally assigned. She does not reflect that the only thing that forces her to stand there in her evening dress is her decision that what she gains by so doing outweighs what she would lose if she chose not to. Finally, in a long passage of reflection, punctuated again by references to the mystical old woman across the way, Clarissa puts Septimus away entirely, concluding paradoxically that she is "glad" he has killed himself:

> Oh, but how surprising!—in the room opposite the old lady stared straight at her! She was going to be . . . It was fascinating to watch her, moving about, that old lady, crossing the room, coming to the window. Could she see her? It was fascinating, with people still laughing and shouting in the drawing-room, to watch that old woman, quite quietly, going to bed alone. She pulled the blind now. The clock began striking. The young man had killed himself; but she did not pity him; with the clock striking the hour, one, two, three, she did not pity him, with all this going on. There! the old lady had put out her light! the whole house was dark now with this going on, she repeated, and

the words came to her, Fear no more the heat of the sun. She must go back to them. But what an extraordinary night! She felt somehow very like him— the young man who had killed himself. She felt glad that he had done it; thrown it away while they went on living. The clock was striking. The leaden circles dissolved in the air. But she must go back. She must assemble. (205–06)

The incongruity of this affirmation and of the procedure by which she arrives at it escapes Clarissa entirely. She does not see the glaring discontinuities between her own experiences and Septimus' which make her self-identification with him absurd and wholly unfunny. She does not reflect that the very society she believes herself to be "assembling" by her parties is the same society that sent Septimus Warren Smith (and many others like him) to the trenches to be shell-shocked, and then had no way of incorporating his experience into itself when he returned. She does not reflect that the society to which she gives her allegiance is the same society that has amassed an empire and drained the material resources of continents so that its own extravagant ballrooms might be amply lit, its furniture plushly upholstered, its windows curtained with the most delicate lace. It is significant that the question of England's far-flung Indias is only discussed in *Mrs. Dalloway* in an undertone in another room, by Lady Bruton, an old woman whose eccentricities are matters of gossip and condescension. Clarissa cannot let herself feel the extent to which she participates in Septimus' death. If she did not admit the extent to which she was implicated, she would not easily be restored to serenity by the sight of an old woman climbing stairs, nor would she be able to return with such assurance to the vacuities of her party. Her whole precarious selfhood and her deeply self-contradicting way of life hinge on the denial.

If human intercourse is a meeting, above all, of minds, the structure of those meetings is nevertheless governed by the fact that they must occur within the axes of social reality. Every other sort of meeting, purporting to transcend material and historical determinatives, locating itself in some imaginary, mystical moment, will fail. Mrs. Dalloway's "insight" is trumped up; she never connects with her old woman and never escapes the responsibility of her failure to connect with Doris Kilman or Septimus Smith. The structure of a particular historical reality legitimizes certain avenues of communication and response and renders others impossible. In the world summoned into being by the mind of middle-class capitalism, man is alienated from his fellow man, from himself, and from the material world, and the possibility of connection is defined by its perversion or absence. If people are appalled by the shape their relationships take in such circumstances, if they want to connect differently, then they must, since they themselves have created by a series of historical choices the world they deplore, shift the terms of relation, recreate social reality. Mrs. Dalloway, because she tries to suppress rather than to change her morally ambiguous relation to her world, only suffers more rarified states of alienation, more painful degrees of unreality.

NOTES

[1] Lucio Ruotolo, *Six Existential Heroes* (Cambridge: Harvard University Press, 1973), pp. 13–35.

[2] Cf. his discussion in E. D. Hirsch, Jr., "Objective Interpretation," *PMLA*, 75 (1960). Reprinted in Hazard Adams, ed., *Critical Theory since Plato* (New York: Harcourt Brace Jovanovich, 1971), pp. 1177–94.

[3] Lionel Trilling, *Beyond Culture* (New York: The Viking Press, 1965), p. xiii.

[4] Virginia Woolf, *Mrs. Dalloway* (Penguin Books, 1964), p. 6. (All succeeding page references in this essay are to this edition.)

[5] E. M. Forster, *Howards End* (New York: Vintage Books), p. 45.

Robert Kiely

A LONG EVENT OF PERPETUAL CHANGE

Virginia Woolf may not have had Richardson's heroine in mind when she named the protagonist of *Mrs. Dalloway* Clarissa, but the coincidence underlines the contrasting significance of the two titles. It is not merely that one novel deals with the life of an unmarried woman and the other with that of one who is married. Both titles are responses to a literary convention as well as indications of the marital status of their heroines. Richardson, seeming to follow the tradition of popular romance in using his heroine's first name for his title, produced a work that overturned some of the most hallowed premises of that tradition. The narrative does not lead to a happy marriage or any kind of marriage; the conventionally poetic name does not belong to a simple, agreeable character blandly indistinguishable from others of her social class; finally, the first name standing alone goes beyond prettiness to symbolize the character's break with her family, her separation from society, and the impossibility of a respectable marriage. A modern reader can still take *Clarissa* seriously partly because of the heroine's struggle to preserve her chastity becomes a matter less and less of saving family honor (the family name) than of saving her own integrity and identity. In the long course of the novel, she is reduced to being just Clarissa, but then proves to the astonishment of almost everyone that, deprived of all the usual ties and associations, it is a name with an indestructible content of its own.

Whether or not she was thinking of *Clarissa*, Woolf was certainly aware of the conventions governing the titles of novels of English domestic life. While novels with male protagonists ordinarily included both first and family names—*Joseph Andrews, Roderick Random, Tristram Shandy, Guy Mannering, David Copperfield, Henry Esmond, Phineas Finn*—titles of novels with female protagonists—*Amelia, Pamela, Evelina, Emma, Shirley, Romola*—often stopped with first names because one of the primary assumptions of the form was that the last name would change.

From *Beyond Egotism: The Fiction of James Joyce, Virginia Woolf, and D. H. Lawrence* (Cambridge, MA: Harvard University Press, 1980), pp. 119–30.

The symbolism suggests that the unmarried male character, however imperfect morally, represents the stability and completeness of society, while the unmarried female character, however perfect morally, is somehow unstable and incomplete and must find her fulfillment in union with a husband. Unlike a son, the daughter seems only to have borrowed her father's name until the time comes to exchange it for that of another man. By calling her novel, *Mrs. Dalloway,* Woolf breaks an old tradition and advertises the fact that the exchange has already taken place. Like Joyce and Lawrence, she has little interest in presenting marriage as a final solution to life or as a convenient stopping point for narrative fiction.[1]

Far from having given Clarissa Dalloway a settled identity, marriage seems, over the years, to have contributed to her sense of nonbeing. "But often now this body she wore . . . this body, with all its capacities, seemed nothing—nothing at all. She had the oddest sense of being herself invisible; unseen; unknown; there being no more marrying, no more having of children now, but only this astonishing and rather solemn progress with the rest of them, up Bond Street, this being Mrs. Dalloway; not even Clarissa any more; this being Mrs. Richard Dalloway"(14).

At the novel's beginning, Clarissa Dalloway has obviously already given up something of the separate integrity that Clarissa Harlowe fights to retain. Yet the Dalloways' marriage, while not ecstatic, is not depicted as oppressive or unhappy. Richard Dalloway is not shown to be a particularly interesting husband, but he is not possessive enough to keep Clarissa from doing largely as she pleases and leading an interior life separate from his own. As in the case of Bloom and Molly, the Dalloways are seen more often apart than together; this permits the reader to trace in their interior monologues their movements back and forth between separation and mutual involvement. What the modern Clarissa faces is not a choice between marriage and an honorable death but the task of discovering life between the poles of individual separateness and relationship with others.

Woolf's protagonist alternates between concentrating so intensely on herself that she loses sight of her surroundings and emptying herself so completely in the lives of others that she loses sight of herself. While looking at her face in her bedroom mirror, she compares herself with a diamond, sharp, concentrated, and hard. But at other moments, she thinks of herself as a mist mingling in the branches of other lives. In her ordinary day, she experiences countless minor births and deaths, marriages and divorces. Though she may feel herself to be a part of the general and "rather solemn progress" up Bond Street, the plot of her own life and day is not one of progression but of movement back and forth between isolation and relationship, the diamond and the mist, Clarissa and Mrs. Dalloway.

The "solemn progress" describes not Clarissa's actions or thoughts but the background or context within which they occur. Just as images of space—the vast plains, the "roaring" skies, the Gothic arches, the rainbow—dominate Lawrence's novel of marriage, images of time dominate Woolf's. Recollections of the past—missed opportunities, momentary joys, unbearable losses—are juxtaposed with Clarissa's plans for her party and the anxiety of Septimus and Rezia for their future. Throughout it all, Big Ben tolls the hours in a constant reminder that time is running out with equal speed and inevitability for them all.

Lawrence's imagery suggests that marriage is a sign of man's essential connection with the earth and his best means of affirming and sustaining that connection. A good marriage is a sacrament, an embodiment of a power greater than the individual, because it imitates the active resolution of natural discord and the creation of new life. Marriage has no such significance for Woolf because for her human life seems to have no sustainable relationship with earth. All connections, good and bad, are continually diminished and destroyed by the passage of time. Marriage, like all other forms of human ordering, is an expression of a fond wish with little firm basis in reality. Insofar as it has its source in the human will and imagination, it is genuine; but insofar as it presumes a field of stability and permanence outside itself, it is an illusion. Yet since absolute isolation, like absolute intermingling, is a form of death, marriage, like much else in life, is a willed compromise, a constructed form in constant need of alteration and reshaping—not so different from Peter Walsh's adventures, Richard's committees, Rezia's hats, and Clarissa's parties.

These are all forms of communication, languages through which the self is recreated by a process of objective simplification and projection. Whatever effectiveness such languages have, whatever meaning is shaped, flows between poles of no meaning. On one side, there is a conventionality so extreme that it goes beyond its function as conveyer of meaning and becomes its own content; on the other is an unconventionality so extreme that it loses all contact with recognizable networks of communication. One is a language so excessively "for others" as to be incapable of referring intelligibly to the particularity of the speaker; the other is one so excessively "for the self" as to be incapable of referring intelligibly to others.

As a novel about marriage and other forms of communication, *Mrs. Dalloway* explores the movements of life and partial meaning snatched from the shifting field between these two dead poles. The altogether "conventional" Mrs. Dalloway and the mad Septimus Smith feel the attractions of these opposite poles so keenly that they meet (without having seen one another or spoken) in the common experience of death in life. Like Bloom and Dedalus on another level, they are, by all the usual standards of society and realistic fiction, a hopelessly incongruous, unrelated pair. Yet without the intervention of Dickensian coincidence or secret blood ties, a kinship deeper than words and stronger than social classification is shown to exist between them. Though Clarissa survives it and Septimus does not, both are harrowed by a private, incomprehensible, and incommunicable mixture of pain and joy that is derived from human contact but, at the same time, makes further human contact seem impossible.

The primary difference between them is not sex or class, but time. Septimus's incommunicable experience is the love and sudden loss of a friend in the war, a quick and violent collision of attachment and detachment that he cannot understand, put in order for himself, or arrange into words and actions presentable to others.

His madness takes the form of trying over and over to convey a message: "the supreme secret must be told," "I must tell the whole world," "the message hidden in the beauty of words," "the secret signal." In fact, except for a series of disconnected declarations, Septimus can tell nothing. When his wife, Rezia, asks him the time, he promises to tell her but cannot because his own time has been stopped by the death of his friend, whose uniformed ghost summons him to a world without time. "'I will tell you the time,' said Septimus, very slowly, very drowsily, smiling mysteriously. As he sat smiling at the dead man in the grey suit the quarter struck—the quarter to twelve" (106).

In sharp contrast with Septimus, Clarissa has led a life without catastrophe, need, or passion. Her feelings for her husband are, from the very first, affectionate rather than intense. There is a reticence, a coolness that she regrets but cannot seem to help. Even her adolescent infatuation with Sally Seton was marked by restraint and timidity on her part. The return of Peter Walsh, a former suitor, fills her with nostalgia and wistful memories of the past, but she is not sorry she refused to marry him. Yet, like Septimus, Clarissa tastes and smells and feels death, the end of time, not in a split second at the bursting of a shell, but gradually narrowing her existence, reducing her possibilities, and shaping her interior life so that she, too, begins reading and interpreting signs in ways that cannot easily be explained to others.

Soon after Septimus is seen trying to decipher sky-writing, Clarissa returns home, reads a simple message to her husband on the telephone pad (an invitation to lunch with Lady Bruton), and translates the words into a confusion of emotions and thoughts that are consistent enough with her inner life but would appear nearly as insane as the ravings of Septimus if spoken: ". . . as a plant on the river-bed feels the shock of a passing oar and shivers: so she rocked: so she shivered. . . . No vulgar jealousy could separate her from Richard. But she feared time itself, and read on Lady Bruton's face, as if it had been a dial cut in impassive stone, the dwindling of life; how year by year her share was sliced; how little the margin that remained was capable any longer of stretching" (44).

Woolf's technique of third-person narrated monologue suits the situation perfectly. Since communication is one of the major subjects of the book, as well as one of the difficulties for the characters, it is appropriate that Clarissa's inner reactions be approximated by the author rather than imitated literally in what Woolf called the "ventriloquist" style. It is not necessary that the images of the "river-bed" or the "impassive stone" be articulated by Clarissa to herself, as happens in many of the interior monologues in *Ulysses.* The narration is a rendering not of what the character might just as well say for herself, but precisely of what the character experiences but cannot say. Woolf obviously would not agree with Wittgenstein that one can only experience what can be said. If Clarissa has, like Septimus and Bloom, a touch of the poet, it is not revealed in her choice of words, which is as conventional as her choice of husband, furniture, and friends, but in the depth and honesty of an inner life that qualifies and refines those commonplace choices.

Throughout the day, as Clarissa shops, receives Peter Walsh, speaks with her husband and daughter, and prepares for her party—all ordinary outgoing activities—she returns again and again to a private self that seems to have almost nothing to do with these routine gestures. In her life, there is a spare moral reality (reminiscent of *Everyman* without the Christian theology) of a journey that must be taken unaccompanied, a passage through which husbands, friends, servants, silver, and fine pictures cannot come. This experience does not occur for Clarissa at the end of life, but episodically throughout life in rhythmic alternation with ordinary daily activity. Again, there is no doubt that the awareness is Clarissa's, even though the highly imagistic verbalization of it is Woolf's. "Like a nun withdrawing, or a child exploring a tower, she went upstairs . . . There was an emptiness about the heart of life; an attic room. . . . The sheets were clean, tight stretched . . . Narrower and narrower would her bed be. The candle was half burnt down and she had read deep in Baron Marbot's *Memoirs*" (45–46).

When Clarissa's awareness of the continuous juxtaposition of life and death, attachment and detachment, is expressed in thoughts and words of her own, a certain meaning is abstractly conveyed, but it is so barren of nuance and particularity that the reader experiences a linguistic frigidity that nearly kills what it captures. For example, when Richard brings her roses after lunch, she explains his awkward formality to herself in words consistent with her reputation for prim aloofness: "And there is a dignity in people; a solitude; even between husband and wife a gulf; and that one must respect, thought Clarissa, watching him open the door; for one would not part with it oneself, or take it, against his will, from one's husband, without losing one's independence, one's self-respect—something, after all, is priceless" (181).

Put in this way, the subject nearly goes dead; suddenly it seems dry and tedious, a dull justification for an upper-middle-class marriage of convenience. That is certainly the way Peter Walsh sees it, and there are indications that Clarissa herself entertains similar suspicions. But a particular grouping of words or thoughts does not settle matters any more firmly than marriage itself does. The effort to communicate is identical with the effort to live. Both are subject to prolonged spells of incoherence and vacuity; both are capable of sudden unexpected successes.

The reader is able to believe that Clarissa and Richard's marriage is more than empty formality not so much because of what Clarissa says to Richard (they talk about the party, their daughter's friend, Miss Kilman, and his committees), or what they are shown doing together (he gives her flowers and holds her hand), but because of her genius for sympathetic identification. She is like a mute poet, capable of sending her self into another body and then returning to her own, filled with understanding, sorrow, and a kind of love beyond words and action.

The process may produce a descriptive lyricism of sorts, but the poetic text is Woolf's, not Clarissa's. Her attempts to generalize about the old woman at the window of the opposite house are as barren as her thoughts about the dignity of marriage. Clarissa's remarkable gift is not her ability to reflect on the old lady or speak of her (which she never does) but in her being able to *see* her and imaginatively *be* with her. "How extraordinary it was, strange, yes, touching, to see the old lady ... move away from the window ... Clarissa tried to follow her as she turned and disappeared, and could still just see her white cap ... that old lady, she meant, whom she could see going from chest of drawers to dressing-table. She could still see her. And the supreme mystery ... was simply this: here was one room; there another" (193).

Clarissa, who is hostile to and ignorant of religion, politics, and philosophy, cuts across these categories to be momentarily with the old woman in her solitude. It is an imaginative leap without apparent meaning or practical issue. "Here was one room; there was another" is so baldly concrete and unanalytical a statement as to defy coherent systems—like Miss Kilman's religion or Sir William Bradshaw's psychology—that presume causation and comprehensive meanings. It reflects a view of life in which there is much to be experienced and little to be said or done. To imagine that Clarissa would rush out of her room and embrace the old woman, offer her money, reform her life, cure her lumbago, discover her to be a long-lost grandmother, or hire her as a laundress is not merely to conjure up Victorian plots but to be reminded of the fictions of a lost world, in which networks of meaning had validity only insofar as they could be translated into action.

In most nineteenth-century novels, despite varieties of viewpoint, there was a fundamental text, provided by the author and apparent to the reader, which it was the task of the good characters to discover and harmonize with their own text. Through the tolling of Big Ben, the selection of characters, and the preparation for the party, Woolf provides the outlines of a single text, but she does not offer a ground against which all else is to be judged and understood. The realization that there is no "ground," no given or permanent sense of structure, is Clarissa's peculiar weakness and gift. Of all the characters, she and Septimus are the only ones who have not found a single coherent and recognizable language through which to express themselves. Throughout the day, she comes in and out of focus (for herself as well as the reader), dissolves and materializes, lapses into dull conventionality, and bursts into exquisite originality. She needs a narrator as she needs a husband, friends, a household, to provide her with semblances of structure, but she does not mistake those structures for her soul. In her virginal aloofness, she is not simply a woman with a sexual problem, but a person, like all others, who is not capable of being totally possessed by words, ideas, or people. Her great gift is her recognition of this fact about herself and about Richard, the old woman, and Septimus. The secret and paradox of her attractiveness is that she can share, with an intimacy beyond touch and sound, her acquaintance with the solitude of human nature.

Contact with Clarissa can bring about a momentary release from the carefully composed languages and systems of thought and behavior that most of the other characters use to protect themselves from solitude. Peter Walsh bursts into tears in the midst of his excited talk about himself and his plans, not because of anything Clarissa has said or done but because he is mysteriously moved by her presence.

When he leaves Clarissa and follows a pretty girl on the street, he has a momentary revelation as the girl disappears and Clarissa's voice comes back to him. "Well, I've had my fun . . . And it was smashed to atoms—his fun, for it was half made up, as he knew very well; invented, this escapade with the girl; made up, as one makes up the better part of life, he thought—making oneself up" (81). But when Walsh wanders toward Regents Park, he resumes his old habit of "making up" his life as he narrates to himself the story of Clarissa's refusal of his proposal of marriage and her courtship with Richard. By letting Walsh tell this part of the story in a comic-melodramatic mode reminiscent of Wilde or Shaw, Woolf gives the reader another illustration of the gulf between things ("here was one room; there was another"). The more conventionally "dramatic" the language, the less convinced we are of the sequence, emphasis, and causation it imposes on events: "For of course it was that afternoon, that very afternoon, that Dalloway had come over . . . that was the beginning of it all" (92).

Walsh's recollection of his proposal to Clarissa is like the reconstruction of the setting for a play. He recalls his urgent note to Clarissa asking her to meet him by a fountain "far from the house, with shrubs and trees all around it." He thinks of the moment as "the final scene, the terrible scene which he believed had mattered more than anything in the whole of his life." Even Walsh realizes that this is all an "exaggeration," but it is his habitual way of giving form to his experience. Moreover, it is the only sustained account Woolf gives of the events leading up to Clarissa's marriage to Dalloway. Though we may resist Walsh's theatricality, we have no firmer textual ground on which to base our understanding. "Terrible scenes" and "marriages of convenience" are unsatisfactory labels for rejected proposals and imperfect relationships; if we can see beyond them, however, it is not to a perfect language or a perfect love, but to the desolation that makes even foolish talk tolerable.

Richard Dalloway, member of Parliament and of a number of committees, has also developed a language through which his thoughts and actions are predictably and safely channeled. If anything, it is a language even more limited than Walsh's, the language of the public man, composed of sporting phrases ("Really it was a miracle thinking of the war, and thousands of poor chaps, with all their lives before them, shovelled together"), vague judgments ("our detestable social system and so forth"), good-natured clichés ("you can't deny it a certain dignity"), and sentimental generalizations ("it was a great age in which to have lived"). As he walks home to present Clarissa with a bunch of roses, Richard thinks about how he would like to tell her "in so many words" how he loves her, but when the time arrives the words refuse to come: "(But he could not bring himself to say he loved her; not in so many words.)"

The communication, nonetheless, is achieved. Clarissa understands his meaning, and though they speak of commonplace things, it is as if silent vows have been repeated and the marriage made again. In fact, what happens between them is analogous to what happens between author and reader. It is a collaboration and completion that requires a text but does not end with it. Since the book itself holds together only insofar as the reader is able to "read between the lines" of the various speeches and interior texts, one is prepared to believe that Clarissa has interpreted Richard's meaning correctly even if he has not articulated it "in so many words." The bouquet, the polite words and gestures are the occasions of their coming together without constraint. Neither forces the other to say or do anything in particular. Richard proffers the flowers as a sign Clarissa is free to interpret. That she reads the sign so quickly and correctly gives Richard enormous satisfaction and shows the reader the extent to which she accepts him. The episode reflects an attitude analogous to Sartre's view of the art of writing as an act of trust in human freedom, since it involves offering words that provide guides to meaning but cannot force a particular interpretation or guarantee interest or attention. The author is in the continual state of proposing, while the reader is free to accept, reject, or ignore the proposal altogether.

The marriage that parallels that of the Dalloways throughout the novel is that of Septimus Smith and Rezia, his Italian wife. In fact, almost as soon as the reader sees them together, it becomes clear that there is no marriage, that sharing and communication are absent. Since the death of his friend Evans, time has stopped for Septimus. When his wife speaks to him, he is not there. He is like a reader who has closed the book, leaving her words unread and inert. " 'For you should see the Milan gardens,' she said aloud. But to whom? There was nobody. Her words faded. So a rocket fades. Its sparks, having grazed their way into the night, surrender to it, dark descends" (34).

Rezia tries to tell herself that she is a married woman, that she must stand by her husband and not admit to herself or to anyone else that he is mad. But their scenes together reveal moments of unbridgeable isolation. Their attempts at communication are not filled with the comic irony of Joyce or marked by violent ruptures, as in Lawrence; instead, they are desolate monologues, signs not of mismatching or impending divorce but of nonmarriage. When Septimus notices that Rezia is not wearing her wedding ring, he thinks to himself "with agony, with relief," that "their marriage was over." But as Rezia gradually admits to herself, there never was a marriage. Nothing has been broken because nothing was created between them. "It was not marriage; it was not being one's husband to look strange like that, always to be starting, laughing, sitting hour after hour silent, or clutching her and telling her to write. The table drawer was full of those writings; about war; about Shakespeare; about great discoveries; how there is no death" (212). The picture of Septimus dictating to Rezia provides an important contrast with the shared moment between Richard and Clarissa, in which so little is said and so much meant. Richard's reticence and Clarissa's (felt by both as faults in their own characters) are momentarily seen by the reader as positive qualities. Neither wishes, by uttering "so many words," to force or dictate a response from the other.

Septimus's dictation to Rezia is of course a kind of madness, but, insofar as marriage and communication are concerned, it is madness of a particularly revealing kind. Though the subjects—death, Shakespeare, and war—are much grander than those discussed by the Dalloways, they are not tokens of rapport between two people but rather the funneling of one person's random thoughts through the uninterpreting, nonparticipating vehicle of another. It is one of many examples in the novel of words that have lost the power to communicate meaning, of a coincidental misuse of persons and language.

It is perfectly consistent with the parallelism between the relationships of words and people that, after hearing of the death of Septimus Smith, Clarissa should enter an empty room in her own house while her party is in progress and there, alone, receive a "message" from the dead man in total silence. Without dictation or prompting, Clarissa "reads" Septimus's suicide as no one else can. "A thing there was that mattered; a thing, wreathed about with chatter, defaced, obscured in her own life, let drop every day in corruption, lies, chatter. This he had preserved. Death was defiance. Death was an attempt to communicate ... closeness drew apart; rapture faded, one was alone" (280–281).

Clarissa sees the opposite of life not in death, since it is so much a part of living, but in the denials of death in life, solitude in relationship, detachment within attachment, that are represented by Sir William Bradshaw's and Miss Kilman's denials of reality. "Forcing your soul, that was it." Having encountered a core of absolute solitude within herself, Clarissa employs sentences and social graces as gestures of reverence and consolation toward others rather than as ends in themselves or efforts to conceal the truth by an imposition of will. Returning, as she does over and over throughout the day, to the simple, absolute fact, that "one was alone," is not for Clarissa a melancholy obsession, but the starting point for what she most vitally is, the nuances of meaning in her commonplace talk, the extraordinary revelations of beauty in her ordinary day, the moments of unexpected joy in her unremarkable marriage.

As the party and the novel draw to a close, Peter Walsh is overheard weaving together an exciting narrative once again, trying desperately to make connections between his old life and his new, to bring about coherence in the way storytellers and novelists do. "There was some one in India. He would like to tell Sally about her. He would like Sally to know her. She was married, he said. She had two small children. They must all come to Manchester, said Sally—he must promise before they left" (295).

But it is Clarissa, not at all articulate, in fact rather bad at putting things together in words, who brings about a moment of true communication. She presents herself not as part of a plot or a scene or even a sentence. She imposes no connection whatsoever. The wonder of her appearance, rather like that of the old woman at the window, does not reside so much in where she has been or where she is going, upstairs, downstairs, to India or Manchester, but that she is mysteriously, completely there. "It is Clarissa, he said. For there she was" (296). Mrs. Dalloway is still Clarissa. She is attached but not imprisoned by marriage. The relationship permits her to give (or lend) herself to others, including Peter Walsh, precisely because it does not make the claims on her freedom that Miss Kilman's un-Christian religion and Dr. Bradshaw's pragmatic psychology do.

One does not see Clarissa's intense empathy for Septimus or her magnetic appeal to Peter Walsh as "infidelities" to Richard, partly because such heavy stress is laid on her sexual primness throughout the book and partly because the moments of sharing are not described in sensual or judgmental terms. In both cases, Clarissa cannot help herself. She is what she is. But that is the point. She has a self, apart from Richard, that responds powerfully to others and is capable of calling up responses unknown to him. Molly Bloom's Chaucerian earthiness and Leopold's wandering eye are also more than merely promiscuous; they are signs of separate vitalities, which may be psychologically and morally problematic, but for which we are nonetheless grateful. Tom and Lydia Brangwen are faithful to one another, but as their marriage becomes better, Lawrence tells us, "he went his way, as before, she went her way." Each marriage derives its character and strength not only from what is shared but from its capacity to tolerate whatever in each partner cannot be taken or given.

For Woolf, as for Joyce and Lawrence, the precondition of true espousal is the same as that for a fruitful wedding of author and reader: the acknowledgment of an ultimate core of inviolability. Far from making communication impossible, this awareness defines its limits without restricting the particularity and dignity of the individual. Whether attributed to sex, existential solitude, class, or cultural distinction, the aspects of self that are incommunicable can lead to marital and artistic despair, to a battle of the wills trying to dominate and convert, or, more happily (though not necessarily more simply), to a tentative and respectful proposal of a bond that requires constant renewal and withers without freedom.

NOTES

[1] Quotations are from Virginia Woolf, *Mrs. Dalloway* (New York: Hartcourt, Brace and World, 1925).

Kenneth Moon

WHERE IS CLARISSA? DORIS KILMAN IN *MRS. DALLOWAY*

In the novel which bears her name, Clarissa Dalloway might well be speaking for the author herself when she expresses an awareness that however boldly a character's central consciousness is rendered and displayed, and however cohesive that consciousness might appear, it is still a far-from-adequate representation of the full person. Clarissa speaks of having "parts" to her which are "incompatible," and of a kind of "centre" which is "composed so for the world only...."[1] She theorizes that

> ... our apparitions, the part of us which appears, are so momentary compared with the other, the unseen part.... (*MD*, p. 169)

She distinguishes also between her Clarissa and her Mrs. (Richard) Dalloway selves:

> ... this being Mrs. Dalloway; not even Clarissa any more: this being Mrs. Richard Dalloway. (*MD*, p. 13)

This "theory" of Clarissa's, that an individual is not only the immediate and visible phenomenon, leads her to consider an "unseen part ... which spreads wide" and which, she very significantly adds, might be "recovered somehow attached to this person or that" (*MD*, p. 169).

Two points can be made about this. The first is that the novel *Mrs. Dalloway* might reasonably be approached as an exercise in characterization, as primarily a search for the whole Clarissa—which is not quite as critics customarily deal with it. Yet character *was* certainly a major preoccupation with the author as she moved through *Jacob's Room* and into *Mrs. Dalloway*. In February, 1921, for instance, she had written to Maynard Keynes: "I can't say how much I envy you for describing characters the way you do."[2] Later, she wonders how one captures in language "the delicacy and complexity" of the soul and its "slipperiness";[3] and she notes a reviewer's charge about *Jacob's Room* that "one can't make characters this way"

From *CLA Journal* 23, No. 3 (March 1980): 273–86.

(*WD*, p. 54). And it is of character, apparently, that she asks, "Have I the power of conveying the true reality?" (*WD*, p. 57), worrying that "the doubtful point is, I think, the character of Mrs. Dalloway" (*WD*, p. 61). Perhaps most significant of all, a fragment of "Mr. Bennett and Mrs. Brown"—"I believe that it is for the purpose of giving character that the form of the novel has been devized"—is scribbled on a blank page of the Dalloway manuscript itself (Vol. 2, opposite p. 7).

The second point is that the author might be seen as indicating in this passage a technique of characterization rather different from that suggested through the well-known "tunnelling" metaphor ("I dig out beautiful caves behind my characters: I think that gives exactly what I want; humanity, humor, depth. The idea is that the caves shall connect and each comes to daylight at the present moment" [*WD*, p. 60]), or a technique at least complementary to this. The method is one of centre-expanding-outwards. It locates Clarissa not simply in the central protagonist of "this, here, now . . ." (*MD*, p. 11), of "the moment of this June morning . . ." (*MD*, p. 42), but also in the characters and events which encircle her, which seem to radiate out from her—what the author is referring to perhaps when, after expressing doubts about the characterizing of Mrs. Dalloway, she talks of "bring[ing] innumerable other characters to her [i.e. Clarissa's] support" (*WD*, p. 61). Certainly such a structure of concentricity occurs with unusual frequency throughout the novel, from the intermittent chimes of Big Ben and St. Margaret's, with their rings of sound expanding outwards from their striking centres (e.g., *MD*, pp. 6, 54, 55, 56, 104, 206) to the final party itself, a model with all circling the hostess at degrees of distance.[4] It is to these satellite events and, particularly, characters that one must look for those generating and determining inner complexities which will make Clarissa complete and unique. These embody, as critics have gone some distance towards recognizing,[5] Clarissa's "unseen part," her more remote and less fixed character properties, what is hidden or rejected or suppressed or "incompatible"; even what-might-have-been, potential unrealized, which is also part of what distinguishes one human being from another.

The most obvious and certainly the major source of such character insights into Clarissa is Septimus Warren Smith, and his role has been much written about. But her troubled spirit, with its crises of pain and bewilderment, can be understood better if one looks also to those components of the novel dealing more specifically with passion and the flesh, and if one looks in particular to the role of Doris Kilman in this. In the highly elaborate and intricate patterning of the novel, the correspondences between Kilman and Clarissa can be traced out; and when so isolated, their considerable significances in the illumination of Mrs. Dalloway become apparent.

There are signals aplenty directing us to some measure of simple identification between the two women: minor items of interest and biography, for example. Kilman is an historian, specializing in Russia. Clarissa, somewhat similarly, reads memoirs; and Baron Marbot's, her current reading, deals with the retreat from Moscow. Also, each has a sibling destroyed young: Clarissa's Sylvia by a falling tree, Kilman's brother in the War. There is also the link between them provided by

Elizabeth Dalloway. Kilman, Elizabeth's governess, enters the novel as Clarissa, proceeding up Bond Street, is reminded by a glove shop of her daughter. This leads her to recall Miss Kilman. Almost immediately we are startled to find the apparently composed and entirely predictable Mrs. Dalloway bursting out in some anguish about what she terms "this hatred" within her:

> It rasped her, though, to have stirring about in her this brutal monster! to hear twigs cracking and feel hooves planted down in the depths of that leaf-encumbered forest, the soul; never to be content quite, or quite secure, for at any moment the brute would be stirring, this hatred, which especially since her illness, had power to make her feel scraped, hurt in her spine; gave her physical pain, and made all pleasure in beauty, in friendship, in being well, in being loved and making her home delightful, rock, quiver, and bend as if indeed there were a monster grubbing at the roots, as if the whole panoply of content were nothing but self-love! this hatred! (*MD*, p. 15)

Throughout most of the novel, and most of her life, Clarissa disowns "this brutal monster" grubbing within her; and when it erupts momentarily here, she characteristically attempts to dismiss it as "Nonsense, nonsense!" But a turbulent inner landscape does exist within Clarissa, and monsters do inhabit it. It is the stimulus of Kilman which leads to the irrepressible stirring of this black turbulence which Clarissa to some extent recognizes and confronts. The governess also gives physicality and dramatic form to this. She both provokes the fierce hatred from Clarissa and becomes at the same time the externalizing and informing image of what Clarissa detests and fears in herself.

This can be argued from a comparison of the following two passages in which each confronts Victoria Street. Here is Clarissa's consciousness:

> In people's eyes, in the swing, tramp and trudge; in the bellow and the uproar; the carriages, motor cars, omnibuses, vans, sandwich men shuffling and swinging; brass bands; barrel organs; in the triumph and the jingle and the strange high singing of some aeroplane overhead was what she loved; life; London; this moment of June. (*MD*, p. 6)

Here is Kilman's:

> Beaten up, broken up by the assault of carriages, the brutality of vans, the eager advance of myriads of angular men, of flaunting women, the domes and spires of offices and hospitals, the last relics of this lap full of odds and ends seemed to break, like the spray on an exhausted wave, upon the body of Miss Kilman standing still in the street for a moment to mutter, "It is the flesh." (*MD*, p. 142)

Each woman has come to Victoria Street, ushered in by a striking clock. Each stands catching up the moment: Clarissa, "this moment of June," Kilman, "just for a moment." Each responds to it, and is revealed by it; and what is most interesting, perhaps, is that while both women look on much the same scene, the description associated with Kilman may be read as a sexually charged and threatening one. Carriages *assault,* vans are *brutal* (as was the "hatred" in Clarissa's earlier outburst); men in myriads *advance* eagerly and are *angular;* women *flaunt;* even buildings are seen in sexually suggestive shapes, as domes and spires.

Clarissa sums up her response to Victoria Street as "life, London, this moment of June," and this is the Clarissa initially presented to us—the evidently eager, life-embracing Clarissa. But Kilman's response is of disgust, rejection: "It is the flesh!" The patterning of language and event suggestively contrasts the two. Together in the context in which each "moment" occurs, however, the patterning also forces on us a comparison, one which is reinforced by a certain paralleling of the actions of the two women which occurs not only here but throughout the novel, and by the verbal echoes associated with this paralleling. Thus another Clarissa is being obliquely uncovered, a being little acknowledged even to herself: the Clarissa who, at almost the same moment as she delights in life, London, summer, can also exclaim: "Think of Peter in love . . . Horrible passion! . . . Degrading passion!" (*MD*, p. 140). This reaction is very similar to Kilman's rejection of "the flesh" so nearly juxtaposed to it. Clarissa's thinking then almost immediately proceeds to Kilman: "thinking of Kilman and her Elizabeth walking to the Army and Navy Stores" (*MD*, p. 141). Thus the author links, in Clarissa's own mind, Clarissa's response to Peter and sexual love, with her response to Kilman and Kilman's attachment to Elizabeth. This Kilman-Clarissa, this body-rejecting Clarissa, is the one who attempts to hide her green dress, as Peter runs up the stairs to her, "Like a virgin protecting her chastity" (*MD*, p. 45); who is conscious of Peter tilting his penknife towards it; who opens her scissors only when the erect knife-blade is withdrawn (*MD*, p. 46). This is the Clarissa who calls love "that monster" (*MD*, p. 50)—again, a signpost towards Kilman, whom she sees as the brutal monster of hatred—and who brackets it (love) with religion as "detestable" and "the cruellest things in the world" (*MD*, p. 140). "Love destroyed too," Clarissa asserts. "Everything that was fine, everything that was true went. Take Peter Walsh now . . ." (*MD*, p. 140). This cry of Kilman's—"It is the flesh"—illuminates, above all, the Clarissa who rejects Peter (to whom love is "the most important thing in the world . . ." [*MD*, p. 135]) and marries Richard (who "could not tell her that he loved her" [*MD*, p. 131]). Love to this Clarissa looks like unrestrained, demanding, debasing flesh; like sexuality. Its naked portrait is Kilman.

A reading of the Dalloway manuscript offers what can arguably be seen as reinforcement of the speculation that Kilman's Victoria Street is sexually coloured and that the governess herself is Clarissa's sexual *alter ego.* Woolf seems deliberately to have added sexual reference to the Kilman paragraph as she built it up (Vol. II, pp. 71, 72). In the first version, she wrote:

> the eager swarming advance of myriads of professional men and women.

The only word here which might seem to have any kind of sensual suggestiveness at all is "swarming," and this the author has crossed out; though in the margin is "who appeared to be swarming," which is used in the second version. In this second version, too, the men become "black coated" instead of "professional," which is more sharply physical; and the women, quite significantly, "flaunting" (as well as what seems to be "flowery"—the writing is unclear). In the final version the men are "angular," which might be seen to have some sexual feeling (Cf. in "Modern Fiction," in *The Common Reader,* First Series: "Does the emphasis laid . . . upon indecency, contribute to the effect of something angular . . ." p. 191, Hogarth Press edition); and the mammary domes and phallic spires are here introduced.

One of the suggestively echoic links between Clarissa and Kilman is the word "flaunting." Significantly enough this occurs in relation to the young Clarissa's Sapphic attachment to Sally, in that the flaunting women of Kilman's Victoria Street take one back to the rooks at Bourton when she, Clarissa, was in her state of "excitement" and "ecstacy" over Sally (*MD*, p. 39)—the rooks there are "flaunting up and down." When these tumescent feelings for Sally are not present, however, the rooks are simply "rising, falling" (*MD*, p. 5). (In Vol. II of the Dalloway manuscript these "flaunting" rooks are only "cawing," so the term was later deliberately changed; and in an early version of the novel, to become eventually the short story "Mrs. Dalloway in Bond Street," the rooks are also outside any Sally context and so sexually neutral: "the caw of rooks falling from ever so high, down, down, down through the October air—there is nothing to take the place of childhood" [*Mrs. Dalloway's Party,* Hogarth Press, p. 19].)

In Kilman's covert erotic feelings towards Elizabeth are similarly sketched the more elemental and grossly sexual underpinnings of Clarissa's feeling for Sally (*MD*, pp. 36–40). "And what was this except being in love?" (*MD*, p. 40) Clarissa asks—though the full significance of her question escapes her. Yet when Sally kissed her on the lips, Clarissa continues, the whole world might have turned upside down. Alone with Sally, her love seemed a "diamond," something infinitely precious. But this "diamond" is "wrapped up." If it were unwrapped, if the deep sources of Clarissa's impulses were uncovered, these feelings, whatever their immediate innocence, would look like Kilman's elemental passion, described thus: Kilman, with Elizabeth, felt she was

> . . . about to split asunder . . . the agony was so terrific. If she could grasp her, if she could clasp her, if she could make her hers absolutely and for ever and then die; that was all she wanted . . . The thick fingers curled inwards. (*MD*, p. 146)

This is the crude sexuality from which Clarissa recoils. And the recoil, of course, carries her to the sexlessness of "the bed and Baron Marbot and the candle half-burnt" (*MD*, p. 37).

That we are to understand the Kilman-Elizabeth relationship as providing insight into the sexual natures of the earlier Clarissa-Sally one is reinforced by each woman's cry in response to the ecstasy (for Clarissa) and the agony (for Kilman) of their "love":

> Clarissa: ". . . if it were now to die, 'twere now to be most happy." That was her feeling. (MD, p. 39)

> Kilman: ". . . if she could make her hers for ever and then die; that was all she wanted." (MD, p. 146)

The sentiments here, the vocabulary, the structure and rhythms, echo each other; and Clarissa's exclamation has the additional and significant reverberation into *Othello,* where these words are also something of a romantic "radiance" under which, the play reveals, lie passions "as prime as goats, as hot as monkeys,/As salt as wolves in pride. . . ."[6] As a result of these Kilman-Elizabeth and Clarissa-Sally links we are able the more readily to see and accept the erotic element underlying Clarissa's "cold . . . excitement" and "kind of ecstacy" (MD, p. 39) as she dresses and does her hair before going down to Sally at Bourton. Other verbal and imagistic correspondences, however tenuous, put this sexual dimension beyond much doubt. The use of pink, for instance. (Naked flesh?) As Clarissa sits at her dressing table, the rooks outside are flaunting up and down in the "pink evening light" (MD, p. 39). This pinkness of the sky, which Clarissa remembers, again links her to Kilman through the pink cakes the latter so craves; and also links each woman to her "victim," as both Sally and Elizabeth, at the lesbian moment, wore pink. Elizabeth even turns pink when Kilman arrives, her mother notes (MD, p. 132).

One further illustration: In the passage which precedes and provokes Clarissa's discussion of "this question of love . . . this falling in love with women" (MD, p. 37) and of her relationship with Sally, she confesses that "she could not resist sometimes yielding to the charm of a woman" and that "she did undoubtedly then feel what men felt" (MD, p. 36). Her tumescence, which is certainly a strong blend of "what men felt" as well as what women feel, she describes thus:

> It was a sudden revelation, a tinge like a blush which one tried to check and then, as it spread, one yielded to its expansion, and rushed to the farthest verge and there quivered and felt the world come closer, swollen with some astonishing significance, some pressure of rapture, which split its thin skin and gushed and poured with extraordinary alleviation over the cracks and sores. Then, for that moment, she had seen an illumination, a match burning in a crocus; an inner meaning almost expressed. But the close withdrew; the hard softened. It was over—the moment. Against such moments (with women too). . . . (MD, pp. 36–37)

As one would expect, Clarissa's state is again isolated and mirrored (more physically and more grossly) in Kilman, who, shortly before *her* homosexual declaration, is described as

> . . . fingering the last two inches of a chocolate eclair . . . Miss Kilman opened her mouth, slightly projected her chin, and swallowed down the last inches of

the chocolate eclair, then wiped her fingers, and washed the tea round in her cup. (*MD*, pp. 145–46)

The eclair in the mouth is to the match in the crocus as Kilman is to Clarissa. It is the "something central which permeated; something warm which broke up surfaces and rippled the cold contact of man and woman or of women together" (*MD*, p. 36).

One might notice, too, that each woman has her "party" and that these are in a way central in importance to their lives. Clarissa states, with almost hysterical extravagance, that "anything, any explosion, any horror" would be better than the party "falling flat" (*MD*, p. 186), and even the tolerant Richard remarks it "a very odd thing how much Clarissa minded about her parties" (*MD*, p. 132). Kilman, naturally, asserts a seemingly opposing viewpoint: "I never go to parties" (*MD*, p. 146). Nevertheless, the reality is that she tells Elizabeth that they "must have their tea" (*MD*, p. 144) and reflects that "sometimes lately it had seemed to her that, except for Elizabeth, her food was all that she lived for" (*MD*, p. 143) and that "the pleasure of eating was almost the only pleasure left her" (*MD*, p. 144). Kilman's tea acts as a parody of Clarissa's party, reducing it in substance and dignity. Each follows departure from Clarissa's house, for instance, and is preceded by a period of shopping. But what is more significant is that Kilman's is, as one would expect, a grosser version of Clarissa's. Kilman's is simple satisfaction of appetite—for food, for power and possession, for crushed sexual urges.

It was her way of eating, eating with intensity, the looking, again and again, at a plate of sugared cakes on the table next to them; then, when a lady and a child sat down and the child took the cake, could Miss Kilman really mind it? Yes, Miss Kilman did mind it. She had wanted that cake—the pink one. The pleasure of eating was almost the only pleasure left to her, and then to be baffled even in that! (*MD*, p. 144)

And again, when Elizabeth attempted to leave her:

Ah, but she must not go! Miss Kilman could not let her go! This youth, that was so beautiful, this girl, whom she genuinely loved! Her large hand opened and shut on the table. (*MD*, p. 145)

At her own party, Clarissa keeps the Kilman within her well concealed, although by this stage of the novel we would be quite aware of its presence. But it is not out of sight throughout. At one point she confronts it in her own consciousness, in all its sexually threatening character:

Kilman her enemy. That was satisfying; that was real. Ah, how she hated her—hot, hypocritical, corrupt; with all that power; Elizabeth's seducer; the woman who had crept in to steal and defile (Richard would say, What nonsense!). She hated her: she loved her. (*MD*, p. 193)

Earlier, of course, it was Clarissa herself who had seen these sentiments about Kilman as "nonsense." But presumably no longer, as she transfers the role of scoffer to Richard. This is perhaps some measure of the distance she has come during the day to a recognition of her Kilman component.

The ambivalence of Clarissa's sexual responses are in a general sense articulated in this passage: "She hated her: she loved her" (*MD*, p. 193). There is the attraction towards, the recoil from. The earlier love for Sally had been one which made virtually no overt physical demands. It was imaged perhaps in the cut heads of flowers floating in bowls of water (*MD*, p. 38): lovely, "extraordinary," but proceeding to nothing. But Peter, with his open-bladed knife pointed towards her, was another matter. It demanded a response of the flesh. Better Richard, who brings not an erected weapon but a hot water bottle; and even that, to a separate bed.[7] Kilman, then, is in heavy outline the demands of the flesh within Clarissa. Clarissa's response to her registers her response to this carnal element, as Kilman's own rejection of physicality is a grotesque of Clarissa's and some explanation for the trajectory of her life to this point.

This attempt by Clarissa Dalloway to deny her physicality is, to revert to the novel's structuring metaphor, itself a center of 'fact' which in turn expands into a wider significance. It seems to be part of, and becomes an image for, her flinching from a full embrace of life altogether. Yet we are made aware that at the same time there lie within her certain impulses *towards* life and love, even towards acceptance of "the flesh." These, although not completely counterbalancing Doris Kilman and Septimus Smith, are most obviously represented in Peter Walsh and Sally Seton; but they are subtly suggested also in the aeroplane, whose "strange high singing"[8] first reaches Clarissa as part of "life; London; this moment of June" (*MD*, p. 6)—that is, as she is crossing Victoria Street and so being first linked with Kilman. The aeroplane and Kilman are thus significantly juxtaposed. And because it was in her earlier years that Clarissa came closest to plunging unreservedly into life—in the time of her "love" for Sally and before her rejection of Peter and his passion—because of this, the echoes and imagery and rhythm of the singing aeroplane direct us back to Bourton, the place of youth, of Peter and Sally, of early morning, of delight. "What a lark! What a plunge!"[9] Clarissa exclaims simultaneously of Westerminster and of the Bourton garden where, aircraft-like, she had "plunged into the open air" (*MD*, p. 5). The aircraft, too, larks and plunges: "[I]t roared straight up, curved in a loop, raced, sank, rose ..."—"It swept and fell" (*MD*, pp. 23–25, 32). It also gathers itself to Bourton through the rooks there, which like it are "rising, falling"; and through Sally, "all light, glowing, like some bird or air ball that has flown in" (*MD*, p. 40). Like Sally, too, who could "do anything, say anything" (*MD*, p. 37), the aircraft "turned and raced and swooped exactly where it liked, swiftly, freely" (*MD*, p. 24). Even the aeroplane's smoke, issuing white, curling, twisting and wreathing, catches up Bourton; for there, too, we are told, was smoke, winding off the trees[10] (*MD*, p. 5). This Bourton world, however, was not secure; and the sound of the aircraft boring "ominously" throws back to Clarissa's premonition at Bourton that "something awful was about to happen." So the aeroplane links in Clarissa, and in a tension seemingly without possibility of resolution, "the strange high singing" along with what is ominous and intrusively sinister—as does the brutal monster of hatred within the sunny tranquility of Bond Street. So, too, is linked the "She hated her: she loved her" interior outburst at the party; and, indeed, the party itself holds opposites in tension as death dramatically intrudes upon the celebration (" . . . in the middle of my party, here's death" [*MD*, p. 203]).

The aeroplane, then, brings us the Clarissa who once sought life but discovered it to be, or at least to seem (which is what matters), hot, fleshy, and gross. She chose instead what led her away from blackberrying with others in the summer sun (whose heat she feared), and led her to the wintry—the chill of stretched sheet, narrow bed, shut door, attic room, lone tower and an emptiness about the heart of life (*MD*, p. 35). She found herself, at fifty (and like Septimus), "alone, exposed on this black eminence, stretched out . . ." (*MD*, p. 160). So she weeps for what she fears life offered her and she passed by. She weeps because it is "all over for her" and she is "alone forever" (*MD*, pp. 52, 53). Her impulsive "Take me with you . . ." (*MD*, p. 53) to Peter remains unspoken; as it must, because it is too late. Peter is no longer, like the clouds, moving freely around the aeroplane, "destined to cross from West to East on a mission . . ." (*MD*, p. 24). It is only momentary illusion that she had run away and lived with him. All that is true is that "the five acts of a play . . . (are) now over . . ." (*MD*, p. 53).

The novel, then, presents Clarissa as she struggles, and has struggled, to contain and accommodate herself to the fierce heats of living as well as the arctic annihilation of death. At one epicentrum of this struggle is Kilman, who lights up for us what is barely discernible directly, Clarissa's sexual nature and dilemma. This is part of the achievement of the work, which presents us with Clarissa Dalloway looking back over fifty years; uncertain, strangely moved, divided within herself; questioning; and "in the depths of her heart an awful fear" (*MD*, p. 204). Her triumphs seem to her to have a hollowness; to be at arm's length and not in the heart (*MD*, p. 193). Did she, she wonders, gain the whole world but suffer "the death of the soul" (*MD*, pp. 66, 67)—for which her "privacy of the soul" is mere euphemism? (*MD*, p. 140). Did she allow the Dalloways and the admirable Hugh to turn her into a "mere hostess"? (*MD*, p. 84). She seems to recognize in Sally the free and romantic radicalism of her youth, which she chose not to nourish; in Peter, those driving, passional, life-celebratory forces she too felt but would not, perhaps could not, wholly embrace;[11] and in Kilman, towards the end of that June day, the human sexual landscape, real or imagined, from which she recoiled but which now she feels that she might, with some profit, have comprised with and channelled into acceptable satisfactions, even into love. Such a reading certainly complements and balances the role of Septimus Warren Smith, who "could not feel" (*MD*, p. 96) and who had married his wife without loving her (*MD*, p. 101), suffering something of that profound anesthesia of the spirit which has worked to isolate Clarissa, too, from the deepest springs of life—where the song is "ee um fah um so / foo swee too emm oo" (*MD*, pp. 90, 92), a love song—and impelled her instead towards that uncommitting, unenduring, surface human relationship, the party. Was she right, as she claims quite early in the novel (*MD*, p. 10), not to marry Peter? Perhaps we find the novel's informing irony in her cry, "Oh if she could have had her life over again!" (*MD*, p. 13)—because her conviction at that point was that she wanted to be more like lady Bexborough, "the woman she admired most ..." (*MD*, p. 13)—that is, the woman who had apparently so disclaimed her natural impulses and feelings that she "opened a bazaar, they said, with the telegram in her hand, John, her favourite, killed" (*MD*, p. 7).[12]

The stuff of the novel, then, both human and material, serves from time to time to image what is so fugitive to fiction—the ambiguity and seeming randomness and discontinuity within an apparently fixed and ordered human character. We are led not simply to a statement of Clarissa's successes and failures, but also to an experience of her assurance and her bewilderment, her delights and her griefs, her sensitivities and her brutalities, her "ecstacy" and her "terror" (*MD*, p. 215). One might indeed employ the novel's final words—they are Peter Walsh's—to say of the work as a whole:

It is Clarissa ... for there she was.

NOTES

[1] Virginia Woolf, *Mrs. Dalloway* (1925; rpt. Harmondsworth, England: Penguin Books in association with the Hogarth Press, 1964), p. 42; hereafter cited in the text as *MD*, followed by the page number. Bernard, in *The Waves* (1931; rpt. Harmondsworth, England: Penguin Books, 1951), p. 55, likewise claims that the individual is "not one and simple but complex and many."

[2] Charleston Papers, Kings College Library, Cambridge—Virginia Woolf Letters, Misc.40.3.

[3] Virginia Woolf, *A Writer's Diary* (London: Hogarth Press, Ltd., 1969), pp. 64, 65; hereafter cited in the text as *WD*, followed by the page number.

[4] In fact, the rhythm of much of the imagery manifests the rhythm of the character-revealing process. There is the grey car which "had left a slight ripple which flowed through glove shops and hat shops and tailors' shops on both sides of Bond Street" (*MD*, pp. 20, 21). There are the aeroplane's smoke words which gradually dissolve outwards into the sky; and Peter's cigar smoke rings which "breasted the air bravely for a moment; blue, circular ... then began to wobble into hour glass shapes and taper away ..." (*MD*, p. 63); and the image of words fading as a rocket fades. "Its sparks, having grazed their way into the night, surrender to it ..." (*MD*, p. 27). When Clarissa feels the shock at Lady Burton's having asked Richard but not her to lunch, she shivers "as a plant on a river bed feels the shock of a passing car and shivers" (*MD*, p. 34); and Peter, looking back over his daily activities during his long absence from England, finds that "at once everything seemed to radiate from him; journeys, rides; quarrels, adventures; bridge parties; love affairs; work; work, work!" (*MD*, p. 49).

[5] In *Virginia Woolf: The Inward Voyage* (Princeton: Princeton University Press, 1970), Harvena Richter makes something of this point, for example, on pp. 99–128. She explores the way, throughout the novel in general, "People, objects, landscapes ... become a series of mirrors reflecting the many aspects of the character(s) ..." (p. 99).

[6] *Othello*, III.iii.400–01. Signet Classics.

[7] In the Dalloway manuscript, Richard is presented also as boring—or at least is seen so by Elizabeth.

    ... her father went on boring people ... could be so boring ... people yawning ... his old stories of Chatham and Burke. (II, 88)

[8] "Strange" frequently indicates the life-and-love affirming. For example, in the Dalloway manuscript Clarissa persists in using "strange" in connection with her relationship with Sally—three times on p. 46 of Vol. I, to give an instance.

[9] "Lark," with its link to bird, to aeroplane, is apparently a deliberate choice. The Dalloway manuscript had first "miracle," then "ecstacy" (II, 114). Similarly, the initial manuscript "... stepped out onto the terrace at Bourton" becomes "... plunged at Burton onto the terrace..." which in turn becomes "... plunged at Burton into the open air..." Each change makes Clarissa's action more readily identifiable with that of the aeroplane.

[10] This scene is again linked with life-and-love, "that eternal spring," in the figure of the old woman and her song outside Regent's Park tube station:

> Cheerfully, almost gaily, the invisible thread of sound wound up into the air like the smoke from a cottage chimney, winding up clean beech trees and issuing in a tuft of blue smoke among the topmost leaves. (MD, p. 92)

[11] Amongst the first twenty seven words Peter Walsh speaks in the novel, four are "yes" and four are "will" (MD, p. 45). Affirmation and, in a sense, assertion, imperative. This is what Clarissa sees as "indomitable egotism" (MD, p. 51).

[12] "She had wanted success, Lady Bexborough and the rest of it" (MD, p. 205). Initially, this was stated even more positively: "... wanted success, Lady Bexborough her first thought on waking, and her last" (Dalloway MS., III, 95).

Howard Harper
MRS. DALLOWAY

*J*acob's Room ends with the discovery that the existential space of its central character is now empty. The next novel represents a voyage out from such a view, an effort to discover meaning in the role of "Mrs. Dalloway." Clarissa Dalloway and her husband Richard had suddenly appeared in the third chapter of Virginia Woolf's first novel, dominated the action for three chapters, and then debarked from the *Euphrosyne* at an unnamed port of call. Now, as *Jacob's Room* was being finished, they were beginning to appear again in some short stories.[1] One of these, "Mrs. Dalloway in Bond Street," published in *The Dial* in July, 1923, evolved into the opening sequence of *Mrs. Dalloway*.

There is no reference to any of the events of *The Voyage Out* in the later novel, where the Dalloways themselves, especially Richard, seem rather different. "Pompous and sentimental," Helen Ambrose had called him. Jane Austen put him to sleep, and he loudly opposed women's rights, But he was also sexually attractive to Rachel, and when he suddenly kissed her, she was overwhelmed in "black waves." None of this seems very appropriate for the Richard of *Mrs. Dalloway*, although he is somewhat sentimental and does not, so far as we know, read Jane Austen. His wife in *The Voyage Out* had dressed pretentiously, talked in clichés, and written condescendingly about the other passengers. But her energy, vitality, and her caring for Rachel seemed important too. The differences in Clarissa between the two books arise more from the differences in their perspectives than from differences in Clarissa's personality. In *Mrs. Dalloway* the narrative discovers much greater depth in her.

There are also links between the second and third novels and *Mrs. Dalloway*. Mrs. Hilbery of *Night and Day* and Clara Durrant and her mother of *Jacob's Room* are guests at Clarissa's party. Although these are not important characters, the reflexive connections suggest that *Mrs. Dalloway* is not an entirely independent

From *Between Language and Silence: The Novels of Virginia Woolf* (Baton Rouge: Louisiana State University Press, 1982), pp. 107–17, 122–31.

entity, and perhaps even that it may synthesize what the creative consciousness has discovered so far. Yet it also tries to advance the frontiers of the lifework. In choosing to return to this character from the first novel and to explore her reality more deeply, the creative consciousness turns in an important new direction.

> Mrs. Dalloway said she would buy the flowers herself.
>
> For Lucy had her work cut out for her. The doors would be taken off their hinges; Rumpelmayer's men were coming. And then, thought Clarissa Dalloway, what a morning—fresh as if issued to children on a beach.
>
> What a lark! What a plunge! For so it had always seemed to her when, with a little squeak of the hinges, which she could hear now, she had burst open the French windows and plunged at Bourton into the open air. How fresh, how calm, stiller than this of course, the air was in the early morning; like the flap of a wave; the kiss of a wave; chill and sharp and yet (for a girl of eighteen as she then was) solemn, feeling as she did, standing there at the open window, that something awful was about to happen; looking at the flowers, at the trees with the smoke winding off them and the rooks rising, falling; standing and looking until Peter Walsh said, "Musing among the vegetables?"—was that it?—"I prefer men to cauliflowers"—was that it? He must have said it at breakfast one morning when she had gone out on to the terrace—Peter Walsh. He would be back from India one of these days, June or July, she forgot which, for his letters were awfully dull; it was his sayings one remembered; his eyes, his pocket-knife, his smile, his grumpiness and, when millions of things had utterly vanished—how strange it was!—a few sayings like this about cabbages.
>
> She stiffened a little on the kerb, waiting for Durtnall's van to pass. A charming woman, Scrope Purvis thought her. . . .[2]

Thus *Mrs. Dalloway* opens—into the world of Clarissa's consciousness. In the single sentence of the opening paragraph, the narrative perceives her objectively as "Mrs. Dalloway" and summarizes what she "said." In the next sentences, however, the style becomes more recognizably like what she must be thinking, and in the fourth sentence the narrative acknowledges that with "thought Clarissa Dalloway."

In retrospect, however, even the opening sentence could be seen as a rendering of her consciousness: she could think of herself in the social role of "Mrs. Dalloway," announcing her plans to her household staff. The flowers are also significant. Ordinarily, Lucy, Clarissa's maid, would be sent for them, but Lucy is busy preparing for the party that night. So Clarissa will walk to the florist's shop herself (the depth and delicacy of her feeling for Lucy are confirmed soon after she returns, in the scene in which Lucy offers to help her mend her dress). Then too, it is a beautiful morning, and the walk from Westminster through St. James's Park to Bond Street will be pleasant. Flowers are important in another way too: Richard brings her roses during the afternoon, intending to tell her that he loves her. At the last moment he finds that too awkward, but the roses tell her for him, and during the party the only flowers she notices are "the roses which Richard had given her." The book begins, then, with this simple promise to "buy the flowers herself." Her voyage out to Bond Street keeps that promise. But the promise is fulfilled far beyond its literal meaning. The love which motivates her here multiplies itself throughout her world, and returns to bless her in manifold and mysterious ways.

As her story continues, Clarissa's ambivalence about her role as "Mrs. Dalloway" is revealed more fully. She wishes both to escape from that role and to enter into it more fully. She feels both sheltered and anonymous, useful and trivial, committed and deluded. Her sense of being trapped in the role becomes explicit later in the opening section, as she reaches Bond Street: "She had the oddest sense of being herself invisible; unseen; unknown; there being no more marrying, no more having of children now, but only this astonishing and rather solemn progress with the rest of them, up Bond Street, this being Mrs. Dalloway; not even Clarissa any more; this being Mrs. Richard Dalloway."

The opening passage also shows that, despite her declarations of faith and her acceptance of responsibility, Clarissa looks for the meaning of her life primarily in the past. She is now in her early fifties. But when she thinks of this June morning, in the present, she must also think of summer mornings at Bourton, her family's home in the country, when she was eighteen. She hears now, more than thirty years later, the squeak of the hinges of the French doors there. In contrast, the doors of her home in Westminster are to be removed today—presumably to open up the interior spaces for her party. In the symbology of Virginia Woolf, as we have seen in the earlier books, this signals an expansion of consciousness. The party fulfills that promise too.

Peter Walsh, the young man who had been in love with her then, is the man she must think of now. His "sayings" are more memorable to her now than anything Richard has ever said to her. But Peter's "sayings" never really mature: "I prefer men to cauliflowers," which Clarissa translates as a saying about "cabbages," is repeated at her party, where it becomes "he did not like cabbages; he preferred human beings." And Clarissa seems comforted by her husband's inability to say any but superficial things to her; Peter was threatening because he always said too much. Yet, after thirty years, it is still Peter who dominates her imagination—which lives not in the London of her present, but in the Bourton of her late adolescence. It was there that she had refused Peter and accepted Richard. And it was there that she experienced "the most exquisite moment of her whole life," a kiss on the lips by Sally Seton.

Now, many years later, Bourton remains a mysterious world which in some ways Clarissa, despite her obsession with it, does not wish to think about. There is one striking passage, for example, in which Peter thinks about Clarissa's skepticism:

> her notion being that the Gods, who never lost a chance of hurting, thwarting and spoiling human lives, were seriously put out if, all the same, you behaved like a lady. That phase came directly after Sylvia's death—that horrible affair. To see your own sister killed by a falling tree (all Justin Parry's fault—all his

carelessness) before your very eyes, a girl too on the verge of life, the most gifted of them, Clarissa always said, was enough to turn one bitter. Later . . . she evolved his atheist's religion of doing good for the sake of goodness.

It seems strange that Clarissa herself never thinks of Sylvia's death, even though she does think of her father several times during this day. What she had said about it to Peter must have led to his feeling that it was all her father's fault, and that she later came to believe that "no one was to blame." Did she really believe that? or did she repress her earlier feeling? Her comment that Sylvia was "the most gifted of them" may imply that to be gifted is to be doomed—and could help to explain Clarissa's own reluctance to appear to be different. Unconsciously, she—and the narrative—might feel somehow that Sylvia's fate is that of the "gifted girl," and even that the father may be implicated in that fate.[3]

While we can only speculate about Clarissa's complicated feelings about her father and about her sister's death, we can see more clearly the repressive nature of Bourton. "Sally it was who made her feel, for the first time, how sheltered the life at Bourton was," Clarissa thinks—Sally, who read William Morris, sat up all night talking, smoked cigars, rode a bicycle around the parapets of the terrace, forgot her bath sponge and ran naked down a corridor—for which she was summoned into the commanding presence of Helena Parry. The household had been governed by Aunt Helena (a more elderly Helen Ambrose?), aided by such stalwarts as the "grim old housemaid, Ellen Atkins," entertained by such guests as "old Joseph Breitkopf singing Brahms without any voice," and presided over by the figure whom Peter remembers as "that querulous, weak-kneed old man, Clarissa's father, Justin Parry" (a geriatric evolution of Ridley Ambrose and Mr. Hilbery).

Conspicuously absent from all of this is the mother. Until Mrs. Hilbery mentions her at Clarissa's party, she exists only by implication and indirection and, in one strange moment in Clarissa's mind during Peter's visit: then Clarissa becomes both "a child, throwing bread to the ducks, between her parents, and at the same time a grown woman coming to her parents who stood by the lake," holding out her life for their inspection. What has she made of their gift of life? she wonders—another sign of the pall of guilt which hangs over her. Old Mrs. Hilbery, of course, is a more elderly version of the mother in Night and Day. It is she who mentions Clarissa's mother for the only time in Mrs. Dalloway:

> "Dear Clarissa!" exclaimed Mrs. Hilbery. She looked to-night, she said, so like her mother as she first saw her walking in a garden in a grey hat.
> And really Clarissa's eyes filled with tears. Her mother, walking in a garden! But alas, she must go.

The image of the mother in the garden is more fully developed in the next novel, To the Lighthouse, in which Mrs. Ramsay becomes identified with the garden, especially in the mind of her son James. The edenic quality of the garden is implied here in *Mrs. Dalloway* too, where the memory of the mother walking in the garden "in a grey hat" might almost belong to the dreamlike "Time Passes" part of *To the Lighthouse* ("They had the moth in them—Mrs. Ramsay's things. . . . There was the old grey cloak she wore gardening [Mrs. McNab fingered it]"). It all begins, of course in *The Voyage Out,* where the central fact of Rachel's life is that her mother is dead. And it continues through the devastating death of Mrs. Rose Pargiter in *The Years,* the disappearance of the loving mother into the grey world of nonbeing, with traumatic effects on the daughters who remain. In *Mrs. Dalloway* this crucial experience is repressed by Clarissa, and perhaps suppressed by the narrative consciousness itself, but it is still there. It may be more important than either Clarissa or the narrative recognize, especially in her troubled relationship with her daughter Elizabeth.

From the beginning Clarissa's excitement tends toward expression in imagery of the sea and the wind. This too has been familiar from *The Voyage Out,* and Clarissa's anxieties, as well as her excitement, will take linguistic shapes very similar to Rachel's. In more extreme and bizarre forms, they will express the madness of Septimus Warren Smith.

Although the narrative has become identical with Clarissa's consciousness by the third paragraph of the book, it does not stay there, but shifts in the fourth paragraph to the mind of Scrope Purvis, her next-door neighbor, to place her in another perspective. He thinks about her for two sentences, then vanishes, never to reappear in the book. In the next paragraph the narrative is incarnate in Clarissa once again.

The shifts from one mind to another are often more subtle than this—to the extent that it is sometimes difficult to identify precisely the point where the narrative leaves one mind and enters another. For example, the narrative is clearly within Clarissa's mind when she enters the florist's, but then there is this passage:

> There were flowers: delphiniums, sweet peas, bunches of lilac; and carnations, masses of carnations. There were roses; there were irises. Ah yes—so she breathed in the earthy garden sweet smell as she stood talking to Miss Pym who owed her help, and thought her kind, for kind she had been years ago; very kind, but she looked older, this year, turning her head from side to side among the irises and roses and nodding tufts of lilac with her eyes half closed, snuffing in, after the street uproar, the delicious scent, the exquisite coolness. And then, opening her eyes, how fresh, like frilled linen clean from a laundry laid in wicker trays, the roses looked. . . .

Somewhere in this passage the perception is probably Miss Pym's. She thinks that Clarissa is kind and was "very kind" "years ago" (perhaps when Miss Pym especially needed that kindness), but now she looks much older. But much of the passage could also reflect Clarissa's consciousness of Miss Pym's feelings about her, or even what she hopes that Miss Pym might feel. Where does Clarissa's train of thought end, and where does it begin again? Or does the narrative float between the two women, rendering the ambiance of their feeling for each other? Clarissa's identity depends upon her differentiation from the world around her, but her extraordinary sensitivity to that world tends to dissolve that differentiation.

Except for brief glimpses into the mind of Scrope Purvis and the feelings of Miss Pym, the entire opening section of *Mrs. Dalloway* renders the consciousness of Clarissa. It discloses her feelings about Bourton, Peter Walsh, London, the war, Lady Bexborough, the month of June, Hugh Whitbread, marriage, freedom, memory and immortality, manipulating other people, the mystery of identity, Bond Street, gloves, her daughter and her dog, Miss Kilman the religious fanatic, the flowers ⟨. . .⟩

When the narrative first enters Peter's mind, it is to register his reaction to Clarissa: "She's grown older, he thought." Then it discloses his irritation at her social life, his memory of her in the moonlight at Bourton, his resentment at her haunting him, his wondering whether to tell her of Daisy, the married woman for whom he has given up his career in India. He does tell Clarissa, bursting into tears as he does so. After Elizabeth interrupts this scene, he leaves. On his subsequent walk to Regent's Park, the narrative becomes a long meditation in his consciousness—again focused largely on Clarissa.

Peter isn't very convincing if he is judged by conventional standards of realism. He seems too preoccupied with Clarissa, who rejected him more than thirty years ago. He never thinks of his work in India or of his wife there, and seldom of Daisy, for whom he is said to have given up both his marriage and career. He seems rather unconcerned with the fact that he is now unemployed and in London to try to make some sort of new beginning.

What, then, is the reality that Peter represents? From a psychological standpoint, he embodies a consuming male desire which has been disarmed and transformed into a lifelong devotion. The narrative can't really get inside that desire: Peter never thinks of Clarissa's body, even when he is said to be thinking of the time when he was "passionately" in love with her (for that matter, he never thinks of Daisy's either—and the name itself may relegate her to some vegetable world beneath the serious notice of the narrative). Instead, desire is translated into lyricism. This first floods the story as Peter falls asleep in Regent's Park and becomes the dreaming "solitary traveller," endowing sky and trees with woman-hood. The narrative consciousness itself becomes free to dream, captivated by images typical of visionary moments in Virginia Woolf: sky, trees, breezes stirring the leaves, mermaids riding the waves, the goddess rising from the sea, and so on. "Such are the visions," the narrative insists.

And it is Peter to whom the final visionary moment is assigned at the end of the book:

> "I will come," said Peter, but he sat on for a moment. What is this terror? what is this ecstasy? he thought to himself. What is it that fills me with extraordinary excitement?
>
> It is Clarissa, he said.
>
> For there she was.

Terror, ecstasy, excitement: these are abstractions, not the phenomenal realities of the procession at the end of *The Voyage Out* or of the pair of old, empty shoes at the end of *Jacob's Room*. Even the words *he thought*, while they assign these abstractions to Peter's mind, increase the psychological distance between the narrative and that mind. The narrative doesn't render Peter's stream of consciousness directly; it tells us what "he thought." Stylistically, Peter's epiphany remains in the realm of assertion—though the accretion of detail about Clarissa throughout the book does create a rich background for this final vision. But in the final scene Peter seems less convincing as a separate character than as a reflection of Clarissa.

Peter also expresses an important aspect of the narrative consciousness itself: the passionate, awkward outsider with no background and only a very shadowy identity, "a failure," at once envious and contemptuous of everything that Clarissa's class represents. Peter has no family, comes from nowhere. The narrative can't imagine any background for him; the earliest thing it knows is that he was "sent down" from Oxford—for being a Socialist, apparently. He is more alienated from Clarissa's world than Septimus is, for Septimus was never really close to it. Peter expresses the alienation of the narrative consciousness itself from that world.

The distance of Septimus from Clarissa's world is qualitatively different. The narrative discovers him on Bond Street; the quality which it first recognizes in him is "apprehension." In its next look at him it becomes immersed in the terrors of his paranoia: "And there the motor car stood, with drawn blinds, and upon them a curious pattern like a tree, Septimus thought, and this gradual drawing together of everything to one centre before his eyes, as if some horror had come to the surface and was about to burst into flames, terrified him. The world wavered and quivered and threatened to burst into flames. It is I who am blocking the way, he thought. Was he not being looked at and pointed at; was he not weighted there, rooted to the pavement, for a purpose: But for what purpose?" His perception of the pattern of the tree on the blind draws everything together in his vision, and overwhelms his consciousness. These same feelings have haunted the earlier novels. The "immitigable tree" has been there from the beginning, and the other terrors had been present in Rachel's imagination too: things suddenly bursting to the surface from the depths, the fires of sexuality, the anxieties about "blocking the way," about being "rooted" to one place, unable to move. To some extent Peter in *Mrs. Dalloway* also shares such fears—as in the dreams (also "triggered" by trees) in Regent's Park, from which he awakes with a sudden awareness of "the death of the soul." But Septimus can't awake from his terrors. He lives in a constant state of apprehension. And as we learn in this first evocation of his consciousness, those terrors manifest themselves—as they did for Rachel too—through distortions of perspective.

Aside from Clarissa herself, Septimus is the first of the major characters whose consciousness is evoked. In some ways he represents, as Virginia Woolf wrote in her introduction to the Modern Library edition of *Mrs. Dalloway,* Clarissa's "double." But unlike her, he becomes wholly dominated by an inner reality. And that becomes so limited that all he can think to do when Dr. Holmes intrudes upon it is to jump out the window.

Septimus is given a history: he came to London from Stroud, where he lived with his mother, who "lied" and who criticized him for coming to tea "with his hands unwashed"; he confided in his little sister and moved to London, "leaving an absurd note behind him, such as great men have written, and the world has read later." Thus the narrative seems not to be entirely serious about this background, especially his "ethereal and insubstantial" infatuation with Miss Isabel Pole. His volunteering for the war is also viewed as naïve, and his devotion to his superior officer, Evans, is described almost cynically.

The turning point comes after Evans is killed and after the armistice, when Septimus suddenly discovers that "he could not feel." Trying to escape from his ensuing panic, he becomes engaged to Lucrezia. But though she does what she can for him, his condition deteriorates. He rediscovers his literary idols: Shakespeare, Dante, Aeschylus—and their secret message of "loathing, hatred, despair." His wife's desire for a child intensifies that despair, and

> At last, with a *melodramatic gesture* which he *assumed mechanically* and with *complete consciousness of its insincerity,* he dropped his head on his hands. Now *he had surrendered;* now other people must help him. People must be sent for. *He gave in.* [italics added]

Thus the narrative insists that Septimus himself is responsible for this crucial step in his descent into madness. It speaks of the mechanical, melodramatic insincerity of his *gesture,* and discovers the climactic fact that *He gave in.*

The consequences of that surrender are explored in the rest of his story, much more fully than the account of his background. The "world" of Septimus becomes progressively more self-centered, until at last nothing is real to him except his own suffering. Dr. Holmes, with all his hearty advice, seems especially repulsive. Septimus has all the sensitivity of Clarissa and none of her empathy: whatever else she may be guilty of, it is not a lack of feeling, as we see in her reaction to the suicide of Septimus, whom she never knew.

In Septimus, then, the narrative explores the fate of the personality that withdraws from the touch of other people into the abstractions of pure vision. It finds a great deal of self-indulgence in such a personality, and discovers that *giving in* to such a temptation is fatal. The need to "prove" this is so strong the Septimus' story often becomes an essay, an expository "telling" rather than a dramatic "showing." But it does enter deeply into his madness, which is evoked with intensity. The causal chain culminating in that madness, however, tends to be told rather than shown—and told from some distance.

The narrative's immersions in the mind of Septimus are not sustained for as long as those in the minds of Clarissa or Peter, but his consciousness is rendered with more depth and immediacy. And it is linked with Clarissa's consciousness through images and motifs suggesting a larger unity in which they both participate and, at times, can recognize. For example, just before Peter arrives on his morning visit, the narrative hovers between the mind of Clarissa and a more impersonal perspective:

> So on a summer's day waves collect, overbalance, and fall; collect and fall; and the whole world seems to be saying "that is all" more and more ponderously, until even the heart in the body which lies in the sun on the beach says too, That is all. Fear no more, says the heart. Fear no more, says the heart, committing its burden to some sea, which sighs collectively for all sorrows, and renews, begins, collects, lets fall. And the body alone listens to the passing bee; the wave breaking; the dog barking, far away barking and barking.

This is paralleled by a passage in the mind of Septimus very much later in the book:

> Every power poured its treasures on his head, and his hand lay there on the back of the sofa, as he had seen his hand lie when he was bathing, floating, on top of the waves, while far away on shore he heard dogs barking and barking far away. Fear no more, says the heart in the body; fear no more.

The most apparent similarities between the passages have to do with the theme of the "treasures" of experience, the imagery of the waves, the sound of dogs barking, the dirge from *Cymbeline* ("Fear no more the heat o' the sun"), and the phrase "the heart in the body." In the first passage the narrative has been inside Clarissa's consciousness, and whether or not it remains there throughout the passage, it does seem to express the essence of her feelings at this point in the story. But there is also a slight detachment from, and objectification of, that feeling, through a translation of it into a more abstract, figurative language. The quality of the second passage, however, is much more intense and immediate. Septimus, who thinks that he cannot feel, is in reality the victim of his feelings. Clarissa can achieve some distance from her feelings. But when Septimus "gave in," he surrendered to his.

The narrative tries to discover in Septimus' case history some rational explanation for his growing insanity and suicidal impulses. If it can discover the secret of his doom, then perhaps Clarissa can be saved from that same fate. The narrative needs to make Septimus morally responsible for his fate, and it withdraws somewhat from his consciousness at times in order to evaluate it—and also, perhaps, not to become lost in it. To remain immersed in such a consciousness is, as the narrative discovers—and perhaps has known all along—to drown.

The essential dialectical struggle in *Mrs. Dalloway*, then, is between the opposite adaptations to the world which are represented by Clarissa and by Septimus. The configuration of characters in the book gives further definition to these adaptations. Septimus' wife Lucrezia, for instance, is not only a reflector for him but also, in a sense, the symbolic fulfillment of Clarissa's relationship with Peter. Lucrezia submits to a man who demands everything, and to whom she is only an extension of his own personality. He can't relate her feelings to anything real—that is, to anything within his own egocentric reality.

Richard Dalloway remains a rather shadowy figure. The narrative does not enter his consciousness until the second half of the book, and then not in much depth. His thoughts are rather ordinary, except perhaps for his extensive concern with pedigree, with Peter Walsh's love for Clarissa, with his own reticence toward her, and with the "miracle" of their marriage. Elsewhere, Clarissa remembers "Sally Seton saying that Richard would never be in the Cabinet because he had a second-class brain." The limited space given to Richard in the narrative reflects his limited importance in Clarissa's reality, and the curious distance that separates—and, in another way, unites—them. The narrative consciousness sees this distance as essential to a satisfying marriage: Richard gives Clarissa room to be herself.

Their daughter Elizabeth exemplifies that heritage. Caught between the forms of love offered by her mother and by Miss Kilman, Elizabeth instinctively chooses life, and her voyage through the Strand on the omnibus reenacts Clarissa's journey years before (when she told Peter of her theory of immortality). Elizabeth chooses her mother's commitment to life, rather than the commitment to absolutes, and Elizabeth's choice validates her mother's commitment.

Miss Kilman reflects Clarissa in another way; the sexual inhibitions of Clarissa find their grotesque extreme in Miss Kilman. She also reflects Septimus: as his female counterpart, her denial of the flesh is, like his, a denial of life itself.

Sally Seton, whose kiss on the lips had brought Clarissa an ecstasy unequaled thereafter, enters the story in person at the party. The narrative enters into her mind, but primarily to look at the past, and at other people—Clarissa, Peter, Richard. What Sally sees confirms what we already know about them, and adds little to what we know about her. That comes mostly from other perspectives, and isn't very interesting: she is now Lady Rosseter, rich, married to an industrialist in Manchester, the mother of five sons, and so on. Here is still another feminine destiny—and one which the narrative consciousness views from some distance.

Each of these characters, then, reflects the changing aspects of the narrative's struggle toward a final, definitive adaptation to its world. As always, the struggle is reflected through a series of perspectives. And the sequence of perspectives is significant. First, after the evocation of Clarissa's consciousness in her walk to Bond Street, the narrative discovers her antithesis, Septimus, and catches a few frightening but fascinating glimpses of his madness, his withdrawal from the shared reality of Bond Street. Then in Peter's interview with Clarissa, his walk, and his dream, the narrative explores a personality which is opposite to that of Septimus in the sense that it longs not for total transcendence of the need for love, but for total expression of that need. The next major sequence shows Septimus at Sir William Bradshaw's, a confrontation which reveals that their realities too are wholly opposite and irreconcilable. That scene is then succeeded by the luncheon at Lady Bruton's, in which people conscious of their differences act together in reasonable harmony. Then, from his public role at Lady Bruton's, Richard returns to his home and to his private role, his relationship with Clarissa. In that ambiance the previous themes begin to converge, and from it they will radiate. Elizabeth and Miss Kilman, Septimus' female counterpart, leave the house, where Clarissa worries about losing her daughter. But in the next sequence Elizabeth leaves Miss Kilman and, like her mother years before, makes her own pilgrimage through the Strand. This affirmation is in turn succeeded by the sequence in which Peter reminisces and has dinner, and leaves at last for the climactic party. In that final sequence Clarissa survives her experience of Septimus' death, and returns to her primary role as "Mrs. Dalloway": "For there she was." That is the final revelation toward which the dialectical struggle moves, the realization of the nature of Clarissa's existence, a unity emerging at last from this long series of diversities.

Until the very end of the book, and beyond, a fate like that of Septimus seems possible for Clarissa, whose *joie de vivre* seems rather manic and frequently threatened by intimations of despair. In its last penetration into her consciousness, the narrative follows her as she hears of the death of a "young man" from the Bradshaws and as she moves at once into the "little room" where she experiences, in her imagination, the physical sensations of Septimus' death. She feels that she knows, intuitively, why he did it. She knows somehow that Sir William Bradshaw is also responsible. She knows also that "Somehow it was her disaster—her disgrace." She sees the old woman in the house opposite the window going to bed: for a moment the woman stares straight at her—a vision, perhaps of her own old age. And Clarissa feels "glad that he had done it; thrown it away while they went on living. The clock was striking. The leaden circles dissolved in the air. But she must go back. She must assemble. She must find Sally and Peter. And she came in from the little room."[4] The narrative has followed Clarissa from the noise and confusion of her party into the silence of the "little room" of her innermost awareness. Septimus' final melodramatic gesture of defiance ("I'll give it you!" he cried as he plunged) also turns out to be, when it is perceived by the consciousness of Clarissa, a genuine, generous, even beautiful gift. It redeems and renews her life. Perhaps Peter also becomes aware of that somehow when he feels his final "terror," "ecstasy," and "extraordinary excitement," which he attributes to Clarissa.

The first words of the book announce its subject: "Mrs. Dalloway." It develops like a fugue. The various narrative perspectives constitute the thematic elements which evolve toward a resolution, reached at last in the dominant chord at the end: "For there she was." Clarissa's meaning is completed, as she recognizes in her "transcendental theory," by the people—and even the places—that she has touched. The party at the end brings together the people who complete her. Even the dead are suddenly and unexpectedly present: the mother whose reappearance in the garden of Clarissa's childhood moves her to tears; an unknown young man whose final "gift" suddenly forces her to confront her own innermost nature and sweeps her on to epiphany. As these manifold meanings converge, they confirm the richness of her life. And yet, a poignant distance remains between her and the people she loves.

The fullest and the final embodiment of this distance is Peter Walsh. Like the lover in Keats's "Grecian Urn," he exists only in his perpetual pursuit of his beloved: the essence of Peter Walsh is his eternal love for, and eternal rejection by, Clarissa. In the larger context of the *oeuvre,* he continues the line of final visionaries which had begun with St. John Hirst of *The Voyage Out* and which will end with Miss La Trobe of *Between the Acts*—characters whose origins and backgrounds are obscure, whose existence is on the fringes of the established social order, whose relations with other people are inhibited, whose sexual nature is troubled, yet whose distance from all of the conventional norms provides a special perspective on them.

The emergence of this perspective into dominance at the end of *Mrs. Dalloway* consigns Clarissa's life to the realm of the past: "For there she was." From the very beginning of her story there has been a feeling, first expressed by Clarissa herself and then confirmed by Peter's perspective, that the most meaningful time in her life has been the time at Bourton, especially the summer when she refused Peter and accepted Richard. The need to justify that choice recurs again and again in the present. Although she courageously accepts the present, she remains haunted by the past. This inescapable past-ness of Clarissa's innermost reality gives *Mrs. Dalloway* its nostalgic, almost elegiac tone, as if her present existence were a posthumous life.

This sense of the relentless flow of time, and of the longing for the past, is like that of Quentin's section of Faulkner's *The Sound and the Fury.* Like Septimus and Clarissa, Quentin is dominated by the past and tempted toward suicide. Like Septimus, he finally gives in—though another part of his schizophrenic awareness knows that giving in is futile too. Quentin knows what his father would say about the inescapable past: "was the saddest word of all there is nothing else in the world its not despair until time its not even time until it was." The last word of *Mrs. Dalloway* reverberates with a similar sadness.

As we have seen, several antiphonal voices of time are present in the book. The one which remains dominant is the voice of Big Ben, which bears Clarissa, Peter, and the narrative consciousness as well, ceaselessly into the past. Its voice is heard for the last time as Clarissa contemplates the suicide of "the young man" whom we have known as Septimus. As Big Ben strikes, Clarissa stops counting the hours after the third stroke. As she continues to think of the young man's death she is aware only that "The clock was striking. The leaden circles dissolved in the air." If the "leaden circles" are a reminder of mortality, the fact that they dissolve in the air may imply that a single human life and death never really ends, but is absorbed instead into a larger, more timeless and universal form of life. Clarissa knows the meaning of the young man's final gesture, though she had not known Septimus himself: "Death was an attempt to communicate. . . ."

NOTES

[1]"Mrs. Dalloway in Bond Street" appeared in *The Dial*, LXXV (July, 1923), 20–27. It is much fuller and more specific in its references to persons and places than the corresponding section of the novel. For a more detailed discussion of this and of the genesis of *Mrs. Dalloway*, see my essay "Mrs. Woolf and Mrs. Dalloway" in *The Classic British Novel* (Athens: University of Georgia Press, 1972), 220–39. Some aspects of my present essay, especially the discussion of characters, echo that earlier one.

Other stories involving the Dalloways include "The New Dress," first published in *Forum*, LXXVII (May, 1927), 704–11, and "The Man Who Loved His Kind," "Together and Apart," and "A Summing Up," all published posthumously in *A Haunted House and Other Short Stories* (1944). Another story, "The Introduction," was published more recently in *Mrs. Dalloway's Party*, ed. Stella McNichol (London: Hogarth, 1973), 37–43, a volume which reprints the other stories also.

[2]My quotations throughout this chapter are from the first English edition. In the present quotation the American edition adds a comma after *her* in the third sentence of the third paragraph.

There is one significant difference in the apparent structure of the two editions. The American edition consists of eight sections, separated by an additional line space in the text. In the original Hogarth edition there are twelve sections, also separated by space breaks. For the convenience of readers who may wish to correct their American editions, I list these breaks below:

Paragraph opening	Page in Harvest paperback ed.
"'Poor old woman,' said Rezia Warren Smith."	125
"It was precisely twelve o'clock; twelve by Big Ben...."	142
"One of the triumphs of civilization, Peter Walsh thought."	229
"'But where is Clarissa?' said Peter."	284

In some respects the American edition seems preferable; most of the textual changes from the English edition are improvements, and most seem designed to clarify meanings or to correct mistakes. Nevertheless, the textual divisions in the Hogarth edition seem preferable. The four divisions missing in the American text mark important turning points in the novel: (1) from the view of the old street singer through the eyes of Peter Walsh to the view of her by Rezia, i.e., from an inflated mythologization to a simple human view—and also from the story of the Dalloways to that of the Warren Smiths, (2) at the symbolically important moment of noon, when the actions of Clarissa and the Warren Smiths are linked in the same sentence for the first and only time in the book, (3) as Rezia drifts into a drugged sleep after her husband's suicide and Peter hears the ambulance bell which tolls, presumably, for Septimus, and thinks of the "triumphs of civilization"—which, ironically, have just claimed another victim, and (4) as Clarissa returns from her vivid reexperiencing of Septimus' suicide—and from the temptation toward her own—to her party and her role as "Mrs. Dalloway."

[3]If there is an autobiographical parallel for the death of Sylvia, it is the death of Stella, the half-sister whom Virginia loved very much. Her death is reflected more clearly in Prue's death in *To the Lighthouse*. If Virginia felt that her father was in any way responsible for Stella's death, she might have felt that Stella married to escape from his domination and demands. When Stella died of peritonitis a few months later, the fact that she was pregnant may have reinforced Virginia's feeling about the death of her mother: that the demands of the male were ultimately lethal.

Death is important in the genesis of *Mrs. Dalloway*. The death, perhaps by suicide, of Kitty Maxse, the prototype for Clarissa, in October, 1922, probably stimulated a search for the deeper significance of her life (see Quentin Bell, *Virginia Woolf: A Biography* [New York: Harcourt, 1972], II, 87). Kitty Maxse, née Lushington, became engaged under the jackmanii at Talland House in St. Ives (Bell, I, 33); thus she may also be a prototype for Minta Doyle of *To the Lighthouse*. The possibility of suicide must have suggested depths in Kitty that had not been seen before, and may have aroused some guilt because of that. Her death must have made the earlier portrait of Clarissa in *The Voyage Out* seem shallow, or at least unfinished.

[4]The American edition changes this quotation to "glad that he had done it; thrown it away. The clock was striking. The leaden circles dissolved in the air. He made her feel the beauty; made her feel the fun. But she must go back," etc.

Susan M. Squier

CARNIVAL AND FUNERAL

Since her days at 22 Hyde Park Gate, London had seemed to Woolf a public world of intellectual work, whether it limited women to the marginal role of passive spectators or permitted them active involvement in its cultural pursuits. In her earliest years, as *Night and Day* testifies, Woolf saw retreat from the city as the primary solution to the conflict between social and intellectual duties in a woman's life.[1] Yet in 1924, when she and Leonard Woolf bought 52 Tavistock Square and returned to London from a ten-year suburban exile, Woolf was beginning her most celebrated London novel. *Mrs. Dalloway* would approach the relationship between work and social life from a new angle. While London society was the chief lure in the decision to return to the city, "society" had taken on a dramatically different, expanded meaning to Woolf, as a diary entry of June 1923 reveals:

> For ever to be suburban. L. I don't think minds any of this as much as I do. . . . There is, I suppose, a very different element in us; my social side, his intellectual side. This social side is very genuine in me. Nor do I think it reprehensible. It is a piece of jewellery I inherit from my mother—a joy in laughter, something that is stimulated, not selfishly wholly or vainly, by contact with my friends. And then ideas leap in me. Moreover, for my work now, I want freer intercourse, wider intercourse, & now, at 41, having done a little work, I get my wages partly in invitations. [*D*, II: 250–51]

This diary entry reveals Woolf's new interest in the social side of London life, which she now saw as tinged with maternal associations and thus as an environment nurturing both her work and her life.

Several circumstances contributed to Woolf's new perspective on London. First, she had known significant success as a writer during her nearly ten years of residence in suburban Richmond, publishing *Night and Day* (1919), *Kew Gardens*

From *Virginia Woolf and London: The Sexual Politics of the City* (Chapel Hill: University of North Carolina Press, 1985), pp. 91–104, 108–10, 121.

(1919), *Monday or Tuesday* (1921), and *Jacob's Room* (1922). Possibly her intellectual accomplishments made her more eager to explore the social side of life, less likely to resent the intrusion of what seemed obligatory "womanly" duties into her chosen work as a writer. Having established, in *Night and Day* and in her critical essays, her ability to write within the literary and critical tradition of her forefathers, Woolf now gladly turned to the maternal heritage she had earlier avoided. On the anniversary of her mother's death, 5, May 1924, she recalled her "impressions of that day," decided "enough of death—its life that matters," and dedicated herself to just the sort of life her mother had valued: the social side of London. She vowed to "write about London, & how it takes up the private life & carries it on, without any effort" (*D*, II: 300–301). So, in the above-quoted diary entry of June 1923, she expressed her new awareness of the intellectual importance to her of London's social life; her image has a metaphoric subtext revealing her new sense of self as both writer and woman, pregnant with her work, having been fertilized by the stimulating intercourse available in London. "And then ideas leap in me. Moreover, for my work now, I want freer intercourse, wider intercourse" (*D*, II: 250).

　　While the female, social, private side of London life newly preoccupied Woolf as she was composing *Mrs. Dalloway*, she remained concerned with London's male, professional, public side. Contemplating the novel's impending publication, she speculated: "Very likely this time next year I shall be one of those people who are, so father said, in the little circle of London Society which represents the Apostles . . . on a larger scale. Or does this no longer exist? To know everyone worth knowing. . . . just imagine being in that position—if women can be" (*D*, II: 319). As this passage suggests, Woolf anticipated that her literary accomplishment in *Mrs. Dalloway* would win her a social position analogous to that in the cloistered masculine world of the Apostles Society in Cambridge. Yet that fantasy raises several questions with which Woolf was concerned in *Mrs. Dalloway:* What does it feel like to be an insider in society? Can a woman be an insider? Does the social organization epitomized by the Apostles Society—"an ideal community, a secret elite . . . a kind of superior fraternity" of "insiders"—still exist?[2] Although in this diary entry Woolf does not specify what might have destroyed the exclusive circle of London society which she imagines herself penetrating upon publication of *Mrs. Dalloway*, we can speculate that she is thinking of World War I, which not only devastated an entire generation of young men but also brought an end to the entire system of social relations they had known. Both the Great War and the sexually segregated society of the wartime and prewar eras—when men were manly and women womanly—are of major significance to *Mrs. Dalloway*, for the novel explores the roots of war and sexual oppression in the sexually polarized society of early modern London.

　　Woolf described her plans for the novel in insistent dualities: "I want to give life & death, sanity & insanity; I want to criticise the social system, & to show it at work, at its most intense" (*D*, II: 248). Yet careful study of the novel suggests that she wanted to do more than merely juxtapose two opposed ways of living; rather, she wanted to transcend the very habit of thinking in dualities, and to criticize a society based upon such habitual polarization. The novel examines two domains—the private world of women like Clarissa Dalloway, and the public world of men like Peter Walsh and Richard Dalloway. More than that, it calls into question the social polarization that divides female domain from male, private world from public. And *Mrs. Dalloway* goes beyond a critique of the private/public distinction to see its relationship to militarism. In linking a consideration of the relationship between women's domestic role and men's public role to the question of the origins of war, furthermore, the novel anticipates several of Woolf's later essays, most notably *A Room of One's Own* (1929), *Three Guineas* (1938), and "Thoughts on Peace in an Air Raid" (1941), all of which consider some facet of the relationship between woman's ancillary, nurturant social role and man's aggressive drive.

These concerns were not originally apparent in the short story from which the novel grew. "Mrs. Dalloway in Bond Street," written while Woolf was still exiled in suburban Richmond and first published in 1923 in *Dial,* offers a portrait of a woman smoothly integrated into London society.[3] Like its successor, the story is set in Westminster, Whitehall, and Bond Street, but it limits itself to anatomizing the flawed bourgeois civilization surrounding its title character. In a narrative that undercuts Mrs. Dalloway's smugly self-centered perspective on the city around her, the story juxtaposes her thoughts with sketches of the surrounding city in order to reveal the impending changes in class and gender relations seething beneath the smooth surface of London society.

Like the earlier short story, *Mrs. Dalloway* uses urban scenes to explore and embody the privileged world of prewar and wartime London, to portray and criticize a society segregated by class and gender. But while composing the novel Woolf introduced the character of Septimus Smith, the shell-shocked veteran of the Great War, and thus opened up the larger question of the relationship between social polarization (by sex and class) and war between societies. The French feminist theorist Hélène Cixous has recently argued that at the root of any insistently polar way of thinking that depends upon "dual, *hierarchized* oppositions" lies "a male privilege," revealed "in the opposition by which it sustains itself, between *activity* and *passivity*." She further argues that struggle is an implicit part of the duality sustaining male superiority: "the movement by which each opposition is set up to produce meaning is the movement by which the couple is destroyed. A universal battlefield. Each time a war breaks out."[4] This conflict between activity and passivity, which Cixous argues is reflected in all aspects of human experience, "whether we are reading or speaking, through literature, philosophy, criticism, centuries of representation, of reflection,"[5] appears in vivid specificity in the dilemma of Septimus Smith. The two systems of "hierarchized oppositions" (to borrow Cixous's phrase) clash in the experience of that shell-shocked veteran, to replicate the "universal battlefield" that links sexual oppression to militarism, male privilege to war.

While Woolf expanded the novel's focus from the story's single protagonist to three major characters—Clarissa Dalloway, Peter Walsh, and Septimus Smith—she continued to use the urban environment and in particular the city street to initiate consideration of her chosen themes. Not only does Woolf use the city as a public world to which the three characters have differing responses (for example, Clarissa feels "invisible" as she walks up Bond Street, while both Peter and Septimus feel prominent to different degrees as they move through the city), but she also uses aspects of the physical environment to introduce thoughts into the characters' streams of consciousness (for example, when the sight of Gordon's statue initiates Peter Walsh's impulse to follow the attractive woman he sees in Trafalgar Square) and as a realistic corrective to the characters' fantasies (for example, when we can compare Septimus's perceptions of the sky-writing airplane's message with the reality of "Glaxo Kreemo"). Consideration of the novel's three focal street scenes—Clarissa's opening walk up Bond Street to buy flowers for her party (*MD*, 3–19), Peter's stroll from Clarissa's home in Westminster to Regent's Park (72–83), and Septimus's hallucinatory ramble down Bond Street to Regent's Park (20–31)—reveals that all three characters are defined by the streets through which they pass. The buildings, people, and events of their common urban surroundings establish their characters and social circumstances for themselves, for each other, and for the reader; furthermore, the three street scenes compactly present in these early pages the novel's major issues, and they anticipate its conclusion. Finally, what emerges with careful study of these three street scenes is Woolf's reliance on the urban scene to raise two issues of paramount importance to her: the consequences of the public/private dichotomy, and the origin therein of both sexual oppression at home and war abroad.

Clarissa Dalloway's walk up Bond Street in the novel's opening pages establishes a crucial fact about her character: Clarissa thinks of herself not as an important figure, but as part of the background. Woolf controls syntax, style, and theme to emphasize Clarissa's feeling of merging with her environment in the pages charting Clarissa's progress from her house in Westminster to Mulberry's in Bond Street. The narrative interweaves Clarissa's thoughts as she strolls through London, with the surroundings prompting and amplifying them: "For having lived in Westminster—how many years now? over twenty,—one feels even in the midst of the traffic, or waking at night, Clarissa was positive, a particular hush, or solemnity; an indescribable pause; a suspense (but that might be her heart, affected, they said, by influenza) before Big Ben strikes. There! Out it boomed" (*MD*, 4–5). As this passage demonstrates, Clarissa confuses internal (individual) events with external (general) occurrences; she cannot distinguish the pause between heartbeats from the silence before Big Ben strikes, the heart beating from the bell ringing. In fact, she seems unable to separate the beloved city around her from her love for life itself:

Heaven only knows why one loves it so, how one sees it so, making it up, building it round one, tumbling it, creating it every moment afresh; but the veriest frumps, the most dejected of miseries sitting on doorsteps (drink their downfall) do the same; can't be dealt with, she felt positive, by Acts of Parliament for that very reason: they love life. In people's eyes, in the swing, tramp, and trudge; in the bellow and the uproar; the carriages, motor cars, omnibuses, vans, sandwich men shuffling and swinging; brass bands; barrel organs; in the triumph and the jingle and the strange high singing of some aeroplane overhead was what she loved; life; London; this moment of June. [*MD*, 5]

There is a social consequence to Clarissa's tendency to merge with her surroundings. Rather than feeling individual importance as the well-groomed wife of a socially prominent member of Parliament, she accepts kinship with all citydwellers based on their common love of "life; London; this moment of June." This transcendence of class boundaries, affirming a community including even the "veriest frumps" and drunks "sitting on doorsteps," suggests in fiction what Woolf expressed also in her essays—that the urban environment, by its disparate, varied nature, nurtures egalitarian social relations. Clarissa's highly empathetic response to other people, a result of her experience of fluid, shifting city life, makes her unwilling to judge or categorize them:

> She would not say of any one in the world now that they were this or were that. She felt very young; at the same time unspeakably aged. She sliced like a knife through everything; at the same time was outside, looking on. She had a perpetual sense, as she watched the taxi cabs, of being out, out, far out to sea and alone; she always had the feeling that it was very, very dangerous to live even one day. Not that she thought herself clever, or much out of the ordinary.... She knew nothing; no language, no history; she scarcely read a book now, except memoirs in bed; and yet to her it was absolutely absorbing; all this; the cabs passing; and she would not say of Peter, she would not say of herself, I am this, I am that.
>
> Her only gift was knowing people almost by instinct, she thought, walking on. If you put her in a room with some one, up went her back like a cat's; or she purred. [*MD*, 11]

Yet Clarissa's self-declared unwillingness to "sum up" others does not prevent her from feeling an almost instinctive dislike or liking for people. There is, for example, the woman she admired most, Lady Bexborough, "who opened a bazaar, they said, with the telegram in her hand, John, her favourite, killed" (*MD*, 5). And there is Miss Kilman, her daughter's history teacher and unmistakably the woman she admires least:

> for Miss Kilman would do anything for the Russians, starved herself for the Austrians, but in private inflicted positive torture, so insensitive was she, dressed in a green mackintosh coat . . . she was never in the room five minutes without making you feel her superiority, your inferiority; how poor she was;

how rich you were; how she lived in a slum without a cushion or a bed or a rug or whatever it might be, all her soul rusted with that grievance sticking in it, her dismissal from school during the War—poor embittered unfortunate creature! For it was not her one hated but the idea of her . . . for no doubt with another throw of the dice, had the black been uppermost and not the white, she would have loved Miss Kilman! [*MD*, 16–17]

Several differences between these two women, both of whom Clarissa thinks about during her walk to the flower shop that June morning, help us to establish the values informing her life through the qualities of which she approves. First, Lady Bexborough pleases her by keeping private experience comparmentalized, while Miss Kilman irks her by confusing a private grievance with a public wrong. Then, while both women have been severely injured by the War—one losing her son and the other losing her profession—their styles of response to that injury are dramatically different. Lady Bexborough rises above it, to attend to her social duty; Miss Kilman loses all social sensitivity under the pressure of her growing bitterness. Clarissa clearly approves of one set of qualities—compartmentalization and separation of private world and public world—which she does not herself practice. Yet the other aspect of Lady Bexborough, her attention to her social responsibilities, anticipates Clarissa's behavior in *Mrs. Dalloway*'s culminating pages, when she cuts short her musing over the suicide of Septimus Smith in order to return to her party. One final point may be made about the comparison between Miss Kilman and Lady Bexborough as potential examples of female behavior for Clarissa Dalloway; in thinking about Miss Kilman, Clarissa realizes that, with another throw of the dice, things could be entirely different. She expresses this in terms of one set of oppositions—hatred changing to love—yet the image suggests another, more fundamental opposition—identity and difference. I am suggesting that, although Clarissa nowhere actually articulates it, beneath her realization that "with another throw of the dice . . . she would have loved Miss Kilman" lies the even more important recognition that with another throw of the dice she would have *been* Miss Kilman.

Not only does a sense of social plurality and equality result from Clarissa's empathetic union with her surroundings, leading her to feel potential kinship even with such people as Miss Kilman, but a spiritual posture results as well. Once again, the vision—here of an afterlife—is shaped by the urban environment and is introduced during the novel's opening pages, on Clarissa's Bond Street walk. Clarissa imagines human lives being linked and perpetuated by the city around her: "somehow in the streets of London, on the ebb and flow of things, here, there, she survived . . . she being part, she was positive . . . of the house there . . . part of people she had never met" (*MD*, 12). Identifying herself with the city around her, Clarissa extends that identification to others, too, imagining such an atmospheric afterlife even for Peter Walsh although, as we shall see, his whole character proclaims not passive merging with his surroundings, but active intrusion into them.

Clarissa's walk up Bond Street establishes several important facets of her character and experience for readers of *Mrs. Dalloway*, then: her tendency to confuse inner and outer, self and other; her tendency to empathize with other people, whether of her social class or not, rather than distinguishing herself from them; her refusal to categorize herself or other people; her paradoxical dislike for people who (like herself) confuse public and private realms; her possession of a spiritual vision of human relatedness and endurance firmly grounded in the daily reality of the city around her. All of these qualities seen together reveal that Clarissa Dalloway is the classic female product of a patriarchal culture, with the strengths and weaknesses of that position: great ability to bond with others (particularly women) but a diffuse sense of identity; a mind infused with the instrumentalist, misogynistic values of her patriarchal culture yet in conflict with her instincts and actions, which reflect the desire for intimacy and fusion born of her female psychic structure.[6]

The most significant, and most characteristic, aspect of Clarissa Dalloway that is introduced in her walk up Bond Street is the natural extension of this conflict as well as the novel's motivating force: her love of party-giving. Unlike most of the men in the novel, who see themselves as important figures (Peter Walsh as a colonial administrator and a lover, Richard Dalloway as a legislator), Clarissa thinks of herself as merely background and does not attempt to project herself into the world. Rather, she effaces herself, concentrating instead on creating an atmosphere in which other people can shine. As Clarissa is drawn out into London to buy flowers for her party, her plans for the evening's festivities color her perception of the city around her:

> And everywhere, though it was still so early, there was a beating, a stirring of galloping ponies, tapping of cricket bats; Lords, Ascot, Ranelagh and all the rest of it; wrapped in the soft mesh of the grey-blue morning air, which, as the day wore on, would unwind them, and set down on their lawns and pitches the bouncing ponies . . . the whirling young men, and laughing girls in their transparent muslins . . . and she, too, loving it as she did with an absurd and faithful passion, being part of it, since her people were courtiers once in the time of the Georges, she, too, was going that very night to kindle and illuminate; to give her party. [*MD*, 6]

Like her sense of herself, of others, and of life after death, Clarissa's plans for her party are intertwined with their urban setting. Furthermore, her parties are at once conventional and subversive. While they express patriarchal society's relega-tion of women to the private sphere, in their function as "an offering; to combine, to create" they promise to transform not only that private sphere but also the larger public world (*MD*, 185). Clarissa's plans to invite "So-and-so in South Kensington; some one up in Bayswater; and somebody else, say, in Mayfair" promise to bring together not just different people, but different sectors of the city, perhaps even different classes (*MD*, 184–85). So, at the party with which the novel ends, the shabbily genteel Ellie Henderson mingles with Lady Lovejoy and the prime minister (*MD*, 253–61). Clarissa's parties become a private method of transforming public life from its characteristically male dimensions (marked by "denial . . . of relatedness in general") to a more characteristically female world marked by "both the desire and capacity for fusion."[7]

We have seen that Woolf began to feel a new interest in her maternal heritage just as she was composing *Mrs. Dalloway*, and that she linked her mother's joy in social life with her own newly felt appreciation of the pleasures of London society. Clarissa's choice of parties as her vehicle for self-expression and her form of contribution to social betterment similarly reflects and is determined by her maternal heritage—the culturally defined role as a woman in modern patriarchal society. As contemporary feminist theory has established, this role is the result, in part, of a distinctly female psychic structure resulting from the historical and sociological fact that women mother, as well as the related fact of male sexual oppression. Clarissa's stroll through Westminster and up Bond Street in the novel's opening pages reflects her position as a woman unambiguously integrated both into her feminine role and into her society, unquestioningly accepting her confinement in the private sphere and completely identified with the competitive, instrumental values of its patriarchal rulers, even to the point of self-denigration:

> Oh if she could have had her life over again! she thought, stepping on to the pavement, could have looked even differently!
>
> She would have been, in the first place, dark like Lady Bexborough. . . . slow and stately; rather large; interested in politics like a man; with a country house; very dignified, very sincere. Instead of which she had a narrow pea-stick figure; a ridiculous little face, beaked like a bird's. That she held herself well was true; and had nice hands and feet; and dressed well, considering that she spent little. But often now this body she wore (she stopped to look at a Dutch picture), this body, with all its capacities, seemed nothing—nothing at all. She had the oddest sense of being herself invisible; unseen; unknown; there being no more marrying, no more having of children now, but only this astonishing and rather solemn progress with the rest of them, up Bond Street, this being Mrs. Dalloway; not even Clarissa any more; this being Mrs. Richard Dalloway. [*MD*, 14]

Clarissa's odd sensation of invisibility ("there being no more marrying, no more having of children now") is, of course, an accurate rendition of patriarchal society's view of women: unless they are performing their "proper" physical functions of copulation or procreation, they are invisible in that society which grants women no public role. Yet what is important to understand about Clarissa Dalloway is that she *embraces* that invisibility and enjoys her relegation to the private sphere, whether she expresses that enjoyment in her impatience about politics ("she could feel nothing for the Albanians, or was it the Armenians? but she loved her roses") or her preference for solitude in an attic bedroom, reading about the retreat from

Moscow, to a conjugal bed with her husband (*MD*, 182, 46). Clarissa's experience anticipates that to which Woolf would bid farewell in *A Room of One's Own:* the sense of social belonging and harmony experienced by the "typical" woman, while walking down Whitehall. In that later essay the haunts of London's patriarchal power shock the woman into a "sudden splitting off of consciousness," and she discovers herself to be not insider but outsider—not powerful agent but powerless spectator (*AROO*, 101). Until the conclusion of *Mrs. Dalloway*, in contrast, Clarissa accepts—even enjoys, up to a point—her position as an insider in society by virtue of her marriage to Member of Parliament Richard Dalloway. Party-giving is not simply her chosen contribution to society, it is her only gift: "Nothing else had she of the slightest importance; could not think, write, even play the piano. She muddled Armenians and Turks … and to this day, ask her what the Equator was, and she did not know" (*MD*, 185). Clarissa has learned to value herself as an accessory to her husband—for her presentable appearance, her suitability as a consort, her capacity for childbearing—but otherwise to value more highly the "manly virtues" embodied by her friend Lady Bexborough.

As the fashion center of London, Bond Street reiterates the lesson of Clarissa's female heritage: women achieve power by virtue of their relationships to powerful men, and their identities are consequently determined by the physical features that will draw men to them:

> "That is all," she said, looking at the fishmonger's. "That is all," she repeated, pausing for a moment at the window of a glove shop where, before the War, you could buy almost perfect gloves. And her old Uncle William used to say a lady is known by her shoes and her gloves. He had turned on his bed one morning in the middle of the War. He had said, "I have had enough." Gloves and shoes; she had a passion for gloves; but her own daughter, her Elizabeth, cared not a straw for either of them. [*MD*, 15]

Uncle William is no more. Clarissa's musings suggest, furthermore, that gone also is that prewar society in which women and men had distinctly different social roles: while she has a "passion for gloves" and puts her energies into party-giving, her daughter Elizabeth cares "not a straw" for gloves or for shoes and dreams of having a profession. The difference in their social roles is echoed by the different districts of London through which they travel: Clarissa walks through Westminster and up Bond Street, traditionally haunts of male political and female social power, while her daughter takes an omnibus up the Strand, a newly booming center of male and female commercial and professional life: "It was quite different here from Westminster, [Elizabeth] thought, getting off at Chancery Lane. It was so serious; it was so busy. In short, she would like to have a profession. She would become a doctor, a farmer, possibly go into Parliament, if she found it necessary, all because of the Strand" (*MD*, 207). The contrasting perspectives on London of Clarissa and Elizabeth Dalloway reveal the changing status of women in postwar England. While for Clarissa, as for her creator Virginia Woolf, London "takes up the private life and carries it on, without any effort," for Elizabeth, London encourages dreams of a public life (D, II: 301).[8] As she rides through the city on the omnibus, the buildings she passes suggest to her the appeal of a professional life:

> The feet of those people busy about their activities, hands putting stone to stone, minds eternally occupied not with trivial chatterings (comparing women to poplars ...) but with thoughts of ships, of business, of law, of administration, and with it all so stately (she was in the Temple), gay (there was the river), pious (there was the Church), made her quite determined, whatever her mother might say, to become either a farmer or a doctor ... It was the sort of thing that did sometimes happen, when one was alone— buildings without architects' names, crowds of people coming back from the city having more power ... than any of the books Miss Kilman had lent her, to stimulate what lay slumbrous, clumsy, and shy on the mind's sandy floor to break surface ... an impulse, a revelation, which has its effects for ever, and then down again it went to the sandy floor. [MD, 207–8]

What is apparent in the contrast between Clarissa Dalloway's view of London and that of her daughter is the relationship between woman's experience of the city and her conception of herself. While Clarissa feels invisible, part of the background of her society during her travels through London, Elizabeth is both visible and highly capable: "Suddenly Elizabeth stepped forward and most competently boarded the omnibus, in front of everybody" (MD, 205). Furthermore, the contrast between the mother's and the daughter's views of the city reveals that the choice of a meaningful occupation is determined by one's sense of self as either passive background or active figure—which, in turn, is shaped by the extent of one's compliance with the maternal heritage of patriarchal society. Clarissa feels herself as background and spends her time giving parties; Elizabeth, rebelling against "whatever her mother might say," feels an important figure in society and contemplates a profession. Elizabeth's aspirations highlight her mother's dedication to the private world of female concerns, just as Clarissa's London walk emphasizes her ancillary position as an insider in the male, public world. Moved to explore the positive and negative aspects of her maternal heritage, Woolf created in Clarissa Dalloway the embodiment of the traditional female role. ⟨...⟩

Mrs. Dalloway is far from being a novel "about" sexual behavior, much less about sexual pathology, yet it is concerned with the impact of gender and sexuality upon the professional, political, social, and spiritual lives of women and men. For both Peter Walsh and Clarissa Dalloway the quality of sexual life reflects the quality of those more general social relations. Clarissa is castigated by Peter for being "cold, heartless, a prude," yet in reality her "frigidity" toward men reflects her position— revealed in her walk up Bond Street—as passive background to the active male figures in her life. The label "frigid," generally applied only to women, itself reflects woman's restricted social position, as the psychoanalyst Roy Schafer has pointed out: "*Frigidity* means extreme coldness; it is a word specifically suited for describing a milieu. . . . Although a milieu may be said to have effects, it cannot be said to act. Only people act. It follows . . . that the woman is by nature an inactive or passive object."[9] The implications of the label "frigid" highlight the contradictions of woman's position in Western culture: while frigidity is a socially unacceptable quality, the passive sense of self that the condition bespeaks is seen as entirely appropriate: "Strength, force, drive, and power are not for her; nor are intent, initiative, interaction, and control."[10] Yet precisely these qualities are necessary for genuine sexual pleasure for both men and women.

Just as Clarissa's "frigidity" is revealed to be a reflection of her more general sense of self as milieu during her Bond Street walk, so Peter Walsh's walk through London reveals not only his particular sexual problem but also the larger flaw in social relations that his sexual difficulty reflects. What emerges in the episode in which Walsh follows the young woman through London is his tendency to split the object of his emotional regard from the object of his sexual interest. In its narrowly sexual manifestation, this bespeaks *"selective impotence,"* the condition of "being limited to completing the sexual act with only certain types of women; typically . . . 'degraded' women in relation to whom the man may exclude tender, affectionate, and respect feelings."[11] Of course, in using the term "impotence" to describe Peter Walsh I am speaking metaphorically. The label suggests what Peter's street scene reveals: that he can experience his own importance only in response to women whom he can, at least in fantasy, dominate. Furthermore, Peter's desire for domination may be displaced to an interest in the imperialist politics he abjures with his conscious mind. For, as Schafer has observed, "men and women manifest these sexual concerns in areas of life, such as physical, occupational, intellectual, and social fitness and worthiness. Although these areas seem far afield from sexuality, unconsciously they are more or less invested with sexual significance."[12] Peter even seems to be aware of the irony that he should be interested in the continuation of British rule: "Coming as he did from a respectable Anglo-Indian family which for at least three generations had administered the affairs of a continent (it's strange, he thought, what a sentiment I have about that, disliking India, and empire, and army as he did), there were moments when civilisation . . . seemed dear to him as a personal possession; moments of pride in England . . . [in] girls in their security" (*MD*, 82).

The sexual difficulties of Clarissa and Peter, revealed during their solitary walks through London, bespeak a flaw in society as a whole that lies at the root not only of their social discomforts but also of Septimus Smith's suffering. Just as "frigidity" implies an image of the female self as mirroring milieu for man, so "impotence" implies an ideal image of the male self a powerful figure, even if in this case he departs from the ideal. The terms together embody the process of social polarization with which Woolf was concerned in *Mrs. Dalloway:* the opposition between the public, active, male realm and the private, passive, female realm. In establishing Peter and Clarissa as opposites, not only in gender but in sense of self and in relation to society, Woolf showed "society at work, at its most intense" (*D*,

II: 248). With the introduction of Septimus Smith, the shell-shocked veteran in whose painful experience such sexual and social polarities clash, Woolf created a powerful criticism of the social system. While Peter and Clarissa dramatize the workings of society in their enactment of the male/female, public/private dichotomy, Septimus demonstrates its tragic flaw—that such polarized sex roles and limitations on female activity and male passivity breed military aggression. ⟨. . .⟩

Drawing its form and them from the city streets in which it first originated, in "Mrs. Dalloway in Bond Street," *Mrs. Dalloway* examines the "web of associations" that has formed patriarchal society. Like the city streets in which it is grounded, the novel is a creature of opposites: carnival and funeral, protest and celebration. While *Night and Day* derived from Woolf's department from London a response to the conflict between work and society in a woman's life, *Mrs. Dalloway* drew from Woolf's return to London the courage to consider the relationship of woman's traditional social role to the nature and structure of British society.

NOTES

Abbreviations used in the text:
AROO = *A Room of One's Own* (New York: Harcourt, Brace & World, 1957)
D I–IV = *The Diary of Virginia Woolf*, ed. Anne Olivier Bell (New York: Harcourt Brace Jovanovich; I, 1915–19 [1977]; II, 1920–24 [1978]; III, 1925–30 [1980]; IV, 1931–35 [1982])
MD = *Mrs. Dalloway* (New York: Harcourt, Brace & World, 1953)

[1] Although Mary Datchet remains at work in London, she is only a secondary character in *Night and Day*. The protagonist, Katharine Hilbery, plans a retreat from London paralleling her creator's.
[2] Leon Edel, *Bloomsbury: A House of Lions* (Philadelphia and New York: J. B. Lippincott, 1979), 53.
[3] Stella McNichol, "Introduction," *Mrs. Dalloway's Party*, ed. Stella McNichol (New York: Harcourt Brace Jovanovich, 1973), 9. For some "Second Thoughts" on this edition, see John Hulcoop's article thus titled, *Virginia Woolf Miscellany* 3 (Spring 1975); 3–4, 7.
[4] Hélène Cixous, "Sorties," in *New French Feminisms,* ed. Elaine Marks and Isabelle de Courtivron (Amherst: University of Massachusetts Press, 1980), 91.
[5] Ibid., 90.
[6] For the most useful recent discussions of the female psychic structure as it is created in the nuclear family of patriarchal society, see Nancy Chodorow, *The Reproduction of Mothering* (Berkeley: University of California Press, 1978); Elizabeth Abel, "(E)merging Identities: The Dynamics of Female Friendship in Contemporary Fiction by Women," *Signs* 6 (Spring 1981): 413–35; Judith Kegan Gardiner, "The (US)es of (I)dentity: A Response to Abel on (E)merging Identities," *Signs* 6 (Spring 1981): 436–41; and Marianne Hirsch, "Mothers and Daughters," *Signs* 7 (Autumn 1981): 200–222.
[7] Abel, "(E)merging Identities," 417.
[8] Of course, as a writer Woolf was also actively involved in public, professional life.
[9] Ray Schafer, *Language and Insight* (New Haven: Yale University Press, 1978), 150.
[10] Ibid.
[11] Ibid., 144.
[12] Ibid., 141.

Makiko Minow-Pinkney

THE PROBLEM OF THE SUBJECT IN *MRS. DALLOWAY*

Woolf was criticised by her contemporaries for her failure to create 'characters', but clearly she seeks a state of human being prior to its consolidation into personality. Her work thus undercuts

> the masculine point of view which governs our lives, which sets the standard, which established Whitaker's Table of Precedency, which has become, I suppose, since the war, half a phantom to many men and women, which soon, one may hope, will be laughed into the dustbin where the phantoms go, the mahogany sideboards and the Landseer prints, God and Devils, Hell and so forth, leaving us all with an intoxicating sense of illegitimate freedom. (*HH*, 44)

It is only 'reality' or 'character' as defined by this deeply compromised perspective that Woolf is 'unable' to create. 'I dare say it's true, however, that I don't have that "reality" gift. I insubstantiate, wilfully to some extent, distrusting reality—its cheapness. But to get further. Have I the power of conveying the true reality?' (*WD*, 57). The 'true reality' is reality for women; but Woolf is nervous of the censorship and condemnation of men. Julia Kristeva writes: 'In women's writing, language seems to be seen from a foreign land. . . . Estranged from language, women are visionaries, dancers who suffer as they speak'.[1] In a foreign land, one is naturally more cautious about infractions of the law because of the danger of expulsion. So Woolf would never go to extremes as Joyce did, and throughout her career kept a conventional form of narrative writing in the third-person past tense, for 'writing must be formal. The art must be respected' (*WD*, 69). Her literary affirmation of 'true reality' remains well protected by an apparent formality as it subtly undermines the fixed positionalty of the subject in language. Her natural descriptions often emit a lateral message about the process of the novel's own construction, as in this self-reflexive description of a London cloudscape.

From *Virginia Woolf and the Problem of the Subject* (New Brunswick, NJ: Rutgers University Press, 1987), pp. 60–64, 67–72, 80–83.

> Fixed though they seem to be at their posts, at rest in perfect unanimity, nothing could be fresher, freer, more sensitive superficially than the snow-white or gold-kindled surface; to change, to go, to dismantle the solemn assemblage was immediately possible; and in spite of the grave fixity, the accumulated robustness and solidity, now they struck light to the earth, now darkness. (*MD*, 153)

In a similar way, the apparently ordered 'assemblage' of Woolf's own prose may be dismantled in a flash by some disorientating slippage of narrative voice or some 'tunnelling' and mining of the present by the past.

By disrupting linearity and achieving simultaneity, she modifies the status of the subject. For the unified self is only one stage of a 'subject in process/on trial' (as Auerbach seems to have realised instinctively in his reference to 'what is in process' in the depths of the Woolfian 'soul'). The true subject is not a linear 'series of giglamps symmetrically arranged', but is evoked by the more spatial image of 'a luminous halo'. Though the phrase 'from the beginning of consciousness to the end' implies some kind of temporality, yet the image of 'envelope' does not really coincide with the concept of linear continuity. In this image of 'this varying, this unknown and uncircumscribed spirit' with its 'aberration' and 'complexity', Woolf offers us a subject which has no simple unity, no clear boundary between itself and other. The 'envelope' is 'semi-transparent' and therefore not a clear-cut distinction between spirit and world. Woolf's idea of self denies homogeneity: 'she [Nature] let creep instincts and desires which are utterly at variance with his [man's] main being, so that we are streaked, variegated, all of mixture' (*CE*, 4:161).

In writing *Mrs. Dalloway* Woolf aspires to be 'only a sensibility', 'not having to draw upon the scattered parts of one's character' (*WD*, 47), and this is the mode of being the novel itself presents. Phyllis Rose calls it 'the most schizophrenic of English novels'.[2] There is a parallel between the mode of subjectivity that constitutes the stylistic principle of the book, and the state of being of Clarissa and the other characters. Only by a conscious 'assembling' of her scattered parts into one centre can the heroine attain a social identity as Clarissa Dalloway: 'collecting the whole of her at one point (as she looked into the glass). . . . That was her self—pointed; dart-like; definite. That was her self when some effort, some call on her to be herself, drew the parts together' (*MD*, 42). It is not only in her youth that she believed in 'a transcendental theory' that 'the unseen part of us, which spreads wide', might survive. Now as she walks through London she feels herself part of the trees at home, of the house, of people she had never met: 'being laid out like a mist between the people she knew best, who lifted her on their branches as she had seen the trees lift the mist, but it spread ever so far, her life, herself' (11–12). Whether walking through London, alone in her attic, or retiring in the middle of the party into privacy, Clarissa is mostly presented in a state of being where she does not need to 'draw the parts together'. In this context it is interesting to note how obsessive she is about shoes and gloves: 'old Uncle William used to say a lady is known by her shoes and her gloves.... Gloves and shoes; she had a passion for gloves' (13–4). It is as if without this minute 'passionate' attention the extremities of the body cannot be trusted not to fly asunder, acting out the physical dissociation their owner so often experiences!

Clarissa would not say of anyone that 'they were this or were that'. To her, identity is not true; it is impossible for her to be one thing and not the other. 'She felt very young; at the same time unspeakably aged. She sliced like a knife through anything; at the same time was outside, looking on' (10). In a state of constant assemblage and dissolving, 'she would not say of Peter, she would not say of herself, I am this, I am that' (11). 'On the ebb and flow of things', her dispersed parts momentarily fuse with objects she passes as she walks, and she becomes rhythm, sound, colour, shape. Even the sense of the body as a whole disappears: 'this body she wore ... with all its capacities, seemed nothing—nothing at all. She had the oddest sense of being herself invisible; unseen; unknown' (13). In this state of being, she recalls the dirge sung over the apparently dead Imogene in *Cymbeline:* 'Fear no more the heat o' the sun / Nor the furious winter's rages'. With the self 'dead', freed from ego-identity, there is no longer death: 'here, there, she survived, Peter survived, lived in each other, she being part, she was positive, of the trees at home' (11). Later, sitting down to mend her silk dress, the focused 'centre' or 'diamond' (42) of her consciousness dissolves and she becomes one with the physical rhythm of her manual occupation. 'So on a summer's day waves collect, overbalance, and fall; collect and fall; and the whole world seems to be saying "that is all" more and more ponderously, until even the heart in the body which lies on the beach says too, that is all' (44–5). The ego gone, there is only body, movement, colours, sound, pulsing rhythms: 'the body alone listens to the passing bee; the wave breaking; the dog barking, far away barking and barking'.

What is true of Clarissa applies to most of the characters. Septimus naturally experiences a similar state of mind, for his ego has collapsed into psychosis. He no longer retains Clarissa's power to 'collect the whole of her at one point'. He experiences his body as 'connected by millions of fibres' with the leaves of trees (26); everything becomes quickening colour and sounds, rising and falling, rhythms. The sea imagery which evoked Clarissa's experience while mending the dress recurs:

> Septimus Warren Smith lying on the sofa in the sitting-room; watching the watery gold glow and fade with the astonishing sensibility of some live creature on the roses, on the wallpaper. Outside the trees dragged their leaves like nets through the depths of the air; the sound of water was in the room, and through the waves came the voices of birds singing. Every power poured its treasures on his head, and his hand lay there on the back of the sofa, as he had seen his hand lie when he was bathing, floating, on the top of the waves, while far away on shore he heard dogs barking and barking far away. Fear no more, says the heart in the body; fear no more. (153–4)

This recurrent sea imagery figures some great semiotic *chora* traversed by natural pulses, rhythms and currents in which one can lapse out into a state of libidinal bliss. But having asserted the utopian value of the semiotic, the novel then tries to recontain the sensory energies it has released. It does so by what the Russian Formalists term a 'motivation of the device', naturalising and thus "taming" the semiotic impulses it has unleashed. It does so in two ways. First, by locating the events of the novel shortly after the First World War: 'For it was the middle of June. The war was over' (6). After this great disruption of national life, the simplest routines and objects have a vivid novelty they would otherwise lack. The disruptive intensity of the novel's sensory perceptions are rationalised as the simple expression of relief at national survival. Secondly, semiotic intensities are naturalised by being implicitly presented as the effects of a summer heat wave. Under this heat and pressure, sensory impressions become surcharged, almost surreal ⟨. . .⟩ Mrs. Dalloway's utopian impulse to celebrate the semiotic as an end in itself is constrained by a need for naturalistic motivation, just as Woolf mines the laws of writing from *within* rather than brazenly flouting them like James Joyce. ⟨. . .⟩

Feminist theorists argue that the fact that the baby girl's first love-object is a body of her own sex, the mother's, constitutes the basis of woman's narcissistic disposition. It will be difficult for a woman's later relations with men to overcome her original loss of the mother's body. In one sense, narcissism simply marginalises women, reducing them in the male view to the trivia of dress and appearance, to personal vanity. But carried to an extreme, it becomes threatening to men, opening the dangerous prospect of women attaining mutual sexual satisfaction without any need of the male sex. Peter Walsh, who seeks 'compassion, comprehension, absolution' in womanhood, is constantly confronted by Clarissa's total rejection: 'this coldness, this woodenness, something very profound in her . . . an impenetrability' (68). The most vivid image of this is their encounter as she sits mending her dress. There is a mythic resonance as a long-absent Ulysses returns to claim a Penelope whose busy weaving has kept away false suitors. But the scene is more complex than this; there is a compacting of mythic roles. Peter is both Ulysses (newly returned) and false suitor (her true husband, Richard, is away), and Clarissa emphasises his latter role by continuing busily to sew. However, nor is Richard altogether the true possessor. Clarissa often thinks of the extreme joy she might have had if she had married Peter: 'this gaiety would have been mine all day' (52). She thus in a sense rejects both of them. When she hears Walsh at the door 'she made to hide her dress, like a virgin protecting chastity', and a subdued note of sexual violation pervades the scene: ' "And what's all this?" he said, tilting his pen-knife towards her green dress' (45–6). Her sewing up of the dress becomes the restitching into wholeness of a hymen which Walsh constantly threatens to tear.

Because her libido folds narcissistically in upon itself, Clarissa ultimately rejects all relationships. Aware of this cold spirit, she feels 'I am alone for ever' (53), at the same time acclaiming the importance of 'privacy of the soul'. The dialectic within Clarissa between this cold contracting of the self and the schizophrenic dispersal I discussed earlier is obliquely recognised by the novel in its suggestive remark about the negligible figure of Mr. Bowley as he waits at Buckingham Palace: 'Little Mr. Bowley ... was sealed with wax over the deeper sources of life, but could be unsealed suddenly, inappropriately, sentimentally, by this sort of thing' (23). These two impulses are also conveyed in the lines from *Cymbeline:* 'Fear no more the heat o' the sun / Nor the furious winter's rages'. It is the psychic 'heat o' the sun' which melts the sealing wax and unleashes the experience of dissociation. Clarissa's attic is clearly an allusion to that which contains Bertha Mason in *Jane Eyre*, but Woolf has reversed the values traditionally associated with the 'madwoman in the attic'. Whereas Bertha's attic is a place of tropical heat and sexuality, of latent physical violence, Clarissa's has the chill atmosphere of a mortuary.

Yet Clarissa can occasionally overcome the 'contraction of this cold spirit' in her relations with women. She yields to 'the charm of a woman, not a girl' (namely, the mother), and this experience is explicitly sexual:[3]

> It was a sudden revelation, a tinge like a blush which one tried to check and then, as it spread, one yielded to its expansion, and rushed to the farthest verge and there quivered and felt the world come closer, swollen with some astonishing significance, some pressure of rapture, which split its thin skin and gushed and poured with an extraordinary alleviation over the cracks and sores. Then, for that moment, she had seen an illumination; a match burning in a crocus; an inner meaning almost expressed. But the close withdrew; the hard softened. (36)

The culmination of these experiences with women, 'the most exquisite moment of her whole life', is the kiss with Sally Seton (40). Clarissa acclaims this love with Sally for its 'purity' and 'integrity', which are impossible in a relationship with a man, which always becomes domination by the latter. Bonds with men, especially their culmination in marriage, are a menace to the freedom of women. They constitute a kind of delayed repetition of the girl's transition from an active mother-attachment to mere mother-identification, which securely fixes her as a castrated being in patriarchal society.[4] Marriage breaks up the bond between women to prevent them from uniting in a republic of women. Hence 'a sense of being in league together, a presentiment of something that was bound to part them (they spoke of marriage always as a catastrophe), which led to the chivalry, this protected feeling' (39).

The old woman opposite Clarissa's window is a mirror image of herself in her attic, a symbol of both independence and isolation in patriarchal society. With 'a room of her own', she lives up to the demands of Woolf's major feminist tract. 'It was fascinating, with people still laughing and shouting in the drawing-room, to watch that old woman, quite quietly, going to bed alone' (204). This mirror image endows Clarissa with the strength to resist the colonisation of herself by 'the contagion of the world's slow stain',[5] from the 'incessant parties ... blunting the edge of her mind' (87). The characters are continually criticising each other, but the novel implies that there may exist a strong bond between women in spite of differences and hostility:

> her inquiry, 'How's Clarissa?' was well known by women infallibly to be a signal from a well-wisher, from an almost silent companion, whose utterances (half a dozen perhaps in the course of a lifetime) signified recognition of some feminine comradeship which went beneath masculine lunch parties and united Lady Bruton and Mrs. Dalloway, who seldom met, and appeared when they did indifferent and even hostile, in a singular bond. (117).

There is a bond even between such profoundly different types as Clarissa and Miss Kilman. The relationship has a fierce intensity unparalleled in any of her dealings with men: 'she hated her: she loved her' (192).

The problem for woman is to assert a female specificity as difference and to open up a space for this difference in the masculine structure of society. This is not to be achieved simply by the assertion of women's comradeship; it involves, rather, the question of the subject. Having remained close to the maternal body in spite of its enforced repression, the girl or woman inscribes herself naturally within the semiotic, in touch with what Kristeva terms the 'spasmodic force' of the repressed. Her task is then to affirm this force, to find the practices appropriate to it, but this is not a matter of its defining a separate, substantive symbolic of its own. It will rather at best be enacted as a moment *inherent* in the rejection of the process of the ruptures, of the rhythmic breaks. Kristeva writes: 'Insofar as she has a specificity of her own, a woman finds it in asociality, in the violation of communal conventions, in a sort of a-symbolic singularity'.[6] Menaced equally by the paternal paranoia and the mother's schizophrenia, the daughter must maintain herself in a difficult equilibrium between the two.

Women must somehow keep a hold on the symbolic, and thus as if in reinforcement of the mirror phase—the threshold of the formation of the unitary ego—Clarissa needs her own reflection; 'the delicate pink face of the woman . . . of Clarissa Dalloway; of herself' (42). She 'assembles' the self 'when some effort, some call on her self' constrains her, and then becomes conscious of the lack of 'something central which permeated' (36). This lack is the maternal body which she must repress to become a subject in the symbolic. Because of this denial of the maternal and her own body, 'there was an emptiness about the heart of life; an attic room' to which she austerely withdraws 'like a nun' (35). Sally, who more fully owns her body, is quick to detect this absence in Clarissa: 'But—did Peter understand?—she lacked something' (207). The novel stresses this withdrawal from the body in several ways. Clarissa had 'grown very white since her illness'. She is the mere ghost of a woman, cut away by physical infirmity from the energies of bodily life. There is, moreover, 'a touch of the bird about her, of the jay, blue-green, light, vivacious' (6). Such energy as she retains is light and ethereal, more spiritual than physical.

And, finally, she is in her fifties, cut off by the fact of menopause from the fertile biological processes of ovulation and menstruation.

The most positive representation of the body in the novel is the younger Sally Seton, who 'forgot her sponge, and ran along the passage naked' (38). Sally's fascination for Clarissa is 'a sort of abandonment', that is, her different relationship to her own body. Sally teaches Clarissa about sex, speaks of sexual matters in front of men, shocks others by running along the passage naked. She confidently asserts herself as a woman, 'as if she could say anything, do anything' (37). Not that her feminist boldness goes altogether unpunished. Hugh Whitbread's kiss is an act of sexual violence, the rape on a miniature scale of a woman who has dared argue that her sex should have the vote. But to our and Clarissa's disappointment the apparently fearless Sally has married a capitalist millionaire and now has five sons. Maternity is the only female identity which is valorised by patriarchy. Only as a mother is a woman allowed to have her sexuality as difference, to own her body and social place. The novel's arch-rebel becomes a sober conformist, 'Lady Rosseter'.

Repressing the body, Clarissa is given a place in the symbolic order constructed around the Name-of-the-Father:

> this body, with all its capacities, seemed nothing—nothing at all. She had the oddest sense of being herself invisible; unseen; unknown; there being no more marrying, no more having of children now, but only this astonishing and rather solemn progress with the rest of them, up Bond Street, this being Mrs. Dalloway; not even Clarissa any more; this being Mrs. Richard Dalloway. (13)

'Not even Clarissa': once subdued to the laws of the father, a woman is next handed over to another man, the husband, as commodity in the structure of patriarchal exchange relations. Throughout the novel Clarissa's mother is curiously repressed, though her father is always prominent in her memories. Only once, at the party, does a guest exclaim that Clarissa looks that night 'so like her mother'; 'And really Clarissa's eyes filled with tears', but this brief 'return' of her mother is instantly cancelled by her duty as hostess of patriarchy (193). This repression of the mother is also a denial of the maternal in herself, 'unmaternal as she was' (209). Women have to be the daughters of their fathers, not their mothers. Childbirth can no more rupture her hymen outwards than the phallus could inwards; she retains 'a virginity preserved through childbirth' (36). She cannot move from girlhood to full womanhood, and is constantly defensive about her own maternity. Even Walsh notices the over-emphasis with which she declares 'Here is my Elizabeth' (53), and later concludes that the daughter probably does not get on with her mother. Seeing Clarissa, Walsh notes that women 'attach themselves to places; and their fathers—a woman's always proud of her father' (62). In 'Mrs. Dalloway in Bond Street' Clarissa recalls 'A happy childhood—and it was not to his daughters only that Justin Parry had seemed a fine fellow'. Breaking away from the mother, Clarissa accepts the role prescribed by the paternal law, becoming 'the perfect hostess' (9). And this repudiation of the mother is repeated in Elizabeth; Sally could 'feel it by the way Elizabeth went to her father' (213). ⟨...⟩

Clarissa survives despite or perhaps because of her contradictions; Septimus vicariously represents the risk of a total rejection of patriarchal law, and perishes. He is both the absent son, united with the mother only in the Pyrrhic moment of death, and a surrogate for Clarissa, committing suicide on her behalf. In Woolf's original plan Clarissa was herself to die.[7] The invention of Septimus is thus a defensive 'splitting', whereby Clarissa's most dangerous impulses are projected into another figure who can die for her; to this extent, she and he are one composite character. The internal split in Clarissa which worried Woolf—existential anguish versus social superficiality—reveals that the problem of woman opens on to the problems of subjectivity and of writing. How is it possible to recognise and valorise the position of woman as difference? There are two obvious ways open to feminists. One may deny the difference in order to be admitted as subject in the symbolic order, becoming a token man. Or one may refuse the symbolic altogether, and risk being even more marginalised than before or, worse, expelled as mad from society. These alternatives are in a sense represented by Kilman and Septimus; Clarissa must negotiate a precarious balance between them. Either way, a woman is grievously at risk. Clarissa sees her sister Sylvia, 'on the verge of life, the most gifted of them', killed by a falling tree—'all Justin Parry's fault' (87). The Father kills the most gifted girl by means of the Phallus (tree). No wonder then that Clarissa 'always had the feeling that it was very, very dangerous to live even one day' (11). Hence her strategy of wariness: 'her notion being that the Gods, who never lost a chance of hurting, thwarting and spoiling human lives, were seriously put out if, all the same, you behaved like a lady' (87), and we can rewrite 'gods' here as 'men'. To behave 'like a lady', as patriarchy's 'perfect hostess', is thus a cautious programme for survival.

To avoid total submission to the Law of the Father, gaining a place in the symbolic at the price of negating women's difference, but also to avoid expulsion from the symbolic into complete silence: one can only oscillate between these two positions, living a tension which must not be fully resolved in either direction. A woman must reject the frozen identity of the subject but not relinquish subject-hood altogether. This dialectic between stasis and rupture is precisely what the novel's style achieves. Of it, as of the cloudscape, 'Fixed though they seemed at their posts ... nothing could be fresher, freer, more sensitive ... to change, to go, to dismantle the solemn assemblage was immediately possible' (153). Clarissa often experiences the moment of suspense between stasis and rupture: 'How fresh, how calm, stiller than this of course, the air was in the early morning ... and yet ... solemn, feeling as she did, standing there at the open window, that something awful was about to happen' (5). And this momentary pause in the dialectic is memorably repeated in Septimus:

> I went under the sea. I have been dead, and yet am now alive, but let me rest still, ... as, before waking, the voices of birds and the sound of wheels chime

and chatter in a queer harmony, grow louder and louder, and the sleeper feels himself drawing to the shores of life, so he felt himself drawing towards life, the sun growing hotter, cries sounding louder, something tremendous about to happen. (77)

This suspense and adventure of the subject are often evoked in terms of sea imagery: 'an exquisite suspense, such as might stay a diver before plunging while the sea darkens and brightens beneath him, and the waves which threaten to break ...' (34–5). It is a pause or poise or indeterminacy between life and death.[8] Clarissa's heart hesitates between life and death in 'a particular hush, or solemnity; an indescribable pause; a suspense ... before Big Ben strikes' (6). Big Ben in a sense represents the Father (Peter had earlier identified with its 'direct downright' sound). Tolling the hours, it dissects the continuum of life and imposes a structure. *Mrs. Dalloway* was, indeed, titled *The Hours* in the early stages of Woolf's writing (*WD*, 57–62). 'Shredding and slicing, dividing and subdividing, the clocks of Harley Street nibbled at the June day, counselled submission, upheld authority, and pointed out in chorus the supreme advantages of a sense of proportion' (*MD*, 113). Time also introduces death by its measuring out of life, which itself, as sheer semiotic energy, does not know it. Time is alien to the polymorphous mode of being: 'she feared time itself ... how little the margin that remained was capable any longer of stretching, of absorbing, as in the youthful years, the colours, salts, tones of existence' (34). Representing patriarchal law, aligned with the William Bradshaws of the world, Big Ben subjugates even the most recalcitrant subjects to the social order: the old lady 'was forced, so Clarissa imagined, by that sound, to move, to go' (140). As lawgiver, it forces the imperative 'must' on the human subject. As Clarissa lets the hours impose a structure on her life, she collects the dispersed parts of her self into a social entity: 'The clock was striking ... But she must go back. She must assemble' (204–5). Her life is continual dispersion and reassembly. The subject is neither 'this' nor 'that'. Its true 'site' is the very dialectic between dissemination and reconstruction: the melting away of the shell of the self by the sun's heat and the freezing of it again into a hard crust by the thetic winter of Big Ben. 'Fear no more the heat o' the sun / Nor the furious winter's rages'.

In *Anti-Oedipus* Deleuze and Guattari provocatively claim: 'A schizophrenic out for a walk is a better model than a neurotic lying on the analyst's couch'.[9] Clarissa is a decentred subject of flows and part-objects, like Septimus, but she is also the cool, composed hostess of the evening party. Her contradictoriness and internal divisions denote the difficult problem of women's writing itself, since her subjectivity is at the same time the mode of the subject in the writing of the novel. How can a woman give voice to the place of women and reject masculine discourse without being marginalised into madness and silence? If language and the symbolic order are essentially masculine, this is only possible through the repression of the woman. Even the 'martial' Lady Bruton, who talks about politics like a man, has no power of language and logicality. Women have to constitute themselves as split subjects to enter the symbolic and play a man's game. So Woolf never radically destroys the laws of syntax. She lets grammar dissect and regulate the flow of the subject's desire, and keeps the conventional narrative form of third person and past tense. Within this apparent conformism, however, her writing tries to give voice to the specificity of a female subject who is outside any principle of identity-to-self, which can identify with multiple scenes without fully integrating herself into them.

NOTES

Abbreviations used in the text and notes:

CE = Collected Essays, 4 volumes, edited by Leonard Woolf, London, 1966–7
HH = A Haunted House and Other Stories (1944), London, 1962
L = The Letters of Virginia Woolf, 6 volumes, edited by Nigel Nicolson and Joanne Trautmann, London, 1975–80
MD = Mrs. Dalloway (1925), London, 1980
WD = A Writer's Diary, edited by Leonard Woolf (1953), London, 1969

[1] Julia Kristeva, 'Oscillation between Power and Denial' in New French Feminisms, ed. Elaine Marks and Isabelle de Courtivron (Amherst, 1980), p. 166.
[2] Phyllis Rose, Woman of Letters: A Life of Virginia Woolf (London, 1978), p. 125.
[3] To Ethel Smyth, Woolf wrote: 'how can you imagine how much sexual feeling has to do with an emotion for one's mother!' Cited by Jane Marcus in her 'Thinking Back through Our Mothers' in New Feminist Essays on Virginia Woolf, ed. Jane Marcus (London, 1981), p. 14.
[4] Juliet Mitchell, Psychoanalysis and Feminism (London, 1974), p. 116.
[5] The Shelley quotation is in 'Mrs. Dalloway in Bond Street' in Mrs. Dalloway's Party: A Short Story Sequence by Virginia Woolf, ed. Stella McNichol (London, 1973), p. 22. In this short piece, from which the novel developed, the theme of losing integrity and purity as one grows is more explicit.
[6] Kristeva, Polylogue (Paris: Editions du Seuil, 1977), p. 79, cited in Josette Féral, 'Antigone or the Irony of the Tribe', Diacritics (September 1978), p. 12.
[7] See the preface to the first edition of Mrs. Dalloway. In a letter Woolf wrote 'Septimus and Mrs. Dalloway should be entirely dependent upon each other' (L, 3:189).
[8] In the novel, 'life' and 'death' do not have one fixed value; they constantly interchange positive and negative signs. Septimus' suicide is positive, while the 'life' the doctors uphold is corruption and lies. Elsewhere 'life' is joy and pleasure and death their negation.
[9] Gilles Deleuze and Felix Guattari, Anti-Oedipus: Capitalism and Schizophrenia (New York, 1977), p. 2.

CONTRIBUTORS

HAROLD BLOOM is Sterling Professor of the Humanities at Yale University and Henry W. and Albert A. Berg Professor of English at the New York University Graduate School. He is a 1985 MacArthur Foundation Award recipient, served as the Charles Eliot Norton Professor of Poetry at Harvard University (1987–88), and is the author of eighteen books, the most recent being *Poetics of Influence: New and Selected Criticism* (1988). Currently he is editing the Chelsea House series Modern Critical Views and Modern Critical Interpretations, and other Chelsea House series in literary criticism.

REUBEN ARTHUR BROWER was Henry B. and Anne M. Cabot Professor of English at Harvard University and fellow of Churchill College, Cambridge, until his death in 1975. His works include *Alexander Pope: The Poetry of Allusion* (1975), *Hero and Saint: Shakespeare and the Graeco-Roman Heroic Tradition* (1971), and *Mirror on Mirror: Translation, Imitation, Parody* (1974). He also edited *Forms of Lyric* (1970), *Twentieth-Century Literature in Retrospect* (1971), and *I. A. Richards: Essays in His Honor* (1973; with Helen Vendler and John Hollander).

GEOFFREY H. HARTMAN is Professor of English and Comparative Literature at Yale University. Some of his recent works are *Easy Pieces* (1985), *The Unremarkable Wordsworth* (1987), and, as editor, *Bitburg in Moral and Political Perspective* (1986) and *Midrash and Literature* (1986; with Sanford Budick).

BLANCHE H. GELFANT is Robert E. Maxwell Professor in the Arts and Sciences at Dartmouth College. She is the author of *The American City Novel* (1954) and *Women Writing in America: Voices in Collage* (1984) and has published extensively on American literature in scholarly journals and essay collections.

LEE R. EDWARDS is Professor of English at the University of Massachusetts. She has written *Psyche as Hero: Female Heroism and Fictional Form* (1984) and edited *The Authority of Experience: Essays in Feminist Criticism* (1977; with Arlyn Diamond).

DANIEL ALBRIGHT is author of *The Myth against Myth: A Study of Yeats's Imagination in Old Age* (1972) and *Personality and Impersonality: Lawrence, Woolf, and Mann* (1978).

JOHN G. HESSLER is a former Postdoctoral Fellow in the Humanities at Stanford University and a former Visiting Assistant Professor at the University of Hawaii.

ROBERT KIELY teaches Modern Literature and the Novel at Harvard University. He is the author of *The Romantic Novel in England* (1972) and *Beyond Egotism: The Fiction of James Joyce, Virginia Woolf, and D. H. Lawrence* (1980) and editor of *Modernism Reconsidered* (1983; with John Hildebidle).

KENNETH MOON is Senior Lecturer in English at the University of New England in Armidale, New South Wales, Australia. He has published many articles on modern literature.

HOWARD HARPER is author of *Between Language and Silence: The Novels of Virginia Woolf* (1982). He is Professor of English at the University of North Carolina.

SUSAN M. SQUIER is Associate Professor of English at the State University of New York, Stony Brook. She has written *Virginia Woolf and London: The Sexual Politics of the City* (1985) and edited *Women Writers and the City: Essays in Feminist Literary Criticism* (1984).

MAKIKO MINOW-PINKNEY is author of *Virginia Woolf and the Problem of the Subject* (1987).

BIBLIOGRAPHY

Abel, Elizabeth, "Narrative Structure(s) and Female Development: The Case of *Mrs. Dalloway.*" In *The Voyage In: Fictions of Female Development,* ed. Elizabeth Abel, Marianne Hirsch, and Elizabeth Langland. Hanover, NH: University Press of New England, 1983, pp. 161–85.

Bazin, Nancy Topping. *Virginia Woolf and the Androgynous Vision.* New Brunswick, NJ: Rutgers University Press, 1973.

Beja, Morris, ed. *Critical Essays on Virginia Woolf.* Boston: G. K. Hall, 1985.

Beker, Miroslav. "London as a Principle of Structure in *Mrs. Dalloway.*" *Modern Fiction Studies* 18 (1972): 375–85.

Bishop, Edward. "Writing, Speech, and Silence in *Mrs. Dalloway.*" *English Studies in Canada* 12 (1986): 397–423.

Bloom, Harold, ed. *Virginia Woolf.* New York: Chelsea House, 1986.

————, ed. *Virginia Woolf's* Mrs. Dalloway. New York: Chelsea House, 1988.

Bowlby, Rachel. *Virginia Woolf: Feminist Destinations.* Oxford: Basil Blackwell, 1988.

Brown, Keith. "Mrs. Dalloway on Mount Caburn: A Garden Extended." *Cambridge Review,* 29 January 1982, pp. 100–105.

Clements, Patricia, and Isobel Grundy, ed. *Virginia Woolf: New Critical Essays.* Totowa, NJ: Barnes & Noble, 1983.

DiBattista, Maria. *Virginia Woolf's Major Novels: The Fables of Anon.* New Haven: Yale University Press, 1980.

DuPlessis, Rachel Blau. *Writing beyond the Ending: Narrative Strategies of Twentieth-Century Women Writers.* Bloomington: Indiana University Press, 1985.

Fleishman, Avrom. *Virginia Woolf: A Critical Reading.* Baltimore: Johns Hopkins University Press, 1975.

Freedman, Ralph. "Awareness and Fact: The Lyrical Vision of Virginia Woolf." In *The Lyrical Novel: Studies in Hermann Hesse, André Gide and Virginia Woolf.* Princeton: Princeton University Press, 1963, pp. 185–270.

————, ed. *Virginia Woolf: Revaluation and Continuity.* Berkeley: University of California Press, 1980.

Ginsberg, Elaine E., and Laura Moss Gottlieb, ed. *Virginia Woolf: Centennial Essays.* Troy, NY: Whitston, 1983.

Gregor, Ian. "Voices: Reading Virginia Woolf." *Sewanee Review* 88 (1980): 572–90.

Hafley, James. *The Glass Roof: Virginia Woolf as Novelist.* Berkeley: University of California Press, 1954.

Henke, Suzette A. *"Mrs. Dalloway:* The Communion of Saints." In *New Feminist Essays on Virginia Woolf,* ed. Jane Marcus. Lincoln: University of Nebraska Press, 1981, pp. 125–47.

Hynes, Samuel. "The Whole Contention between Mr. Bennett and Mrs. Woolf." *Novel* 1 (1967): 34–44.

Jensen, Emily. "Clarissa Dalloway's Respectable Suicide." In *Virginia Woolf: A Feminist Slant,* ed. Jane Marcus. Lincoln: University of Nebraska Press, 1983, pp. 162–79.

Kelley, Alice van Buren. *The Novels of Virginia Woolf: Fact and Vision.* Chicago: University of Chicago Press, 1971.

Leaska, Mitchell. *The Novels of Virginia Woolf: From Beginning to End.* New York: City University of New York Press, 1977.

Lee, Hermoine. *The Novels of Virginia Woolf*. London: Methuen, 1977.

Leonard, Diane R. "Proust and Virginia Woolf, Ruskin and Roger Fry: Modernist Visual Dynamics." *Comparative Literature Studies* 18 (1981): 333–43.

Love, Jean O. *Worlds in Consciousness: Mythopoeic Thought in the Novels of Virginia Woolf*. Berkeley: University of California Press, 1970.

McLaurin, Allen. "Consciousness and Group Consciousness in Virginia Woolf." In *Virginia Woolf: A Centenary Prespective*, ed. Eric Warner. New York: St. Martin's Press, 1984, pp. 28–40.

Marcus, Jane. *Virginia Woolf and the Languages of Patriarchy*. Bloomington: Indiana University Press, 1987.

———, ed. *New Feminist Essays on Virginia Woolf*. Lincoln: University of Nebraska Press, 1981.

Meisel, Perry. *The Absent Father: Virginia Woolf and Walter Pater*. New Haven: Yale University Press, 1980.

Miller, J. Hillis. "Character in the Novel: A 'Real Illusion.' " In *From Smollett to James: Studies in the Novel and Other Essays Presented to Edgar Johnson*. Charlottesville: University of Virginia Press, 1981, pp. 277–85.

———. "*Mrs. Dalloway*: Repetition as the Raising of the Dead." In *Fiction and Repetition: Seven English Novels*. Cambridge, MA: Harvard University Press, 1982, pp. 176–202.

Moore, Madeline. *The Short Season between Two Silences: The Mystical and the Political in the Novels of Virginia Woolf*. London: Allen & Unwin, 1984.

Naremore, James. *The World without a Self: Virginia Woolf and the Novel*. New Haven: Yale University Press, 1973.

Poole, Roger. *The Unknown Virginia Woolf*. Cambridge: Cambridge University Press, 1978.

Richter, Harvena. *Virginia Woolf: The Inward Voyage*. Princeton: Princeton University Press, 1970.

Rosenbaum, S. P. "The Philosophical Realism of Virginia Woolf." In *English Literature and British Philosophy*, ed. S. P. Rosenbaum. Chicago: University of Chicago Press, 1971, pp. 316–56.

Rosenman, Ellen Bayuk. *The Invisible Presence: Virginia Woolf and the Mother-Daughter Relationship*. Baton Rouge: Louisiana State University Press, 1986.

Rosenthal, Michael. *Virginia Woolf*. New York: Columbia University Press, 1979.

Rowe, Margaret Moan. "Balancing Two Worlds: Setting and Characterization in *Mrs. Dalloway*." *Virginia Woolf Quarterly* 3 (1978): 268–75.

Ruotolo, Lucio P. "Clarissa Dalloway." In *Six Existential Heroes: The Politics of Faith*. Cambridge, MA: Harvard University Press, 1973, pp. 13–35.

———. *The Interrupted Moment: A View of Virginia Woolf's Novels*. Stanford: Stanford University Press, 1986.

———. "*Mrs. Dalloway*: The Journey out of Subjectivity." *Women's Studies* 4 (1977): 173–78.

Scott, Bonnie Kime. "The Word Split Its Husk: Woolf's Double Vision of Modernist Language." *Modern Fiction Studies* 34 (1988): 371–85.

Showalter, Elaine. *A Literature of Their Own: British Women Novelists from Brontë to Lessing*. Princeton: Princeton University Press, 1977.

Slatoff, Walter J. *The Look of Distance: Reflections on Suffering and Sympathy in Modern Literature: Auden to Agee, Whitman to Woolf*. Columbus: Ohio State University Press, 1985.

Spilka, Mark. *Virginia Woolf's Quarrel with Grieving.* Lincoln: University of Nebraska Press, 1980.

Transue, Pamela J. *Virginia Woolf and the Politics of Style.* Albany: State University of New York Press, 1986.

Wade, Michel. "Mrs. Dalloway's Affirmation of Value." *Hebrew University Studies in Literature* 7 (1979): 245–70.

Wyatt, Jean. "Avoiding Self-Definition: In Defense of Women's Right to Merge (Julia Kristeva and *Mrs. Dalloway*)." *Women's Studies* 13 (1986–87): 115–26.

———. "*Mrs. Dalloway:* Literary Allusion as Structural Metaphor." *PMLA* 88 (1973): 440–51.

Zwerdling, Alex. "Mrs. Dalloway and the Social System." *PMLA* 92 (1977): 69–82.

ACKNOWLEDGMENTS

"Mr. Bennett and Mrs. Brown" by Virginia Woolf, from *The Captain's Death Bed and Other Essays* by Virginia Woolf, © 1950 and renewed 1978 by Harcourt Brace Jovanovich, Inc. Reprinted by permission.

"A Note on Technique" by Elizabeth A. Drew, from *The Modern Novel: Some Aspects of Contemporary Fiction* by Elizabeth A. Drew, © 1926 by Harcourt, Brace & Co., Inc., and renewed 1954 by Elizabeth A. Drew. Reprinted by permission of Harcourt Brace Jovanovich, Inc.

"Virginia Woolf: 'Mind' and 'Matter' on the Plane of a Literary Controversy" by Wyndham Lewis, from *Men without Art,* edited by Seamus Cooney, © 1987 by the Estate of Mrs. G. A. Wyndham Lewis by permission of the Wyndham Lewis Memorial Trust. Reprinted by permission of Black Sparrow Press.

"Virginia Woolf" by Dorothy M. Hoare, from *Some Studies in the Modern Novel* by Dorothy M. Hoare, © 1938 by Chatto & Windus, Ltd. Reprinted by permission.

"The Inception of Mrs. Woolf's Art" by N. Elizabeth Monroe, from *College English* 2, No. 3 (December 1940), © by the National Council of Teachers of English. Reprinted by permission.

"Characters and Human Beings" by Joan Bennett, from *Virginia Woolf: Her Art as a Novelist* by Joan Bennett, © 1945 by Harcourt, Brace & Co., Inc. Reprinted by permission of Harcourt Brace Jovanovich, Inc.

" 'My Tunneling Process': The Method of *Mrs. Dalloway*" by Edward A. Hungerford, from *Modern Fiction Studies* 3, No. 2 (Summer 1957), © 1957 by Purdue Research Foundation. Reprinted by permission.

"Virginia Woolf" by David Daiches, from *The Novel and the Modern World* by David Daiches, © 1939, 1960 by the University of Chicago Press. Reprinted by permission.

"Virginia Woolf: Matches Struck in the Dark" by Morris Beja, from *Epiphany in the Modern Novel* by Morris Beja, © 1971 by the University of Washington Press. Reprinted by permission.

"Together and Apart" by Jeremy Hawthorn, from *Virginia Woolf's* Mrs. Dalloway: *A Study in Alienation* by Jeremy Hawthorn, © 1975 by Chatto & Windus, Ltd. Reprinted by permission.

"Mortal Stain: Literary Allusion and Female Sexuality in 'Mrs. Dalloway in Bond Street' " by Judith P. Saunders, from *Studies in Short Fiction* 15, No. 2 (Spring 1978), © 1978 by Newberry College. Reprinted by permission.

"The Metaphysical Hostess: The Cult of Personal Relations in the Modern English Novel" by Peter Conradi, from *ELH* 48, No. 2 (Summer 1981), © 1981 by The Johns Hopkins University Press. Reprinted by permission.

"Identity and Self" by Mark Hussey, from *The Singing of the Real World: The Philosophy of Virginia Woolf's Fiction* by Mark Hussey, © 1986 by Ohio State University Press. Reprinted by permission.

"Split Perspective: Types of Incongruity in *Mrs. Dalloway*" by Herbert Marder, from *Papers on Language and Literature* 22, No. 1 (Winter 1986), © 1986 by the Board of Trustees, Southern Illinois University. Reprinted by permission.

"Deferred Action in *To the Lighthouse*" by Perry Meisel, from *The Myth of the Modern: A Study in British Literature and Criticism after 1850* by Perry Meisel, © 1987 by Yale University Press. Reprinted by permission.

"Something Central Which Permeated" (originally titled "Something Central Which Permeated: Virginia Woolf and *Mrs. Dalloway*") by Reuben Arthur Brower, from *The Fields of Light* by Reuben Arthur Brower, © 1951 by Oxford University Press, Inc., renewed 1979 by Helen P. Brower. Reprinted by permission of Oxford University Press, Inc.

"Virginia's Web" by Geoffrey H. Hartman, from *Beyond Formalism: Literary Essays 1958–1970* by Geoffrey H. Hartman, © 1970 by Yale University Press. First published in *Chicago Review* 14 (Spring 1961), © 1970 by Geoffrey H. Hartman. Reprinted by permission of Geoffrey H. Hartman.

"Love and Conversion in *Mrs. Dalloway*" by Blanche H. Gelfant, from *Criticism* 8, No. 3 (Summer 1966), © 1966 by Wayne State University Press. Reprinted by permission.

"War and Roses: The Politics of *Mrs. Dalloway*" by Lee R. Edwards, from *The Authority of Experience*, edited by Arlyn Diamond and Lee R. Edwards, © 1977 by The University of Massachusetts Press. Reprinted by permission.

"Personality and Impersonality in Virginia Woolf" (originally titled "Virginia Woolf") by Daniel Albright, from *Personality and Impersonality: Lawrence, Woolf, and Mann* by Daniel Albright, © 1978 by The University of Chicago. Reprinted by permission.

"Moral Accountability in *Mrs. Dalloway*" by John G. Hessler, from *Renascence* 30, No. 3 (Spring 1978), © 1978 by Marquette University Press. Reprinted by permission.

"A Long Event of Perpetual Change" by Robert Kiely, from *Beyond Egotism: The Fiction of James Joyce, Virginia Woolf, and D. H. Lawrence* by Robert Kiely, © 1980 by The President and Fellows of Harvard College. Reprinted by permission of Harvard University Press.

"Where Is Clarissa? Doris Kilman in *Mrs. Dalloway*" (originally titled "Where Is Clarissa? Doris Kilman and Recoil from the Flesh of Virginia Woolf's *Mrs. Dalloway*") by Kenneth Moon, from *CLA Journal* 23, No. 3 (March 1980), © 1980 by The College Language Association. Reprinted by permission.

"*Mrs. Dalloway*" by Howard Harper, from *Between Language and Silence: The Novels of Virginia Woolf* by Howard Harper, © 1982 by Louisiana State University Press. Reprinted by permission.

"Carnival and Funeral" (originally titled "The Carnival and Funeral of *Mrs. Dalloway*'s London") by Susan M. Squier, from *Virginia Woolf and London: The Sexual Politics of the City* by Susan M. Squier, © 1985 by University of North Carolina Press. Reprinted by permission.

"The Problem of the Subject in *Mrs. Dalloway*" by Makiko Minow-Pinkney, from *Virginia Woolf and the Problem of the Subject* by Makiko Minow-Pinkney, © 1987 by Makiko Minow-Pinkney. Reprinted by permission of Rutgers University Press and Harvester University Press.

INDEX